Taragona

P. de Ageiros

P. Budion

Ermita

Boiro

Coyanes

P. S. Cristobal

mpou

Abanqueiro

P. Mexadoiro

P. de Frabe

P. Brion

P. de Peiro

Bamio

P. Portomouro

P. Porron

P. Meyclado

P. Fuentesanta

Feria y
P. de la Merced

Vigia de Incados

I. Ostral

Cortegada

P. Pineiros

I. Brina

CARRIL

C. de la Cruz

P. Peniron

I. Con

I. S. Bartolome

I. del Bao

P. del Chazo

Golpella

I. Benza

I. Ostreira

P. Terrazo

VILLAG

P. de Cabio

Sogran

Fontecarmoa

Iugua

Sobradelo

Cornaz

P. Preguntoiro

P. Cubalo

P. Sines

P. Gorma

Rial

A R O S A

P. Barbafeita

VILLANUEVA

ISLA DE AROSA

P. del Puerto

Caleiro

Torre de Lobera

Arosa (S. Julian)

Andras

P. Niño Corbo

P. Agro

P. del Bado

Deiro

Soloberra

P. Camacho

Arenoso

Tremoedo

Rio Umia

P. Pto. Franco

Oubiña

P. de Quilme

P. Conrretallado

Corbillon

Leiro

P. de Corbillon

Pª Acuetas

P. Castrelo

Besomaño

FEFIÑANES

Vilariño

Rivadumia

P. Trayrobe

P. y Torre de S. Saturnino

CAMBADOS

Sta. TOME

Meis

Barrantes

Pequena

Cizan

GROVA

Cobas

P. Ceiro

Castrelo

Padrenda

# COCAINE
# COAST

## The graphic novel

# COCAINE
# COAST
## The graphic novel

## HISTORY AND INDISCRETIONS OF
## THE NARCO TRAFFICKING IN SPAIN

Based on the book by
NACHO CARRETERO

Script, art and color by
LUIS BUSTOS

Letters by
TAYLOR ESPOSITO

FOR ABLAZE

Managing Editor
Rich Young
Editor
Kevin Ketner
Design
Rodolfo Muraguchi

Publisher's Cataloging-in-Publication data

Names: Bustos, Luis, author. | Carretero, Nacho, 1981-, author.
Title: Cocaine coast : a graphic novel / Luis Bustos ; Nacho Carretero.
Description: Portland, OR: Ablaze Publishing, 2021.
Identifiers: ISBN: 978-1-950912-27-8
Subjects: LCSH Cocaine industry—Colombia. | Drug traffic—Spain—Galicia (Region) |
Cocaine industry—Spain—Galicia (Region) | Drug control—Spain—Galicia (Region). |
Graphic novels. | BISAC COMICS & GRAPHIC NOVELS / Nonfiction / General |
TRUE CRIME / Historical | TRUE CRIME / General
Classification: LCC HV5840.S712 G3529 2021 | DDC 364.1/336509461—dc23

10 9 8 7 6 5 4 3 2 1

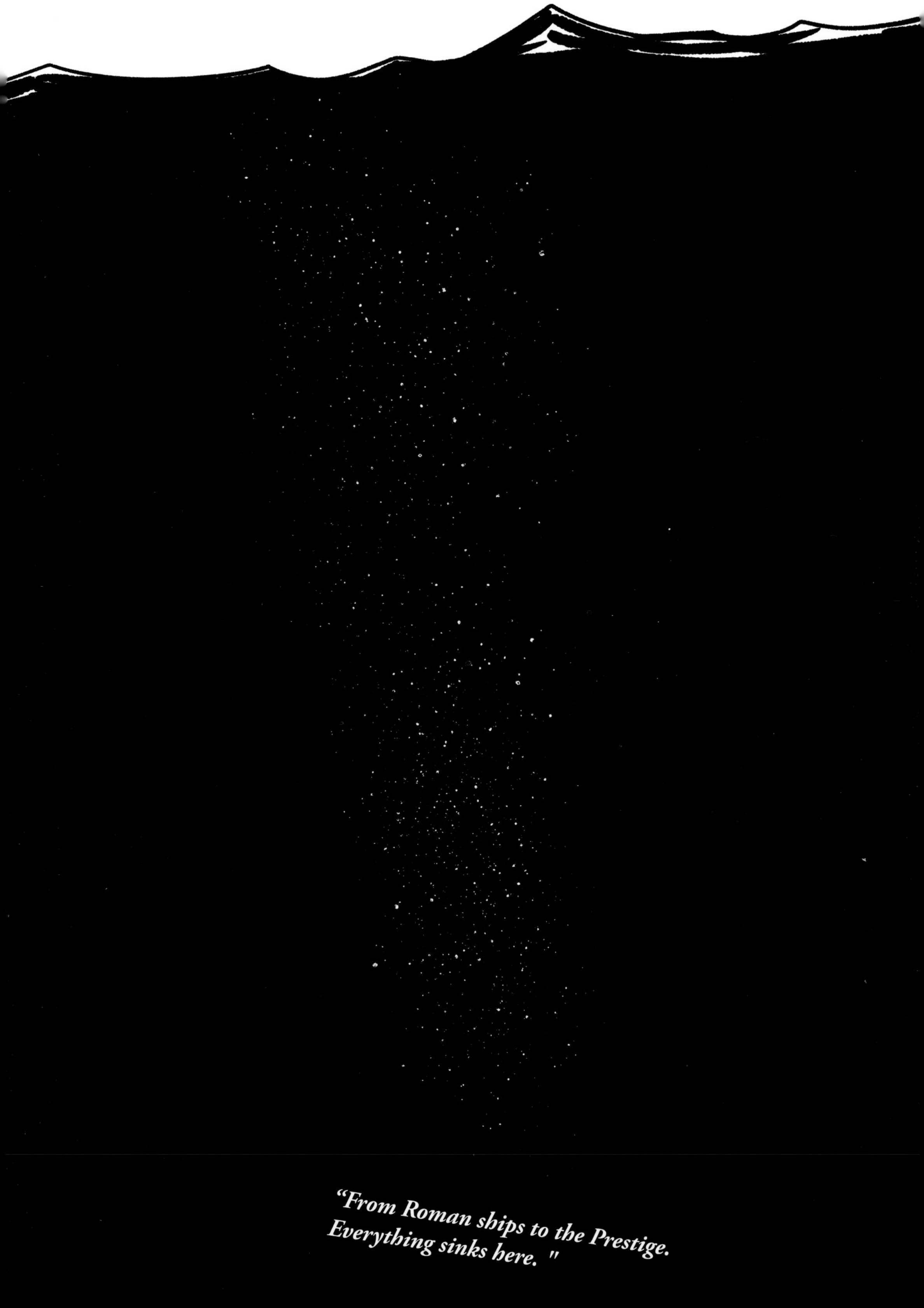
"From Roman ships to the Prestige.
Everything sinks here."

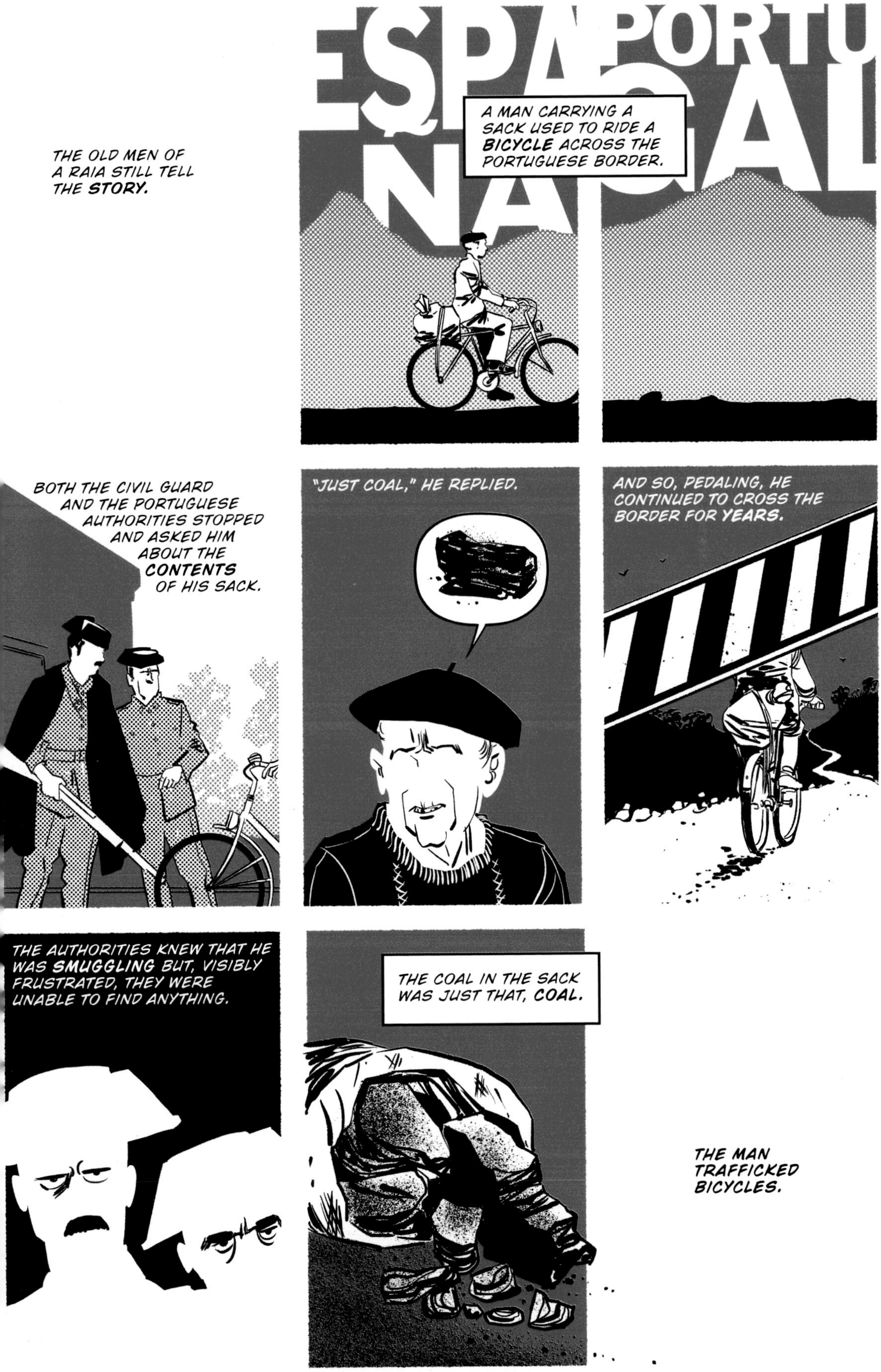

THE OLD MEN OF A RAIA STILL TELL THE **STORY.**
A MAN CARRYING A SACK USED TO RIDE A **BICYCLE** ACROSS THE PORTUGUESE BORDER.
BOTH THE CIVIL GUARD AND THE PORTUGUESE AUTHORITIES STOPPED AND ASKED HIM ABOUT THE **CONTENTS** OF HIS SACK.
"JUST COAL," HE REPLIED.
AND SO, PEDALING, HE CONTINUED TO CROSS THE BORDER FOR **YEARS.**
THE AUTHORITIES KNEW THAT HE WAS **SMUGGLING** BUT, VISIBLY FRUSTRATED, THEY WERE UNABLE TO FIND ANYTHING.
THE COAL IN THE SACK WAS JUST THAT, **COAL.**
THE MAN TRAFFICKED BICYCLES.

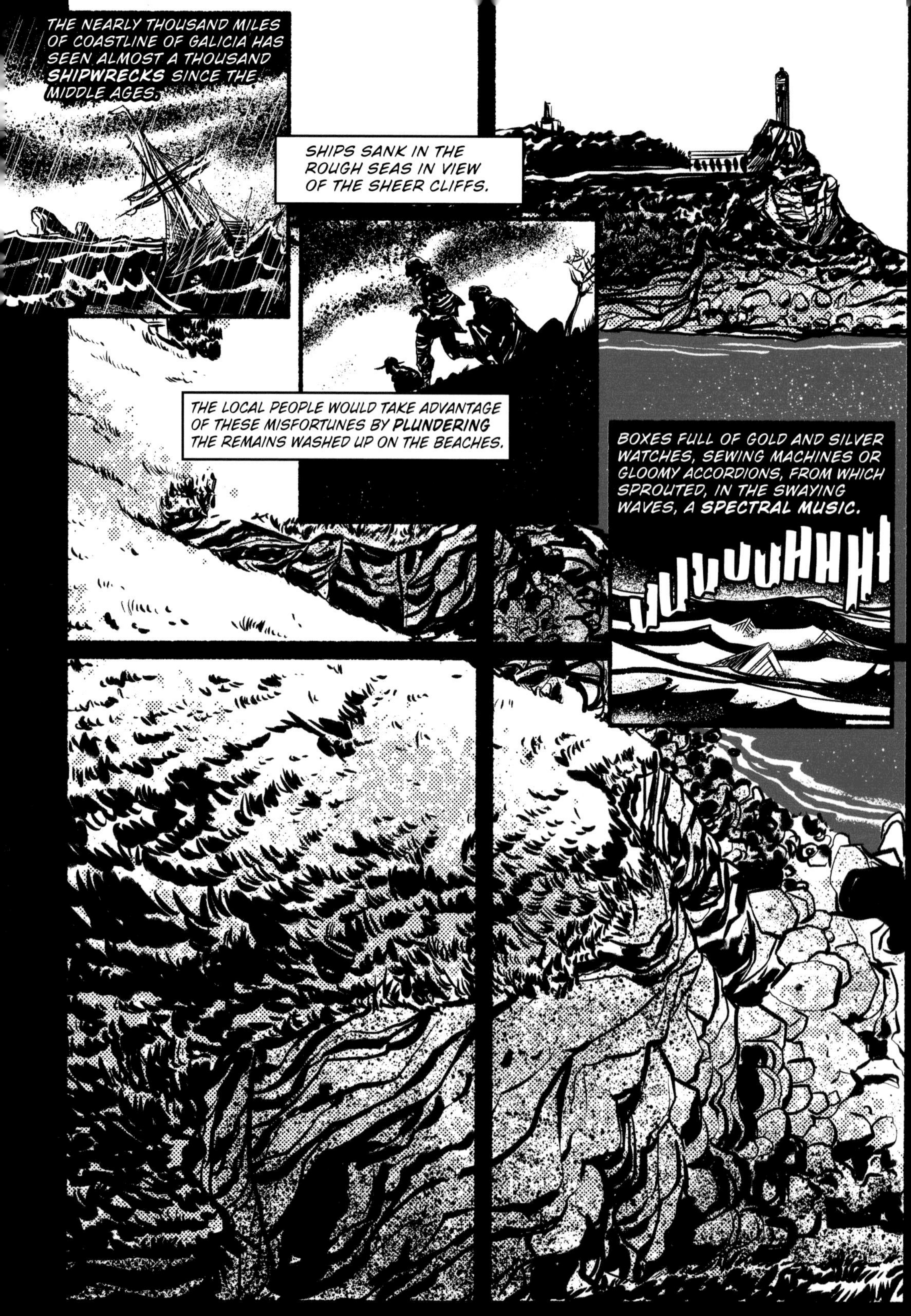
THE NEARLY THOUSAND MILES OF COASTLINE OF GALICIA HAS SEEN ALMOST A THOUSAND SHIPWRECKS SINCE THE MIDDLE AGES.
SHIPS SANK IN THE ROUGH SEAS IN VIEW OF THE SHEER CLIFFS.
THE LOCAL PEOPLE WOULD TAKE ADVANTAGE OF THESE MISFORTUNES BY PLUNDERING THE REMAINS WASHED UP ON THE BEACHES.
BOXES FULL OF GOLD AND SILVER WATCHES, SEWING MACHINES OR GLOOMY ACCORDIONS, FROM WHICH SPROUTED, IN THE SWAYING WAVES, A SPECTRAL MUSIC.
UUUUUUHHHH

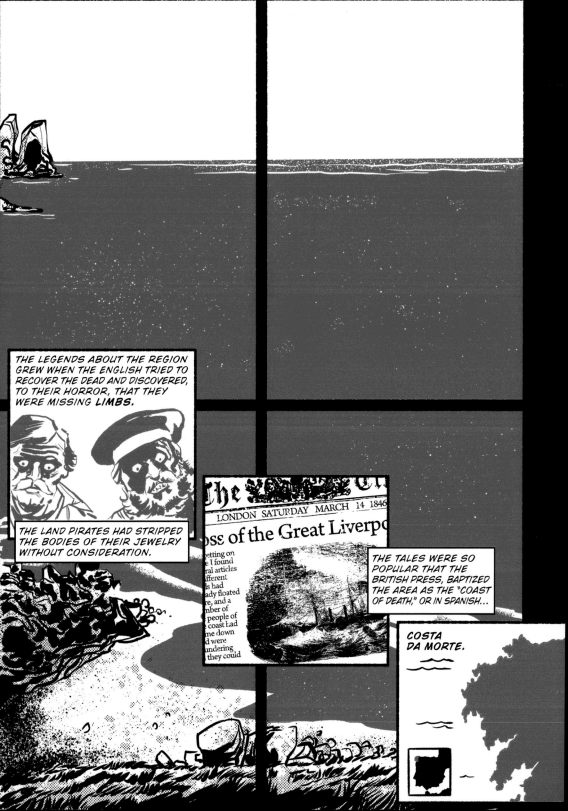

THE LEGENDS ABOUT THE REGION GREW WHEN THE ENGLISH TRIED TO RECOVER THE DEAD AND DISCOVERED, TO THEIR HORROR, THAT THEY WERE MISSING **LIMBS.**

THE LAND PIRATES HAD STRIPPED THE BODIES OF THEIR JEWELRY WITHOUT CONSIDERATION.

The
LONDON SATURDAY MARCH 14 1846
ss of the Great Liverpo

etting on
e I found
ral articles
fferent
s had
dy floated
re, and a
mber of
people of
coast had
me down
d were
ndering
they could

THE TALES WERE SO POPULAR THAT THE BRITISH PRESS, BAPTIZED THE AREA AS THE "COAST OF DEATH," OR IN SPANISH...

COSTA DA MORTE.

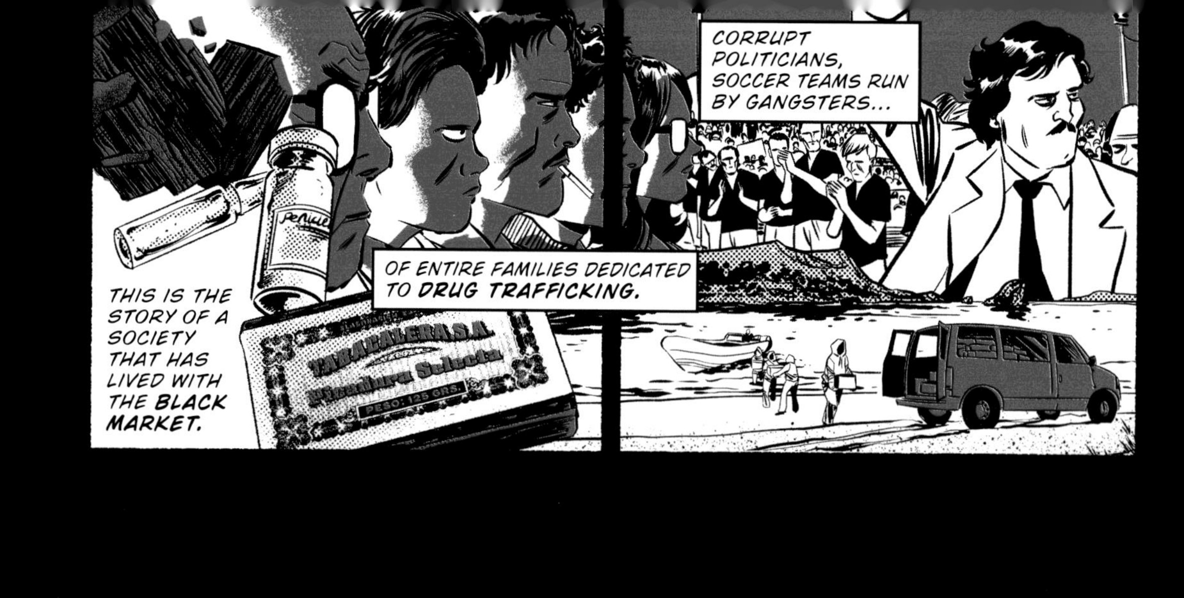
THIS IS THE STORY OF A SOCIETY THAT HAS LIVED WITH THE BLACK MARKET.
OF ENTIRE FAMILIES DEDICATED TO DRUG TRAFFICKING.
TABACALERA S.A.
PESO: 125 GRS.
CORRUPT POLITICIANS, SOCCER TEAMS RUN BY GANGSTERS...

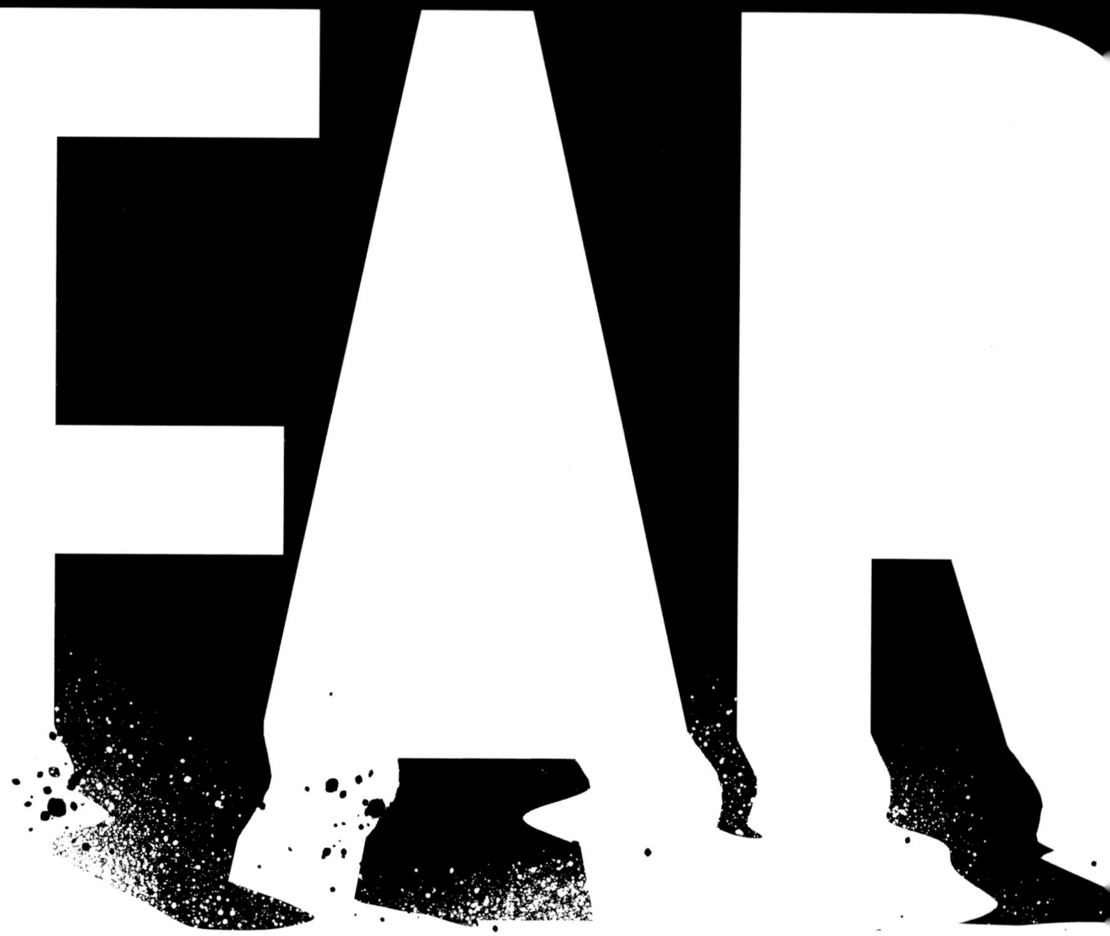

# C O C A I N E

## HISTORY AND INDISCRETIONS OF THE NARCO TRAFFICKING IN SPAIN

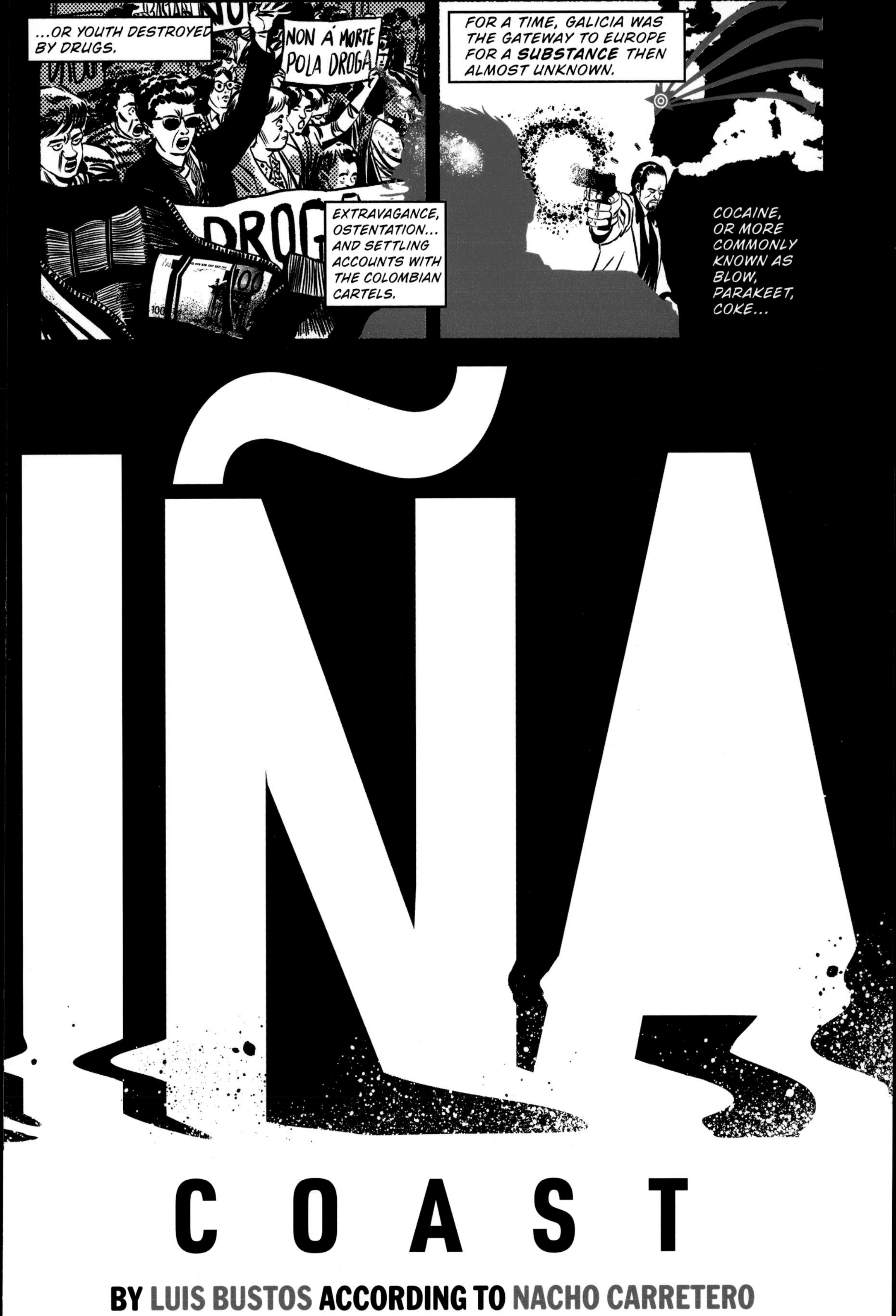
...OR YOUTH DESTROYED BY DRUGS.
NON Á MORTE POLA DROGA
DROG
EXTRAVAGANCE, OSTENTATION... AND SETTLING ACCOUNTS WITH THE COLOMBIAN CARTELS.
FOR A TIME, GALICIA WAS THE GATEWAY TO EUROPE FOR A **SUBSTANCE** THEN ALMOST UNKNOWN.

COCAINE, OR MORE COMMONLY KNOWN AS BLOW, PARAKEET, COKE...

# ÑA

## COAST

**BY LUIS BUSTOS ACCORDING TO NACHO CARRETERO**

Part One

# THE LORDS OF SMOKE

# A RAIA SECA, A RAIA MOLLADA

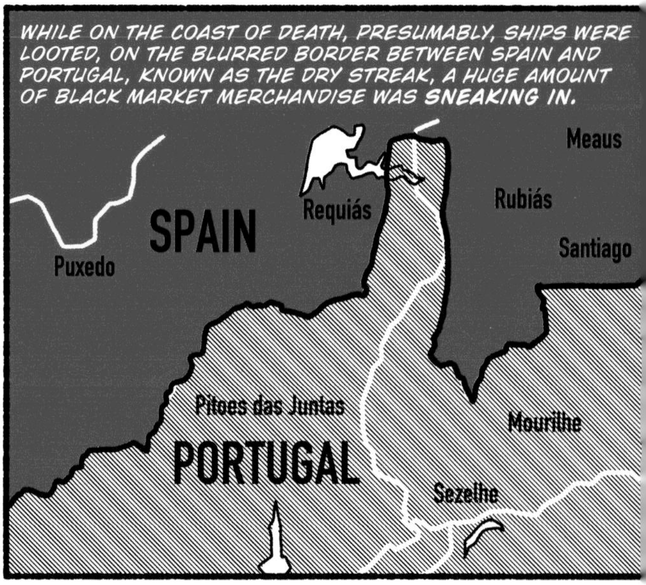
WHILE ON THE COAST OF DEATH, PRESUMABLY, SHIPS WERE LOOTED, ON THE BLURRED BORDER BETWEEN SPAIN AND PORTUGAL, KNOWN AS THE DRY STREAK, A HUGE AMOUNT OF BLACK MARKET MERCHANDISE WAS **SNEAKING IN.**
Meaus
Rubiás
Requiás
SPAIN
Santiago
Puxedo
Pitoes das Juntas
Mourilhe
PORTUGAL
Sezelhe

*BUT LET'S BACK UP TO UNDERSTAND THE PHENOMENON. THE "HOW'S" AND "WHY'S."*

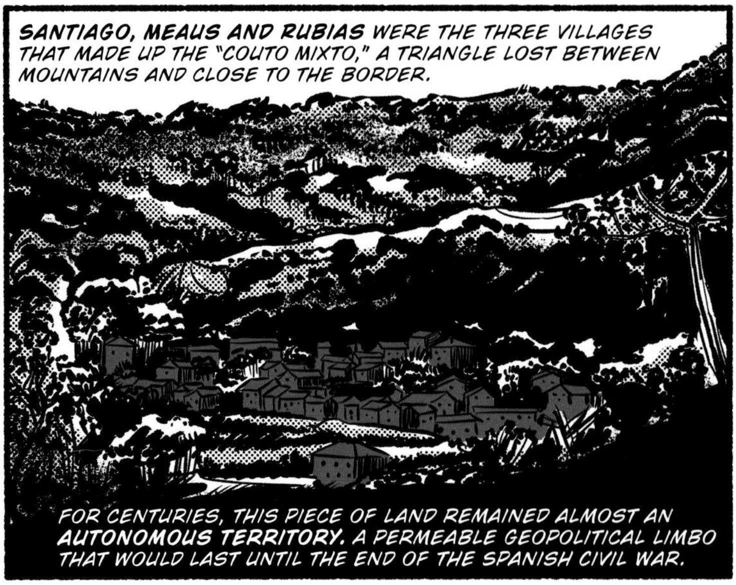
**SANTIAGO, MEAUS AND RUBIAS** WERE THE THREE VILLAGES THAT MADE UP THE "COUTO MIXTO," A TRIANGLE LOST BETWEEN MOUNTAINS AND CLOSE TO THE BORDER.
FOR CENTURIES, THIS PIECE OF LAND REMAINED ALMOST AN **AUTONOMOUS TERRITORY.** A PERMEABLE GEOPOLITICAL LIMBO THAT WOULD LAST UNTIL THE END OF THE SPANISH CIVIL WAR.

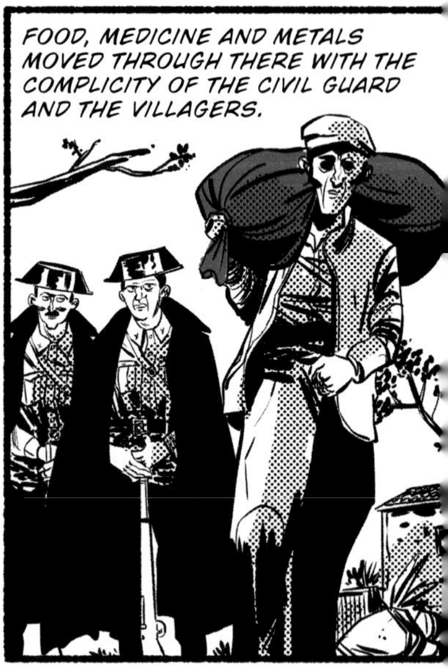
FOOD, MEDICINE AND METALS MOVED THROUGH THERE WITH THE COMPLICITY OF THE CIVIL GUARD AND THE VILLAGERS.

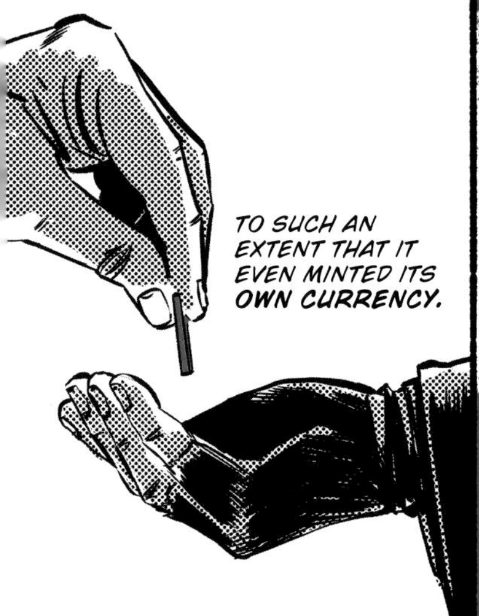
TO SUCH AN EXTENT THAT IT EVEN MINTED ITS **OWN CURRENCY.**

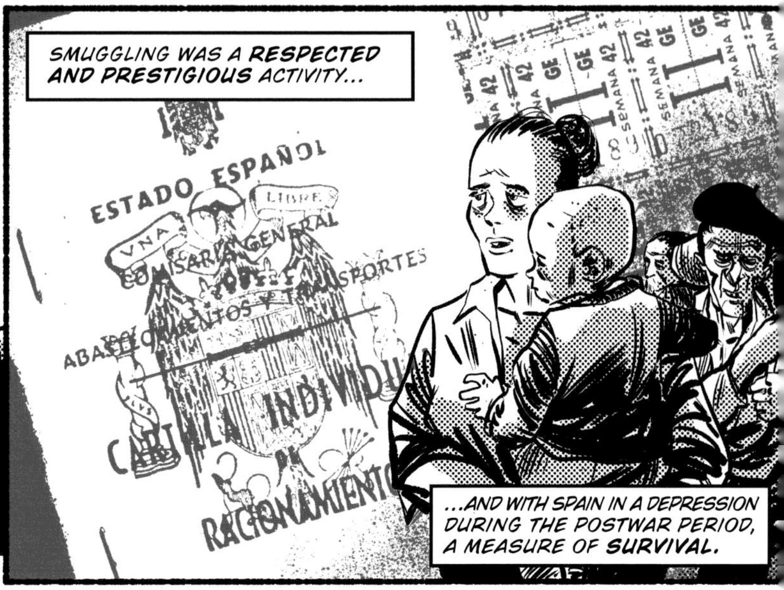
SMUGGLING WAS A **RESPECTED AND PRESTIGIOUS** ACTIVITY...
ESTADO ESPAÑOL
COMISARIA GENERAL
ABASTECIMIENTOS Y TRANSPORTES
CARTILLA INDIVIDUAL DE RACIONAMIENTO
SEMANA 42
...AND WITH SPAIN IN A DEPRESSION DURING THE POSTWAR PERIOD, A MEASURE OF **SURVIVAL.**

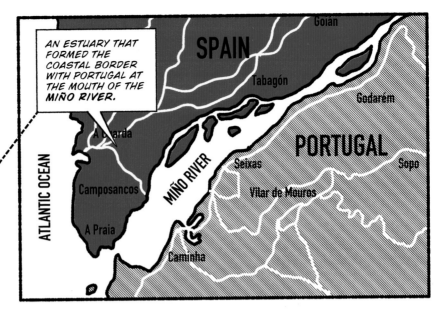

WHILE THE OURENSENS USED THE MOUNTAIN, IN PONTEVEDRA THEY HAD THE SEA, OR...
...THE WET STREAK.
AN ESTUARY THAT FORMED THE COASTAL BORDER WITH PORTUGAL AT THE MOUTH OF THE MIÑO RIVER.
SPAIN
Goián
Tabagón
Godarém
PORTUGAL
Seixas
Sopo
Vilar de Mouros
MIÑO RIVER
ATLANTIC OCEAN
Camposancos
A Praia
Caminha
DURING THE DICTATORSHIP, HUNDREDS OF FAMILIES ENGAGED IN SMUGGLING USING BOATS IN WHAT WOULD UNDOUBTEDLY BE THE BIRTH OF DRUG TRAFFICKING IN SPAIN.
HUNGER AND POVERTY DURING THE FRANCO REGIME MADE LOOTING AND SMUGGLING INTO A NECESSITY.
ON THE OTHER SIDE OF THE BORDER, THERE WAS PROSPEROUS PORTUGAL, WITH ITS LITTLE, WHITE HOUSES, CARS AND ELECTRIC LIGHT...WHILE THE GALICIANS, POORLY LIT, WENT HUNGRY.
IT WAS NOT SURPRISING, UNDER THE CIRCUMSTANCES, THAT MOST PEOPLE LOOKED THE OTHER WAY AND SMUGGLING HAD THE APPROVAL OF THE COMMUNITY...
ESTRAPERLISTAS y NUEVOS RICOS
usos, costumbres y rarezas
Texto y dibujos de
V. CASTANYS
OVER TIME, TUNGSTEN AND THEN PENICILLIN AND, FINALLY, TOBACCO BECAME THE MOST COVETED AND PROFITABLE OF COMMODITIES.

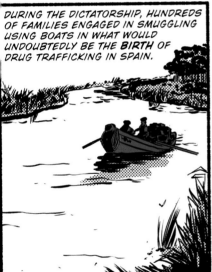

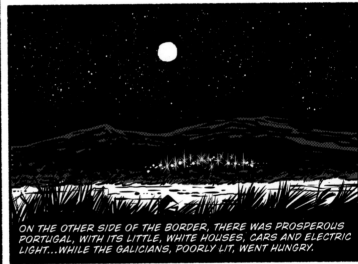

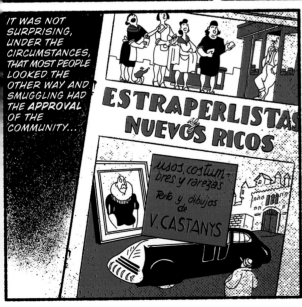

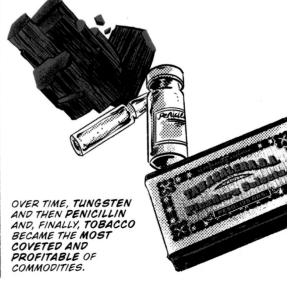

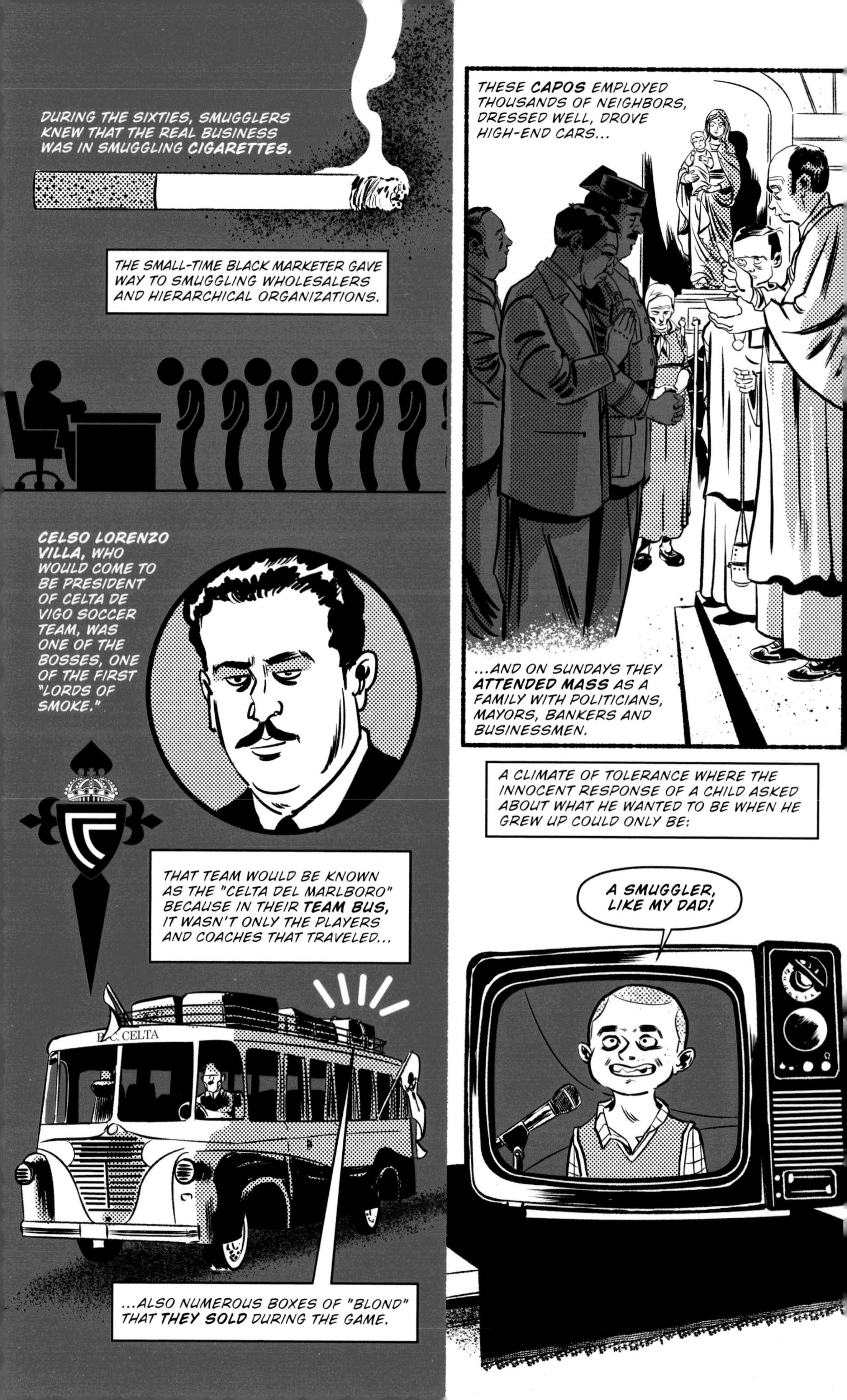
DURING THE SIXTIES, SMUGGLERS KNEW THAT THE REAL BUSINESS WAS IN SMUGGLING CIGARETTES.
THE SMALL-TIME BLACK MARKETER GAVE WAY TO SMUGGLING WHOLESALERS AND HIERARCHICAL ORGANIZATIONS.
CELSO LORENZO VILLA, WHO WOULD COME TO BE PRESIDENT OF CELTA DE VIGO SOCCER TEAM, WAS ONE OF THE BOSSES, ONE OF THE FIRST "LORDS OF SMOKE."
THAT TEAM WOULD BE KNOWN AS THE "CELTA DEL MARLBORO" BECAUSE IN THEIR TEAM BUS, IT WASN'T ONLY THE PLAYERS AND COACHES THAT TRAVELED...
R.C. CELTA
...ALSO NUMEROUS BOXES OF "BLOND" THAT THEY SOLD DURING THE GAME.
THESE CAPOS EMPLOYED THOUSANDS OF NEIGHBORS, DRESSED WELL, DROVE HIGH-END CARS...
...AND ON SUNDAYS THEY ATTENDED MASS AS A FAMILY WITH POLITICIANS, MAYORS, BANKERS AND BUSINESSMEN.
A CLIMATE OF TOLERANCE WHERE THE INNOCENT RESPONSE OF A CHILD ASKED ABOUT WHAT HE WANTED TO BE WHEN HE GREW UP COULD ONLY BE:
A SMUGGLER, LIKE MY DAD!

MANUEL DÍAZ GONZÁLEZ, NICKNAMED "LIGHTWEIGHT," WAS ANOTHER UNEDUCATED CAPO, BUT ADMIRED BY HIS NEIGHBORS AND HARDENED IN THE BLACK MARKET.

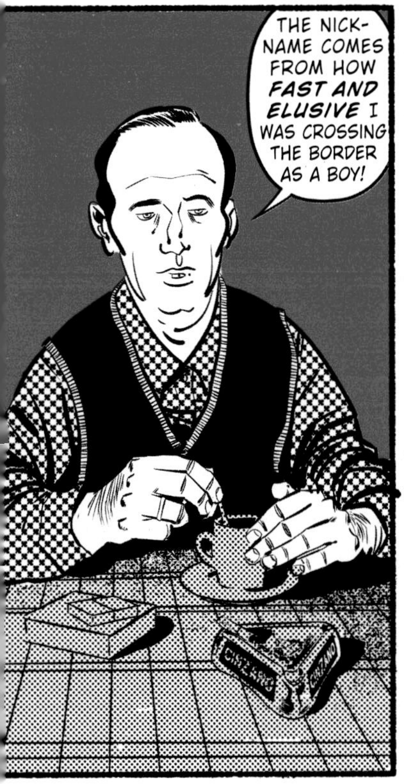
THE NICKNAME COMES FROM HOW FAST AND ELUSIVE I WAS CROSSING THE BORDER AS A BOY!

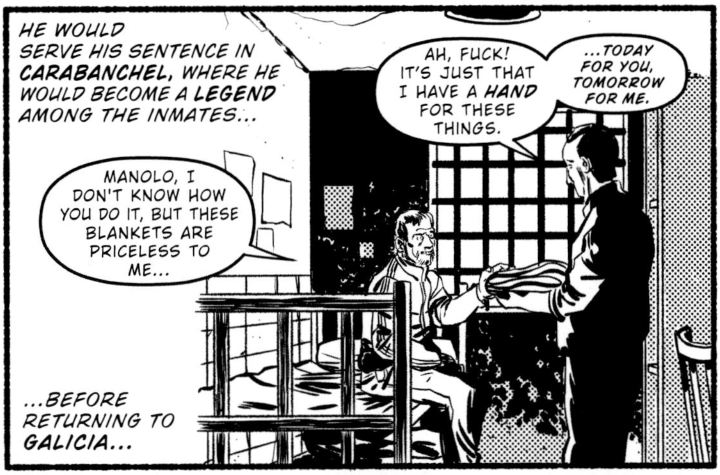
HE WOULD SERVE HIS SENTENCE IN CARABANCHEL, WHERE HE WOULD BECOME A LEGEND AMONG THE INMATES...
MANOLO, I DON'T KNOW HOW YOU DO IT, BUT THESE BLANKETS ARE PRICELESS TO ME...
AH, FUCK! IT'S JUST THAT I HAVE A HAND FOR THESE THINGS.
...TODAY FOR YOU, TOMORROW FOR ME.
...BEFORE RETURNING TO GALICIA...

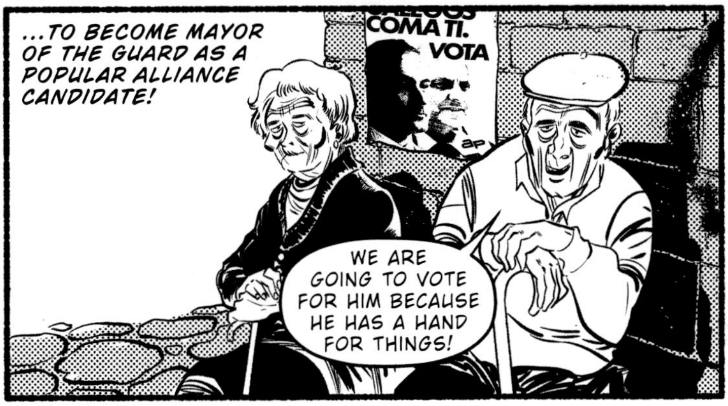
...TO BECOME MAYOR OF THE GUARD AS A POPULAR ALLIANCE CANDIDATE!
COMA TI.
VOTA
WE ARE GOING TO VOTE FOR HIM BECAUSE HE HAS A HAND FOR THINGS!

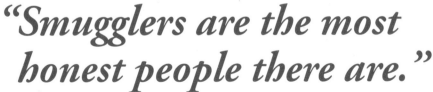

HERE IS HIS HEADLINE...

"Smugglers are the most honest people there are."

AFTER HIS DEATH, THOUSANDS OF PEOPLE ATTENDED THE FUNERAL, INCLUDING DON MANUEL FRAGA, WHO MONTHS LATER WOULD BECOME PRESIDENT OF THE GALICIAN GOVERNMENT.

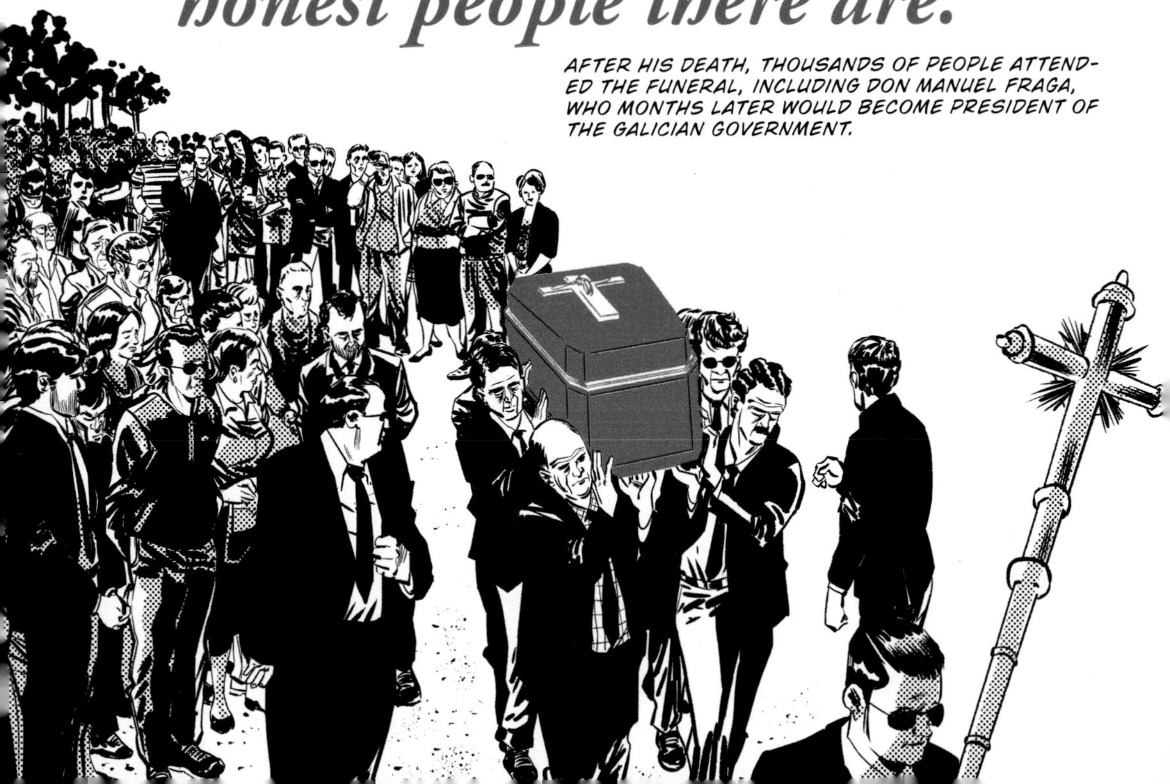

**1982** THE MAN POINTING THE GUN AT LAUREANO OUBIÑA IS VICENTE OTERO, AKA...

I SHIT ON GOD, LAUREANO...

CALM DOWN...

## "TERITO"

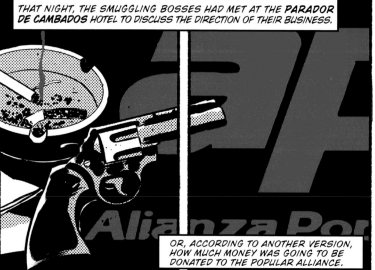

THAT NIGHT, THE SMUGGLING BOSSES HAD MET AT THE **PARADOR DE CAMBADOS** HOTEL TO DISCUSS THE DIRECTION OF THEIR BUSINESS.

OR, ACCORDING TO ANOTHER VERSION, HOW MUCH MONEY WAS GOING TO BE DONATED TO THE POPULAR ALLIANCE.

"TERITO" WAS THE OWNER OF NUMEROUS COMPANIES THANKS TO TOBACCO SMUGGLING AND WAS **THE FIRST CHIEF OF THE RÍA DE AROUSA.**

AND ALSO A STAUNCH SUPPORTER AND **PERSONAL FRIEND OF MANUEL FRAGA.**

WHILE VICENTE GUARANTEED THE MAJORITY OF THE VOTES OF THE REGION, MANUEL DECORATED HIM FROM THE PARTY.

IN THE AREA SURROUNDING THE PARADOR, GUNSHOTS COULD BE HEARD, CARS REVVING IN THE DARK AND THEN...

...SILENCE.

THE RIGHT ARM OF "TERITO" WAS **JOSÉ MANUEL "NENÉ" BARRAL.**

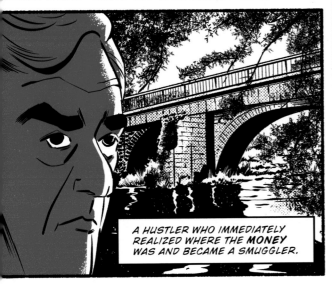

A HUSTLER WHO IMMEDIATELY REALIZED WHERE THE **MONEY** WAS AND BECAME A SMUGGLER.

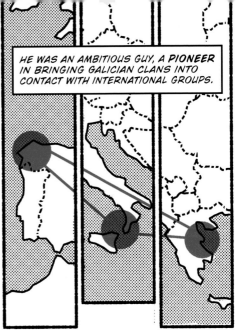

HE WAS AN AMBITIOUS GUY, A **PIONEER** IN BRINGING GALICIAN CLANS INTO CONTACT WITH INTERNATIONAL GROUPS.

"NENÉ" WAS ALSO A POPULAR ACTIVIST, BUT WOULD GO FURTHER BY BECOMING MAYOR OF **RIBADUMIA** IN A LANDSLIDE VICTORY AND ANNOUNCE THAT HE WAS **STOPPING** THE SMUGGLING.

A YOUNG **MARIANO RAJOY,** WHO DISTRUSTED THE TIES THAT THE PARTY HAD WITH THESE BOSSES, COMMUNICATED IT TO FRAGA.

DON MANUEL, VISIBLY **ANNOYED,** ADVISED HIM:

COME ON, MARIANO, GO TO MADRID, LEARN GALICIAN, GET MARRIED AND HAVE CHILDREN.

OVER TIME, THE RESIGNATION OF "NENÉ" WAS PROVEN FALSE AND, DESPITE HIS 18 YEARS AS A MAYOR, HE WAS CAUGHT IN 2001 TRAFFICKING IN PACKS WORTH **1.2 MILLION EUROS\*.**

EVEN SO, HE WOULD DECLARE:

I HAVE BEEN HONORED AND HONEST IN PUBLIC LIFE, MY **MISTAKE** IS PRIVATE.

I APOLOGIZE. I AM LEAVING SO THAT THE NAME OF RIBADUMIA IS NOT LINKED TO **CRIMINAL ACTIVITIES.**

*\*ABOUT $2 MILLION USD TODAY*

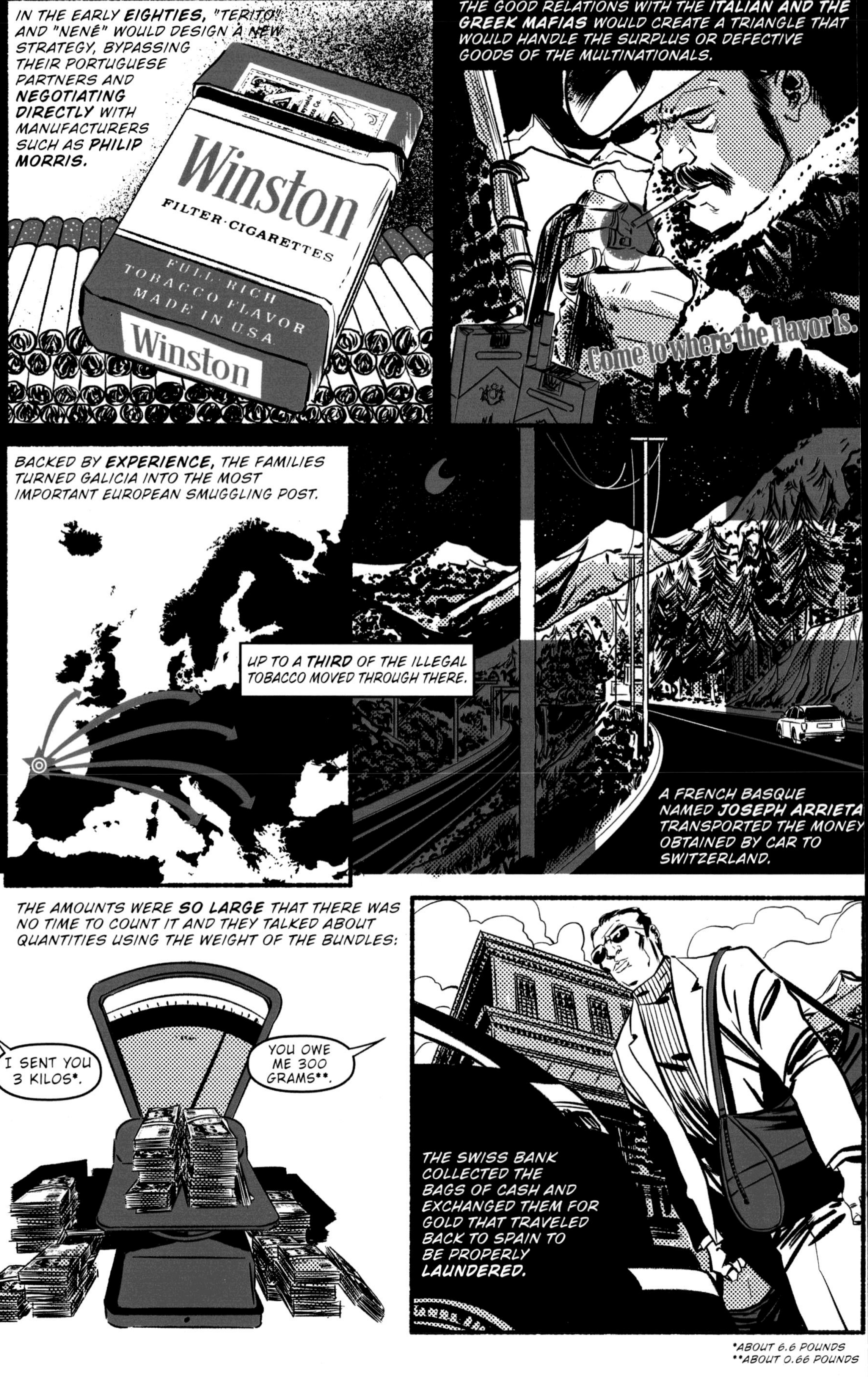
IN THE EARLY **EIGHTIES**, "TERITO" AND "NENÉ" WOULD DESIGN A NEW STRATEGY, BYPASSING THEIR PORTUGUESE PARTNERS AND **NEGOTIATING DIRECTLY** WITH MANUFACTURERS SUCH AS **PHILIP MORRIS.**
Winston
FILTER·CIGARETTES
FULL RICH TOBACCO FLAVOR MADE IN U.S.A.
Winston
THE GOOD RELATIONS WITH THE **ITALIAN AND THE GREEK MAFIAS** WOULD CREATE A TRIANGLE THAT WOULD HANDLE THE SURPLUS OR DEFECTIVE GOODS OF THE MULTINATIONALS.
Come to where the flavor is.
BACKED BY **EXPERIENCE,** THE FAMILIES TURNED GALICIA INTO THE MOST IMPORTANT EUROPEAN SMUGGLING POST.
UP TO A **THIRD** OF THE ILLEGAL TOBACCO MOVED THROUGH THERE.
A FRENCH BASQUE NAMED **JOSEPH ARRIETA** TRANSPORTED THE MONEY OBTAINED BY CAR TO SWITZERLAND.
THE AMOUNTS WERE **SO LARGE** THAT THERE WAS NO TIME TO COUNT IT AND THEY TALKED ABOUT QUANTITIES USING THE WEIGHT OF THE BUNDLES:
I SENT YOU 3 KILOS*.
YOU OWE ME 300 GRAMS**.
THE SWISS BANK COLLECTED THE BAGS OF CASH AND EXCHANGED THEM FOR GOLD THAT TRAVELED BACK TO SPAIN TO BE PROPERLY **LAUNDERED.**

*ABOUT 6.6 POUNDS
**ABOUT 0.66 POUNDS

*HIS WOULD BE KNOWN AS...*

# "PESETA CONNECTION"

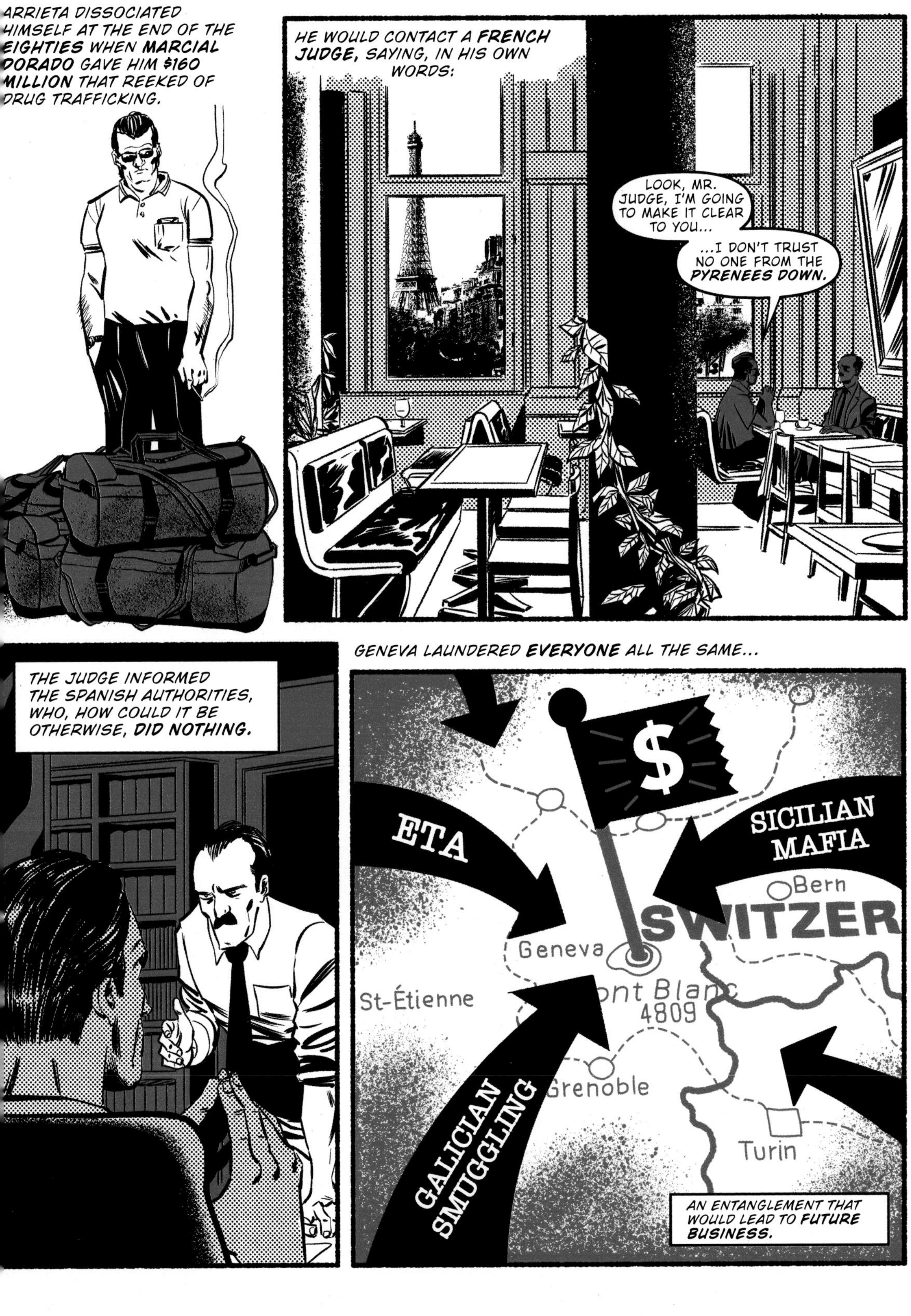
ARRIETA DISSOCIATED HIMSELF AT THE END OF THE EIGHTIES WHEN MARCIAL DORADO GAVE HIM $160 MILLION THAT REEKED OF DRUG TRAFFICKING.
HE WOULD CONTACT A FRENCH JUDGE, SAYING, IN HIS OWN WORDS:
LOOK, MR. JUDGE, I'M GOING TO MAKE IT CLEAR TO YOU...
...I DON'T TRUST NO ONE FROM THE PYRENEES DOWN.
THE JUDGE INFORMED THE SPANISH AUTHORITIES, WHO, HOW COULD IT BE OTHERWISE, DID NOTHING.
GENEVA LAUNDERED EVERYONE ALL THE SAME...
$
ETA
SICILIAN MAFIA
Bern
SWITZER
Geneva
St-Étienne
ont Blanc
4809
Grenoble
Turin
GALICIAN SMUGGLING
AN ENTANGLEMENT THAT WOULD LEAD TO FUTURE BUSINESS.

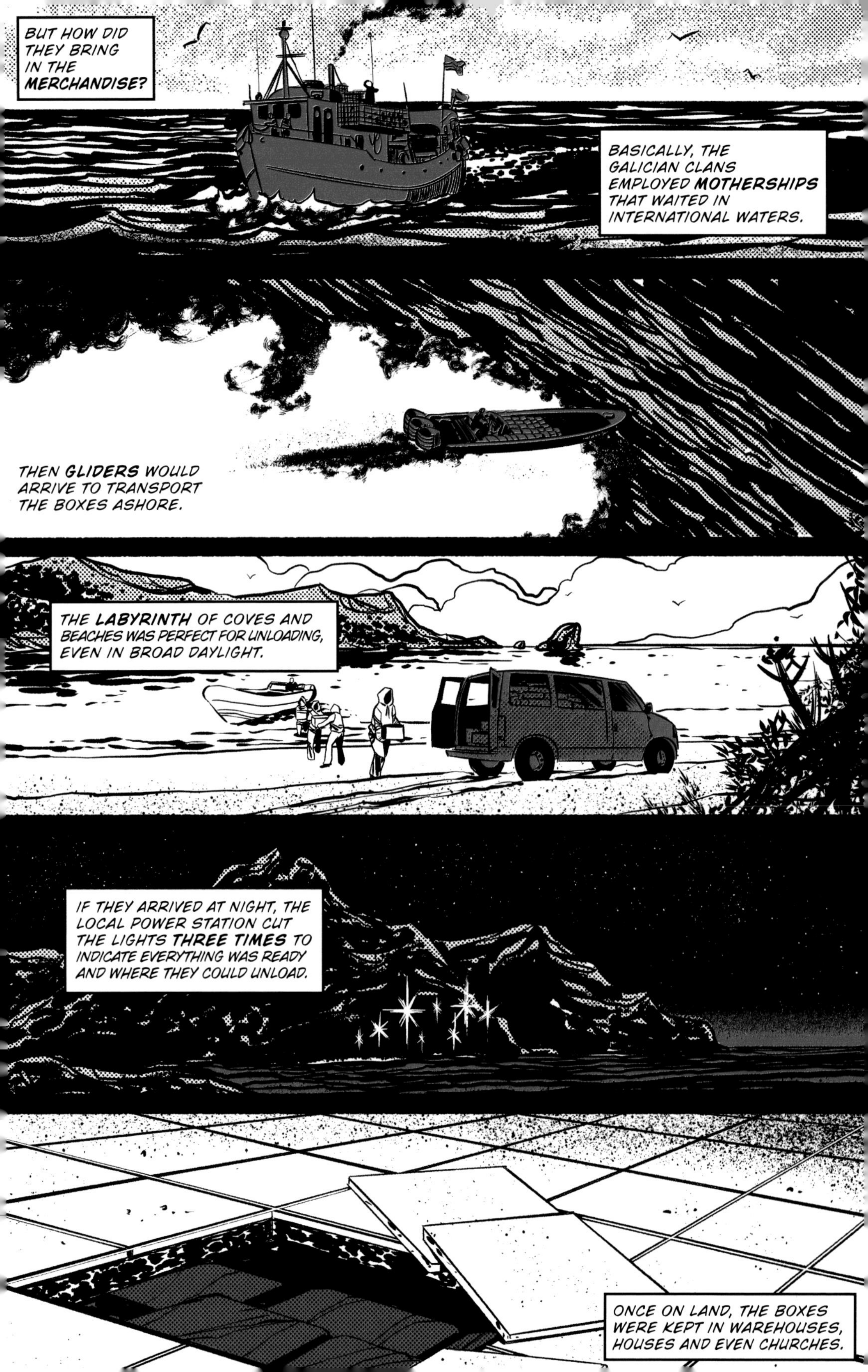
BUT HOW DID THEY BRING IN THE MERCHANDISE?
BASICALLY, THE GALICIAN CLANS EMPLOYED MOTHERSHIPS THAT WAITED IN INTERNATIONAL WATERS.
THEN GLIDERS WOULD ARRIVE TO TRANSPORT THE BOXES ASHORE.
THE LABYRINTH OF COVES AND BEACHES WAS PERFECT FOR UNLOADING, EVEN IN BROAD DAYLIGHT.
IF THEY ARRIVED AT NIGHT, THE LOCAL POWER STATION CUT THE LIGHTS THREE TIMES TO INDICATE EVERYTHING WAS READY AND WHERE THEY COULD UNLOAD.
ONCE ON LAND, THE BOXES WERE KEPT IN WAREHOUSES, HOUSES AND EVEN CHURCHES.

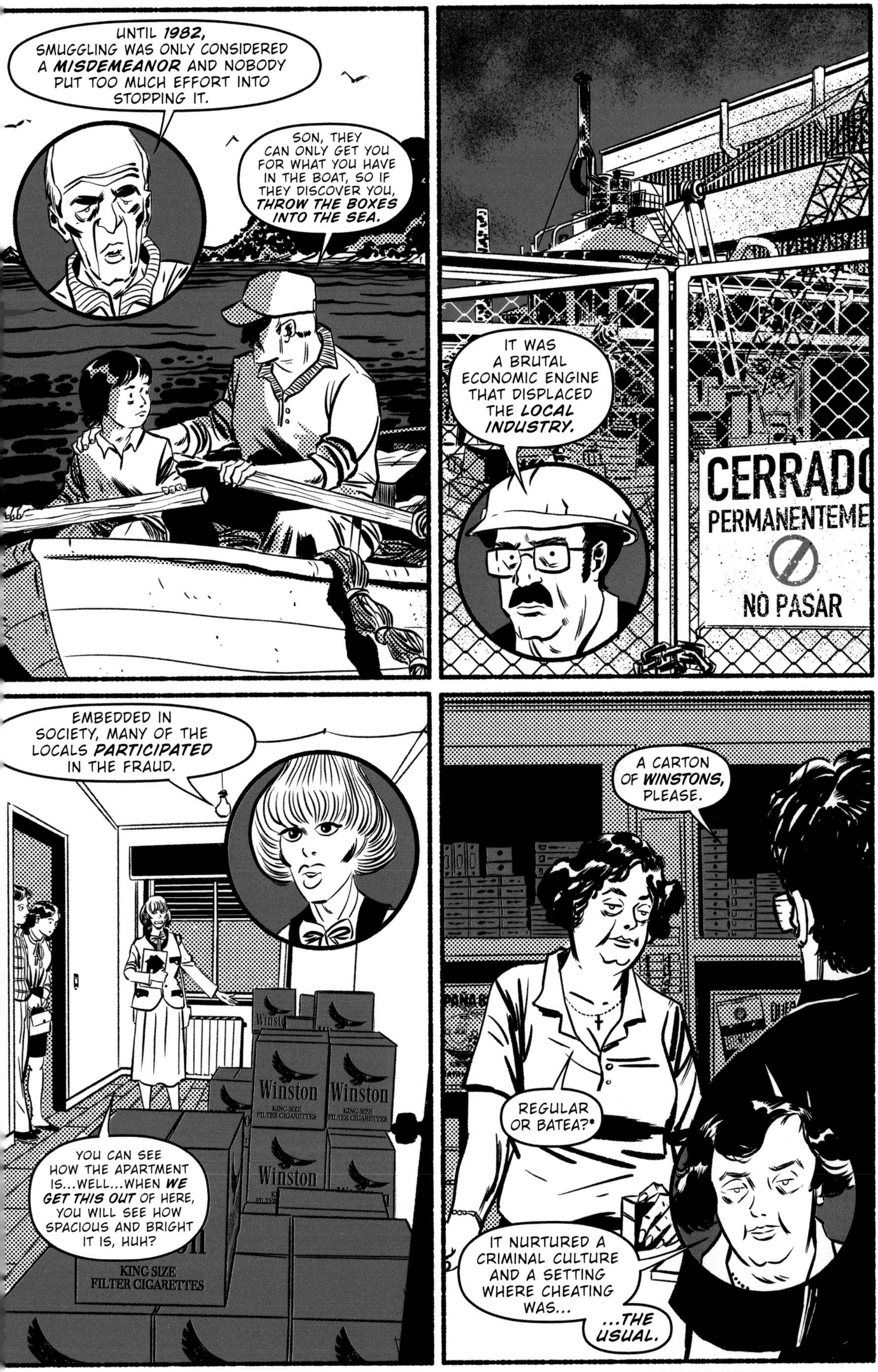
UNTIL 1982, SMUGGLING WAS ONLY CONSIDERED A MISDEMEANOR AND NOBODY PUT TOO MUCH EFFORT INTO STOPPING IT.
SON, THEY CAN ONLY GET YOU FOR WHAT YOU HAVE IN THE BOAT, SO IF THEY DISCOVER YOU, THROW THE BOXES INTO THE SEA.
IT WAS A BRUTAL ECONOMIC ENGINE THAT DISPLACED THE LOCAL INDUSTRY.
CERRADO
PERMANENTEME
NO PASAR
EMBEDDED IN SOCIETY, MANY OF THE LOCALS PARTICIPATED IN THE FRAUD.
Winston
KING SIZE FILTER CIGARETTES
YOU CAN SEE HOW THE APARTMENT IS...WELL...WHEN WE GET THIS OUT OF HERE, YOU WILL SEE HOW SPACIOUS AND BRIGHT IT IS, HUH?
A CARTON OF WINSTONS, PLEASE.
REGULAR OR BATEA?*
IT NURTURED A CRIMINAL CULTURE AND A SETTING WHERE CHEATING WAS...
...THE USUAL.

*BATEA: MUSSEL FARMS USED TO STORE CONTRABAND.

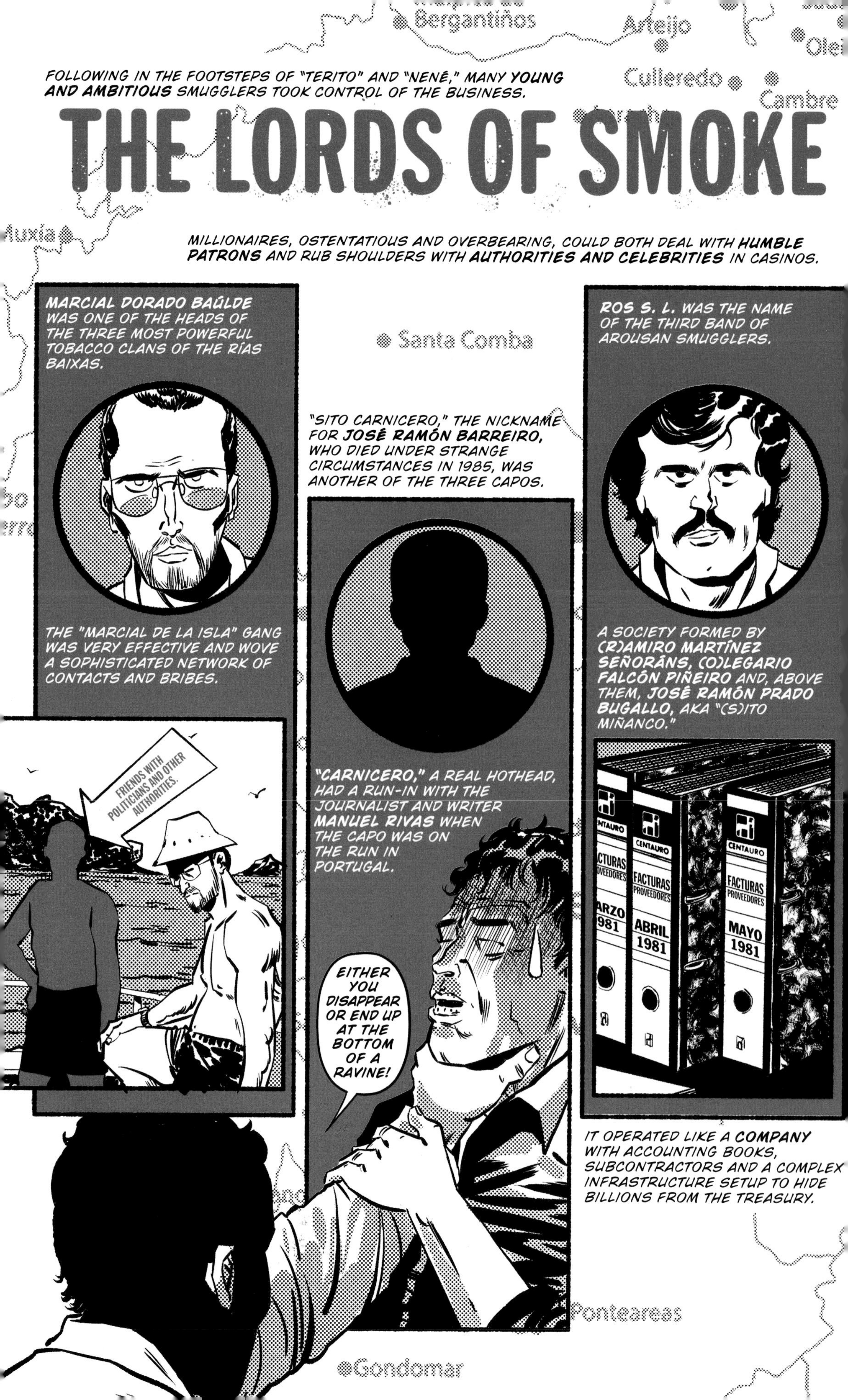

Bergantiños
Arteijo
Culleredo
Cambre
FOLLOWING IN THE FOOTSTEPS OF "TERITO" AND "NENÉ," MANY **YOUNG AND AMBITIOUS** SMUGGLERS TOOK CONTROL OF THE BUSINESS.
THE LORDS OF SMOKE
MILLIONAIRES, OSTENTATIOUS AND OVERBEARING, COULD BOTH DEAL WITH **HUMBLE PATRONS** AND RUB SHOULDERS WITH **AUTHORITIES AND CELEBRITIES** IN CASINOS.
**MARCIAL DORADO BAÚLDE** WAS ONE OF THE HEADS OF THE THREE MOST POWERFUL TOBACCO CLANS OF THE RÍAS BAIXAS.
THE "MARCIAL DE LA ISLA" GANG WAS VERY EFFECTIVE AND WOVE A SOPHISTICATED NETWORK OF CONTACTS AND BRIBES.
FRIENDS WITH POLITICIANS AND OTHER AUTHORITIES.
Santa Comba
"SITO CARNICERO," THE NICKNAME FOR **JOSÉ RAMÓN BARREIRO,** WHO DIED UNDER STRANGE CIRCUMSTANCES IN 1985, WAS ANOTHER OF THE THREE CAPOS.
**"CARNICERO,"** A REAL HOTHEAD, HAD A RUN-IN WITH THE JOURNALIST AND WRITER **MANUEL RIVAS** WHEN THE CAPO WAS ON THE RUN IN PORTUGAL.
EITHER YOU DISAPPEAR OR END UP AT THE BOTTOM OF A RAVINE!
**ROS S. L.** WAS THE NAME OF THE THIRD BAND OF AROUSAN SMUGGLERS.
A SOCIETY FORMED BY **(R)AMIRO MARTÍNEZ SEÑORÁNS, (O)LEGARIO FALCÓN PIÑEIRO** AND, ABOVE THEM, **JOSÉ RAMÓN PRADO BUGALLO,** AKA "(S)ITO MIÑANCO."
CENTAURO
FACTURAS PROVEEDORES
ABRIL 1981
CENTAURO
FACTURAS PROVEEDORES
MAYO 1981
IT OPERATED LIKE A **COMPANY** WITH ACCOUNTING BOOKS, SUBCONTRACTORS AND A COMPLEX INFRASTRUCTURE SETUP TO HIDE BILLIONS FROM THE TREASURY.
Ponteareas
Gondomar

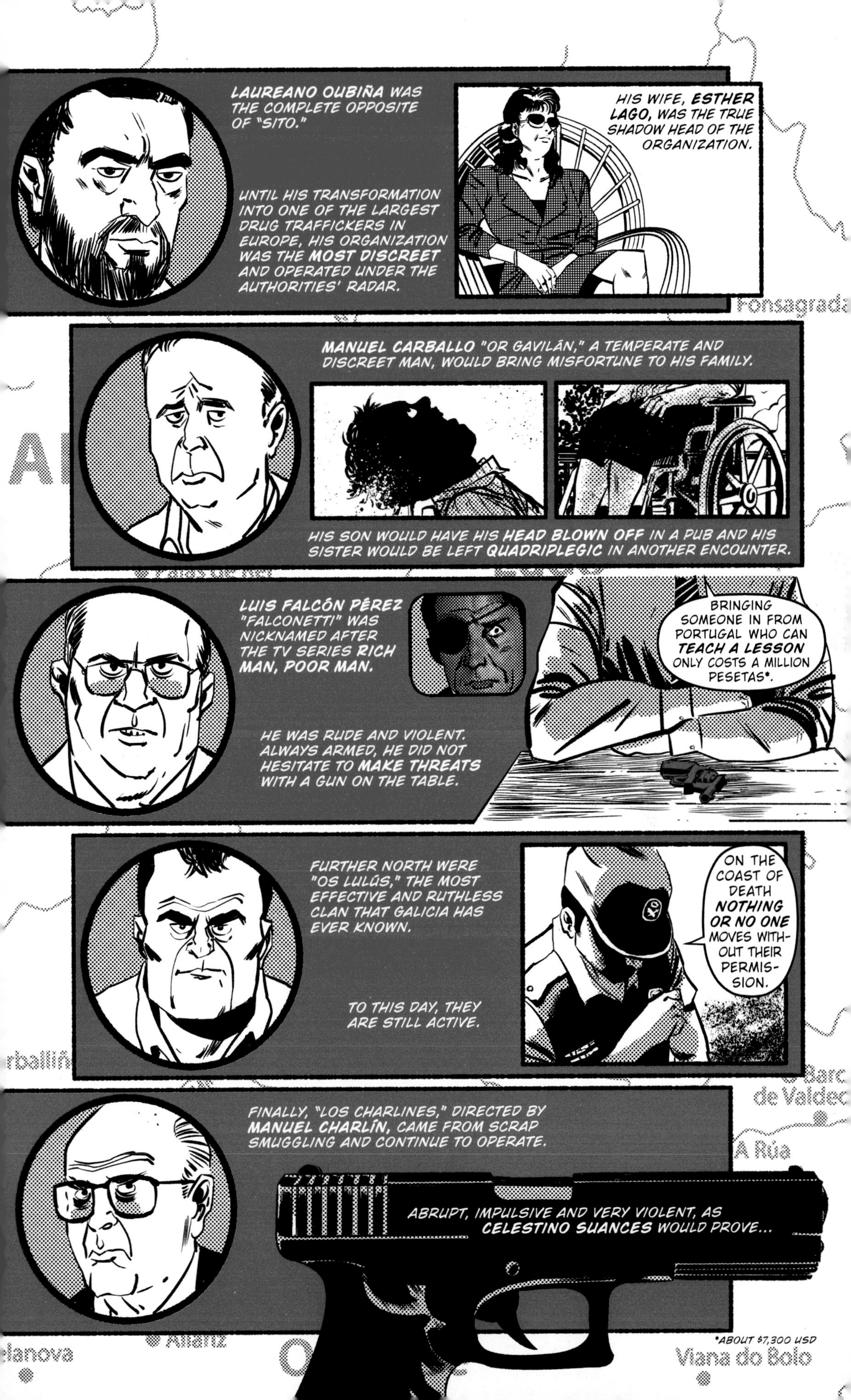

LAUREANO OUBIÑA WAS THE COMPLETE OPPOSITE OF "SITO."
UNTIL HIS TRANSFORMATION INTO ONE OF THE LARGEST DRUG TRAFFICKERS IN EUROPE, HIS ORGANIZATION WAS THE MOST DISCREET AND OPERATED UNDER THE AUTHORITIES' RADAR.
HIS WIFE, ESTHER LAGO, WAS THE TRUE SHADOW HEAD OF THE ORGANIZATION.
MANUEL CARBALLO "OR GAVILÁN," A TEMPERATE AND DISCREET MAN, WOULD BRING MISFORTUNE TO HIS FAMILY.
HIS SON WOULD HAVE HIS HEAD BLOWN OFF IN A PUB AND HIS SISTER WOULD BE LEFT QUADRIPLEGIC IN ANOTHER ENCOUNTER.
LUIS FALCÓN PÉREZ "FALCONETTI" WAS NICKNAMED AFTER THE TV SERIES RICH MAN, POOR MAN.
BRINGING SOMEONE IN FROM PORTUGAL WHO CAN TEACH A LESSON ONLY COSTS A MILLION PESETAS*.
HE WAS RUDE AND VIOLENT. ALWAYS ARMED, HE DID NOT HESITATE TO MAKE THREATS WITH A GUN ON THE TABLE.
FURTHER NORTH WERE "OS LULÚS," THE MOST EFFECTIVE AND RUTHLESS CLAN THAT GALICIA HAS EVER KNOWN.
ON THE COAST OF DEATH NOTHING OR NO ONE MOVES WITHOUT THEIR PERMISSION.
TO THIS DAY, THEY ARE STILL ACTIVE.
FINALLY, "LOS CHARLINES," DIRECTED BY MANUEL CHARLÍN, CAME FROM SCRAP SMUGGLING AND CONTINUE TO OPERATE.
ABRUPT, IMPULSIVE AND VERY VIOLENT, AS CELESTINO SUANCES WOULD PROVE...
*ABOUT $7,300 USD
Fonsagrada
A Rúa
de Valdeo
Viana do Bolo

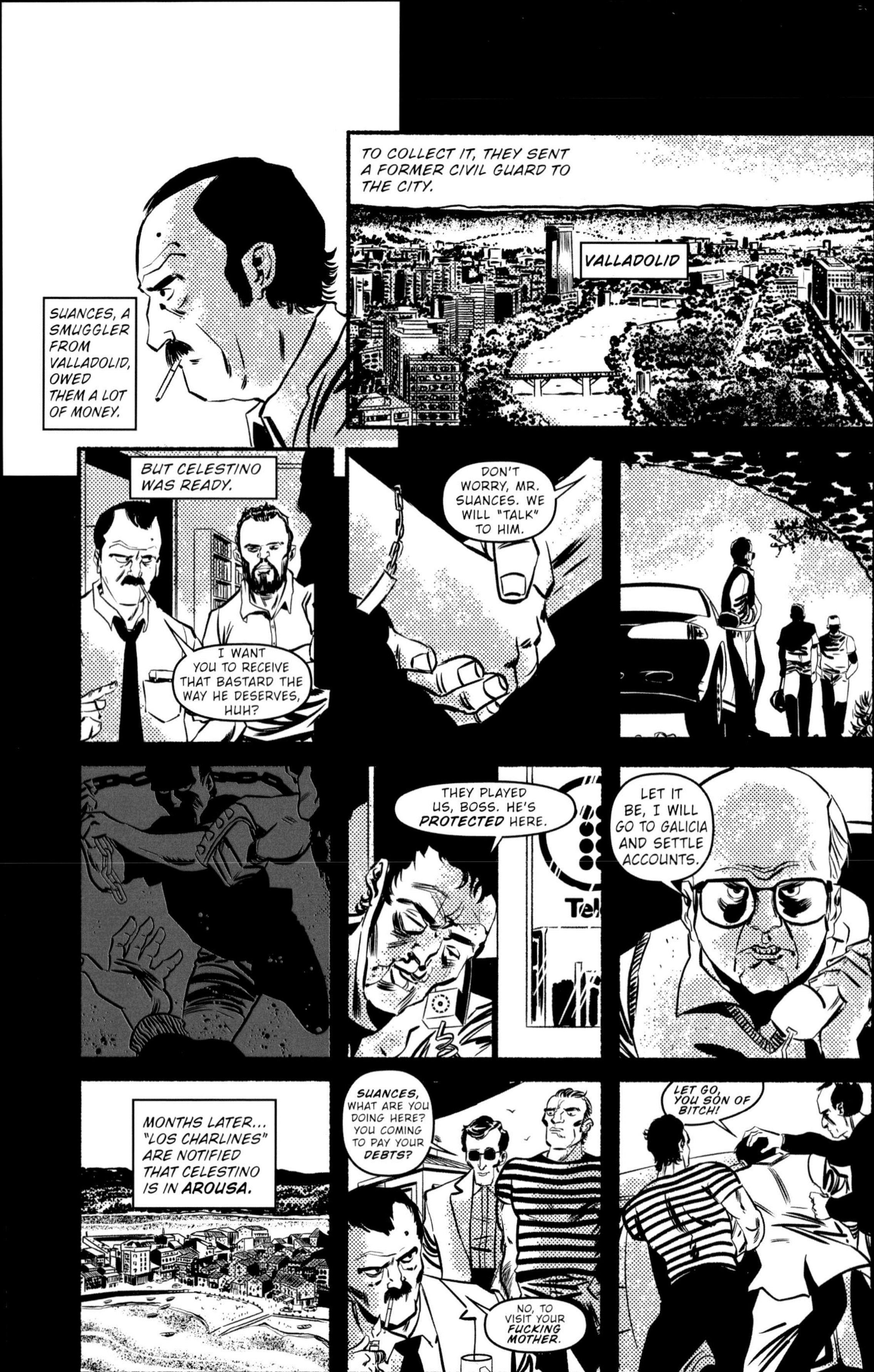
SUANCES, A SMUGGLER FROM VALLADOLID, OWED THEM A LOT OF MONEY.
TO COLLECT IT, THEY SENT A FORMER CIVIL GUARD TO THE CITY.
VALLADOLID
BUT CELESTINO WAS READY.
I WANT YOU TO RECEIVE THAT BASTARD THE WAY HE DESERVES, HUH?
DON'T WORRY, MR. SUANCES. WE WILL "TALK" TO HIM.
THEY PLAYED US, BOSS. HE'S PROTECTED HERE.
LET IT BE, I WILL GO TO GALICIA AND SETTLE ACCOUNTS.
MONTHS LATER... "LOS CHARLINES" ARE NOTIFIED THAT CELESTINO IS IN AROUSA.
SUANCES, WHAT ARE YOU DOING HERE? YOU COMING TO PAY YOUR DEBTS?
NO, TO VISIT YOUR FUCKING MOTHER.
LET GO, YOU SON OF BITCH!

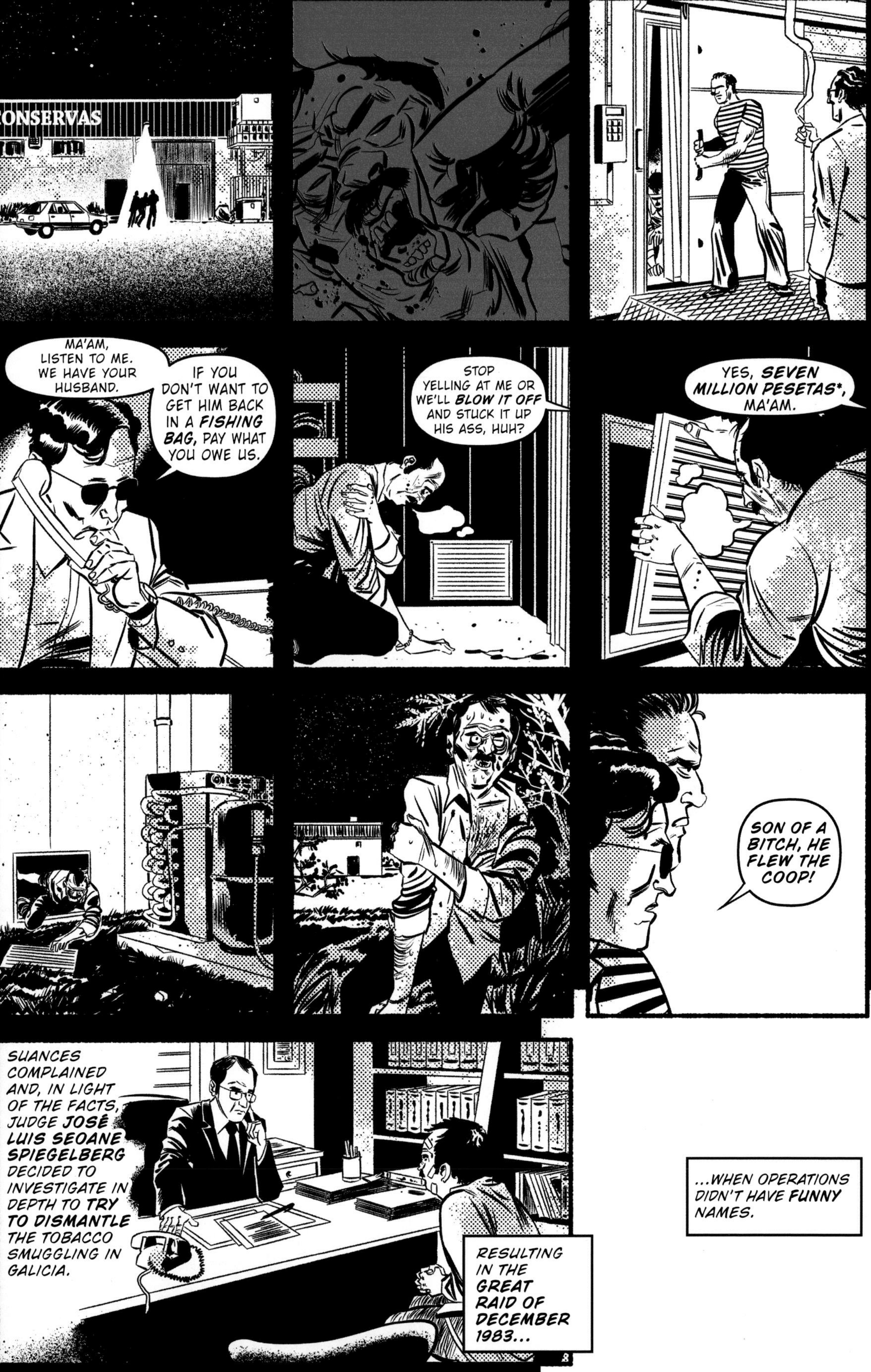
CONSERVAS
MA'AM, LISTEN TO ME. WE HAVE YOUR HUSBAND.
IF YOU DON'T WANT TO GET HIM BACK IN A FISHING BAG, PAY WHAT YOU OWE US.
STOP YELLING AT ME OR WE'LL BLOW IT OFF AND STUCK IT UP HIS ASS, HUH?
YES, SEVEN MILLION PESETAS*, MA'AM.
SON OF A BITCH, HE FLEW THE COOP!
SUANCES COMPLAINED AND, IN LIGHT OF THE FACTS, JUDGE JOSÉ LUIS SEOANE SPIEGELBERG DECIDED TO INVESTIGATE IN DEPTH TO TRY TO DISMANTLE THE TOBACCO SMUGGLING IN GALICIA.
RESULTING IN THE GREAT RAID OF DECEMBER 1983...
...WHEN OPERATIONS DIDN'T HAVE FUNNY NAMES.

*ABOUT $51,000 USD

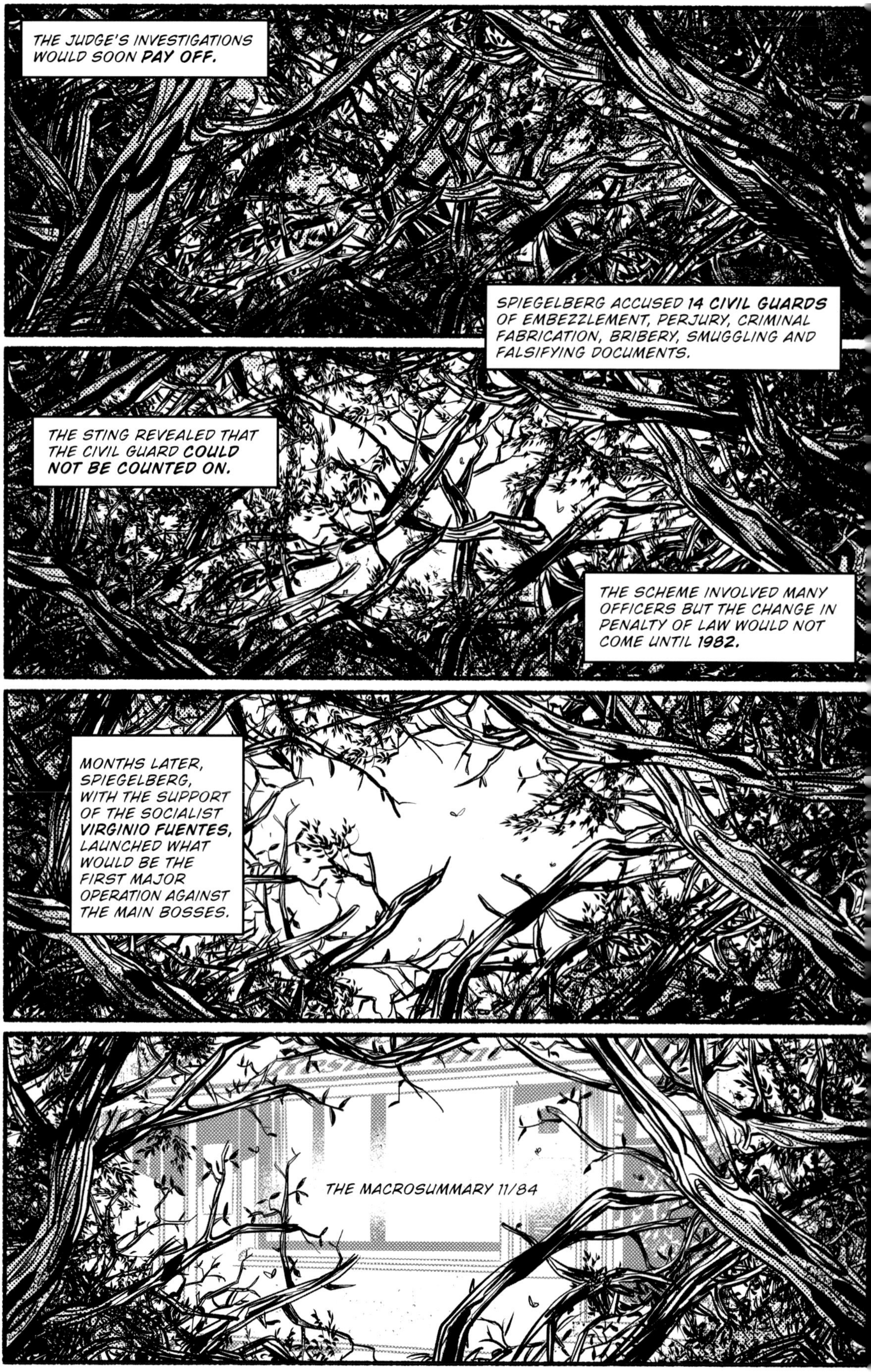
THE JUDGE'S INVESTIGATIONS WOULD SOON PAY OFF.
SPIEGELBERG ACCUSED 14 CIVIL GUARDS OF EMBEZZLEMENT, PERJURY, CRIMINAL FABRICATION, BRIBERY, SMUGGLING AND FALSIFYING DOCUMENTS.
THE STING REVEALED THAT THE CIVIL GUARD COULD NOT BE COUNTED ON.
THE SCHEME INVOLVED MANY OFFICERS BUT THE CHANGE IN PENALTY OF LAW WOULD NOT COME UNTIL 1982.
MONTHS LATER, SPIEGELBERG, WITH THE SUPPORT OF THE SOCIALIST VIRGINIO FUENTES, LAUNCHED WHAT WOULD BE THE FIRST MAJOR OPERATION AGAINST THE MAIN BOSSES.
THE MACROSUMMARY 11/84

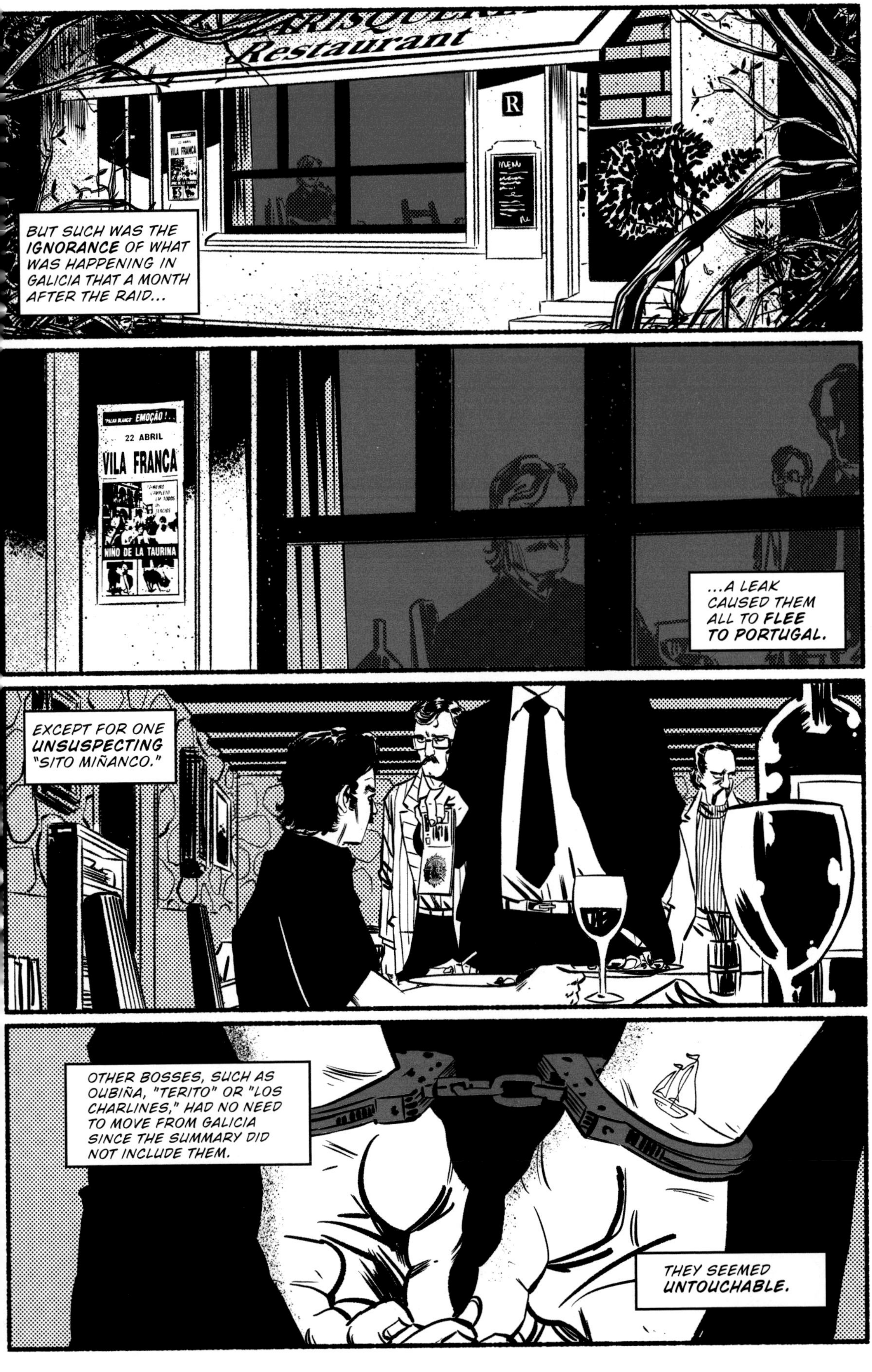
Restaurant
BUT SUCH WAS THE IGNORANCE OF WHAT WAS HAPPENING IN GALICIA THAT A MONTH AFTER THE RAID...
EMOÇÃO !..
22 ABRIL
VILA FRANCA
NIÑO DE LA TAURINA
...A LEAK CAUSED THEM ALL TO FLEE TO PORTUGAL.
EXCEPT FOR ONE UNSUSPECTING "SITO MIÑANCO."
OTHER BOSSES, SUCH AS OUBIÑA, "TERITO" OR "LOS CHARLINES," HAD NO NEED TO MOVE FROM GALICIA SINCE THE SUMMARY DID NOT INCLUDE THEM.
THEY SEEMED UNTOUCHABLE.

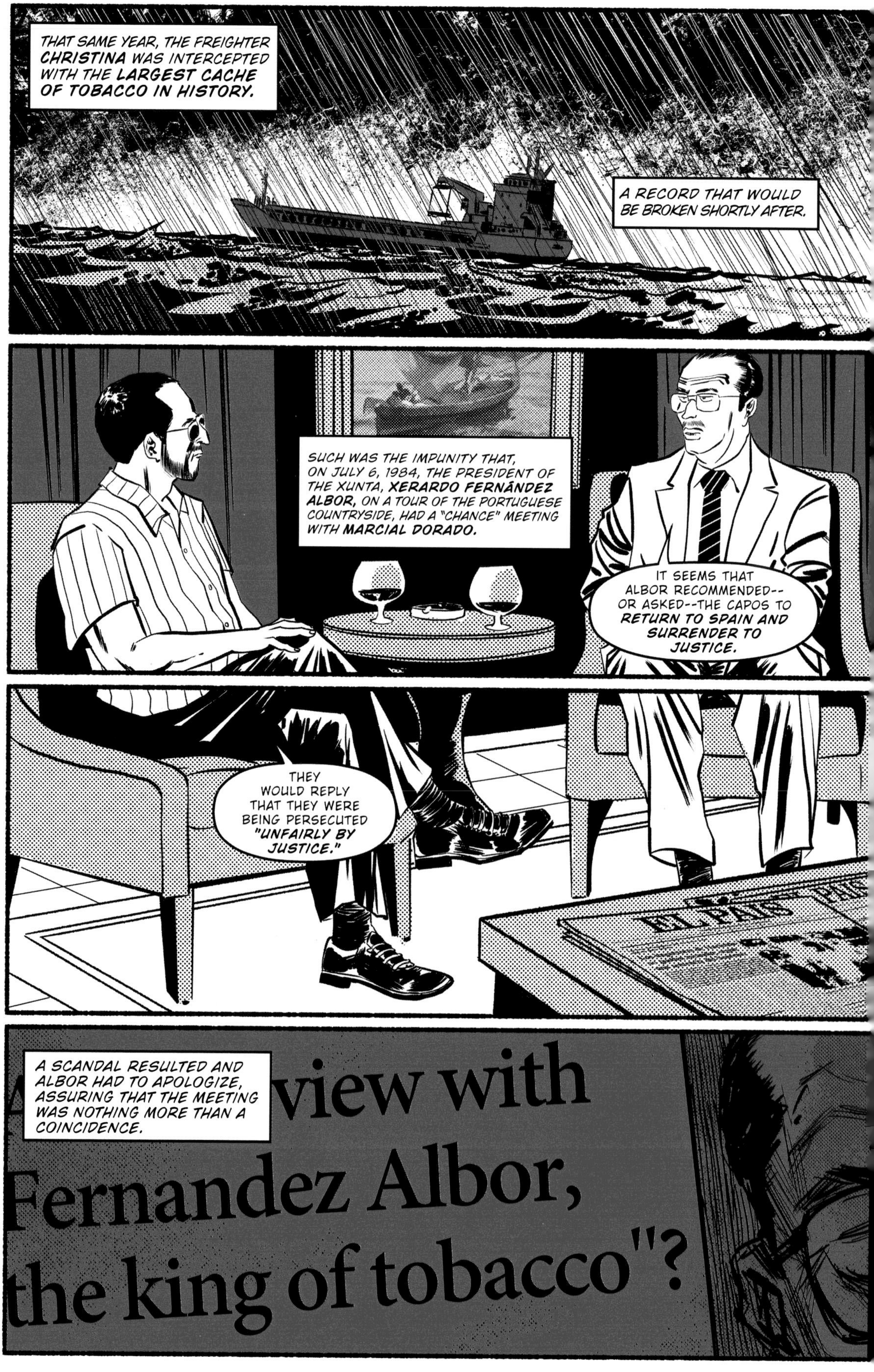

THAT SAME YEAR, THE FREIGHTER **CHRISTINA** WAS INTERCEPTED WITH THE **LARGEST CACHE OF TOBACCO IN HISTORY.**
A RECORD THAT WOULD BE BROKEN SHORTLY AFTER.
SUCH WAS THE IMPUNITY THAT, ON JULY 6, 1984, THE PRESIDENT OF THE XUNTA, **XERARDO FERNÁNDEZ ALBOR,** ON A TOUR OF THE PORTUGUESE COUNTRYSIDE, HAD A "CHANCE" MEETING WITH **MARCIAL DORADO.**
IT SEEMS THAT ALBOR RECOMMENDED--OR ASKED--THE CAPOS TO **RETURN TO SPAIN AND SURRENDER TO JUSTICE.**
THEY WOULD REPLY THAT THEY WERE BEING PERSECUTED **"UNFAIRLY BY JUSTICE."**
EL PAÍS
A SCANDAL RESULTED AND ALBOR HAD TO APOLOGIZE, ASSURING THAT THE MEETING WAS NOTHING MORE THAN A COINCIDENCE.
view with
Fernandez Albor,
the king of tobacco"?

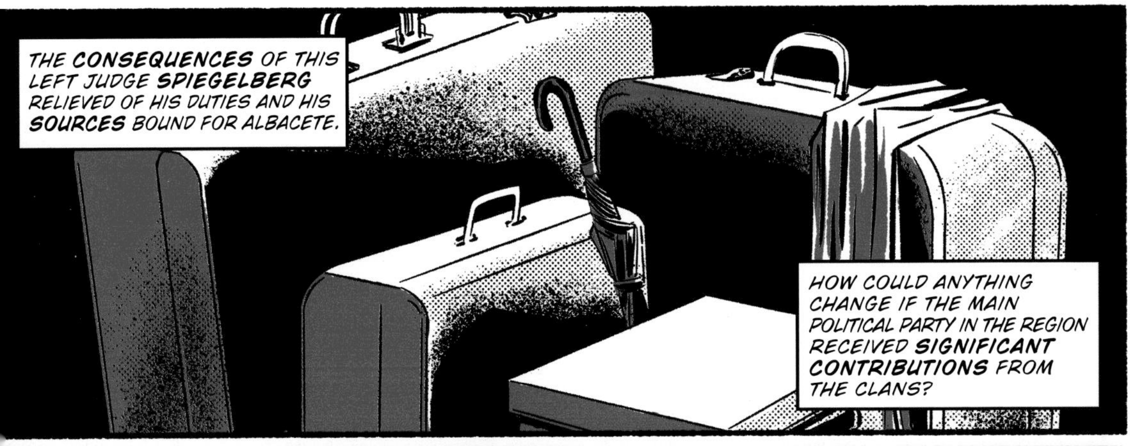
THE CONSEQUENCES OF THIS LEFT JUDGE SPIEGELBERG RELIEVED OF HIS DUTIES AND HIS SOURCES BOUND FOR ALBACETE.
HOW COULD ANYTHING CHANGE IF THE MAIN POLITICAL PARTY IN THE REGION RECEIVED SIGNIFICANT CONTRIBUTIONS FROM THE CLANS?

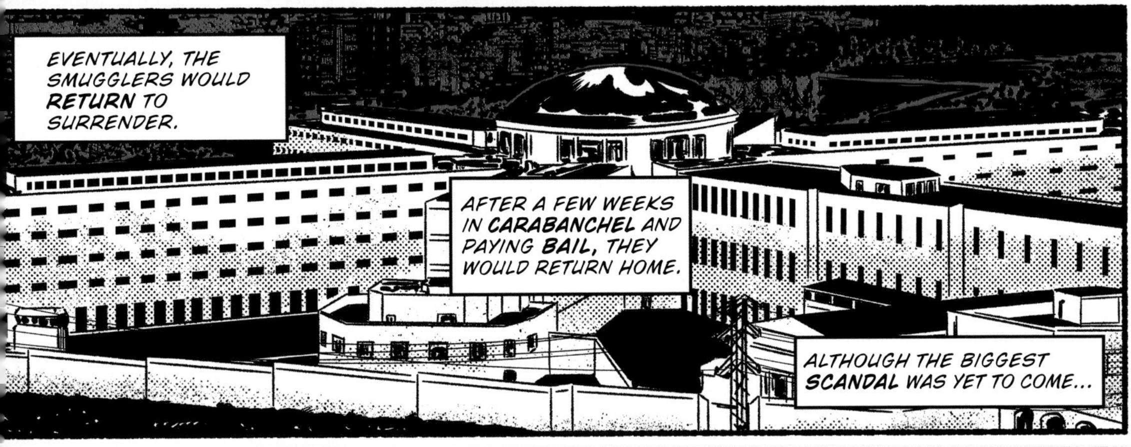
EVENTUALLY, THE SMUGGLERS WOULD RETURN TO SURRENDER.
AFTER A FEW WEEKS IN CARABANCHEL AND PAYING BAIL, THEY WOULD RETURN HOME.
ALTHOUGH THE BIGGEST SCANDAL WAS YET TO COME...

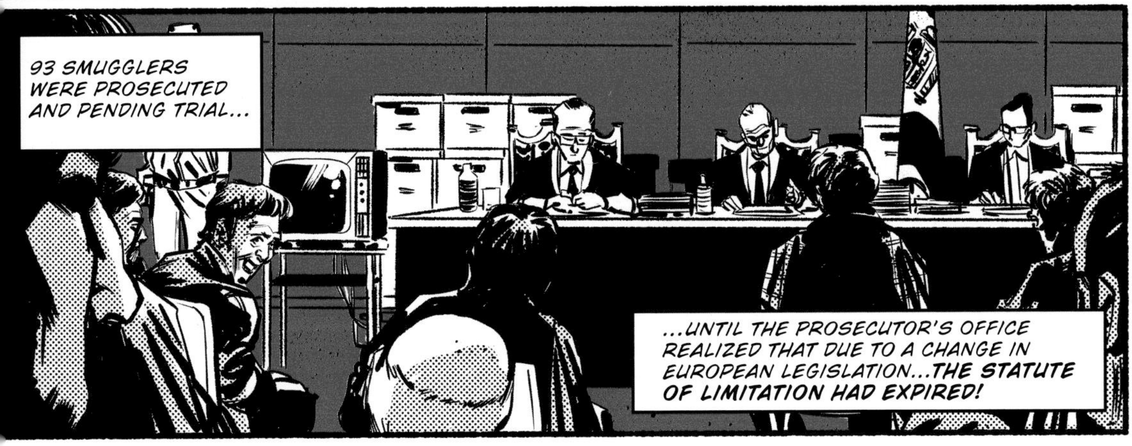
93 SMUGGLERS WERE PROSECUTED AND PENDING TRIAL...
...UNTIL THE PROSECUTOR'S OFFICE REALIZED THAT DUE TO A CHANGE IN EUROPEAN LEGISLATION...THE STATUTE OF LIMITATION HAD EXPIRED!

*THAT IMPUNITY, THE RECENT COLOMBIAN CONTACTS IN CARABANCHEL AND* ***THE AMAZING ABILITY TO PUT CARGO ON THE GROUND*** *WOULD LEAVE EVERYTHING READY FOR ...*

Part Two

# THE BIG JUMP

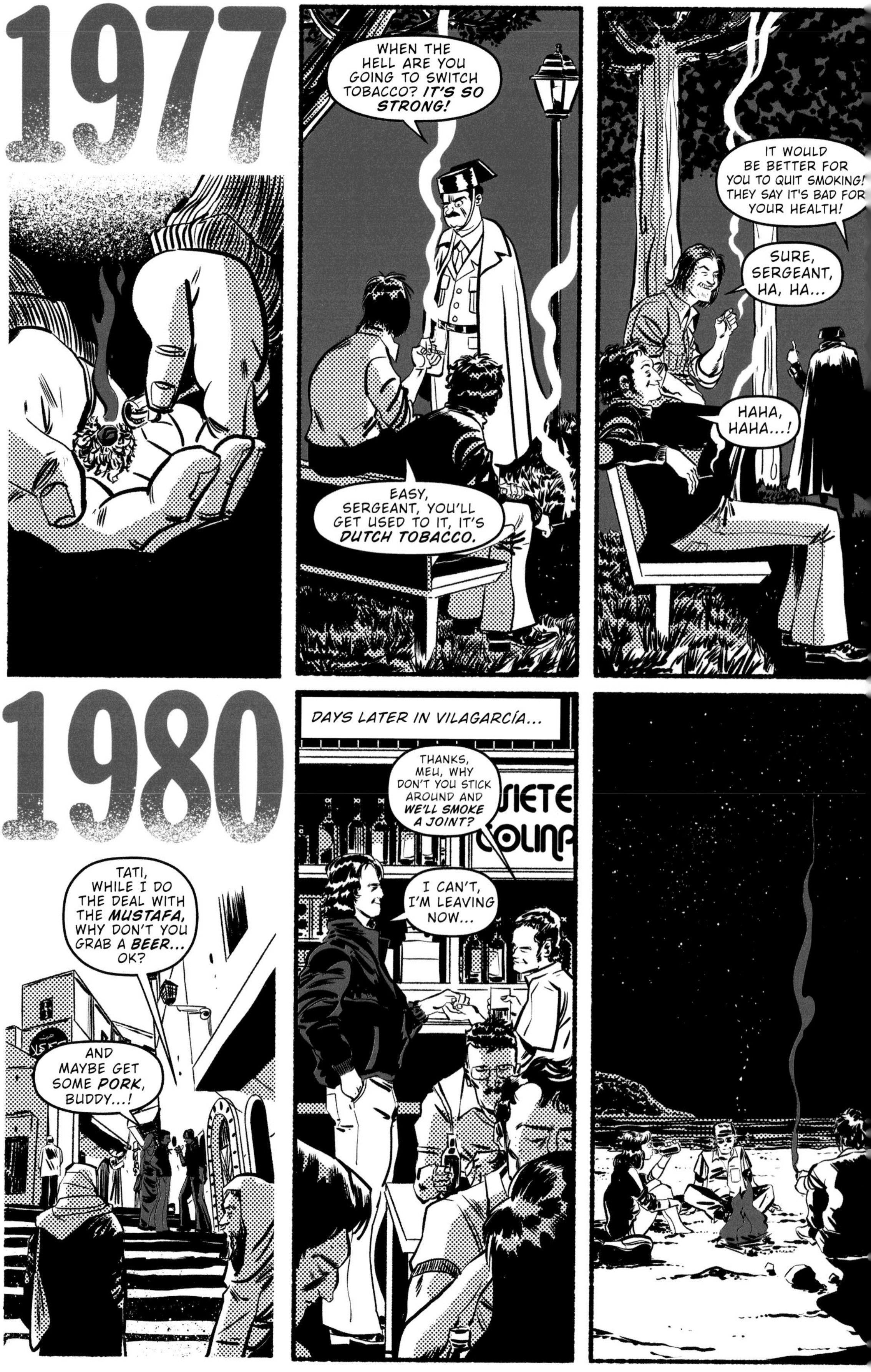
1977
WHEN THE HELL ARE YOU GOING TO SWITCH TOBACCO? IT'S SO STRONG!
EASY, SERGEANT, YOU'LL GET USED TO IT, IT'S DUTCH TOBACCO.
IT WOULD BE BETTER FOR YOU TO QUIT SMOKING! THEY SAY IT'S BAD FOR YOUR HEALTH!
SURE, SERGEANT, HA, HA...
HAHA, HAHA...!
1980
TATI, WHILE I DO THE DEAL WITH THE MUSTAFA, WHY DON'T YOU GRAB A BEER... OK?
AND MAYBE GET SOME PORK, BUDDY...!
DAYS LATER IN VILAGARCÍA...
THANKS, MEU, WHY DON'T YOU STICK AROUND AND WE'LL SMOKE A JOINT?
I CAN'T, I'M LEAVING NOW...
SIETE COLINA

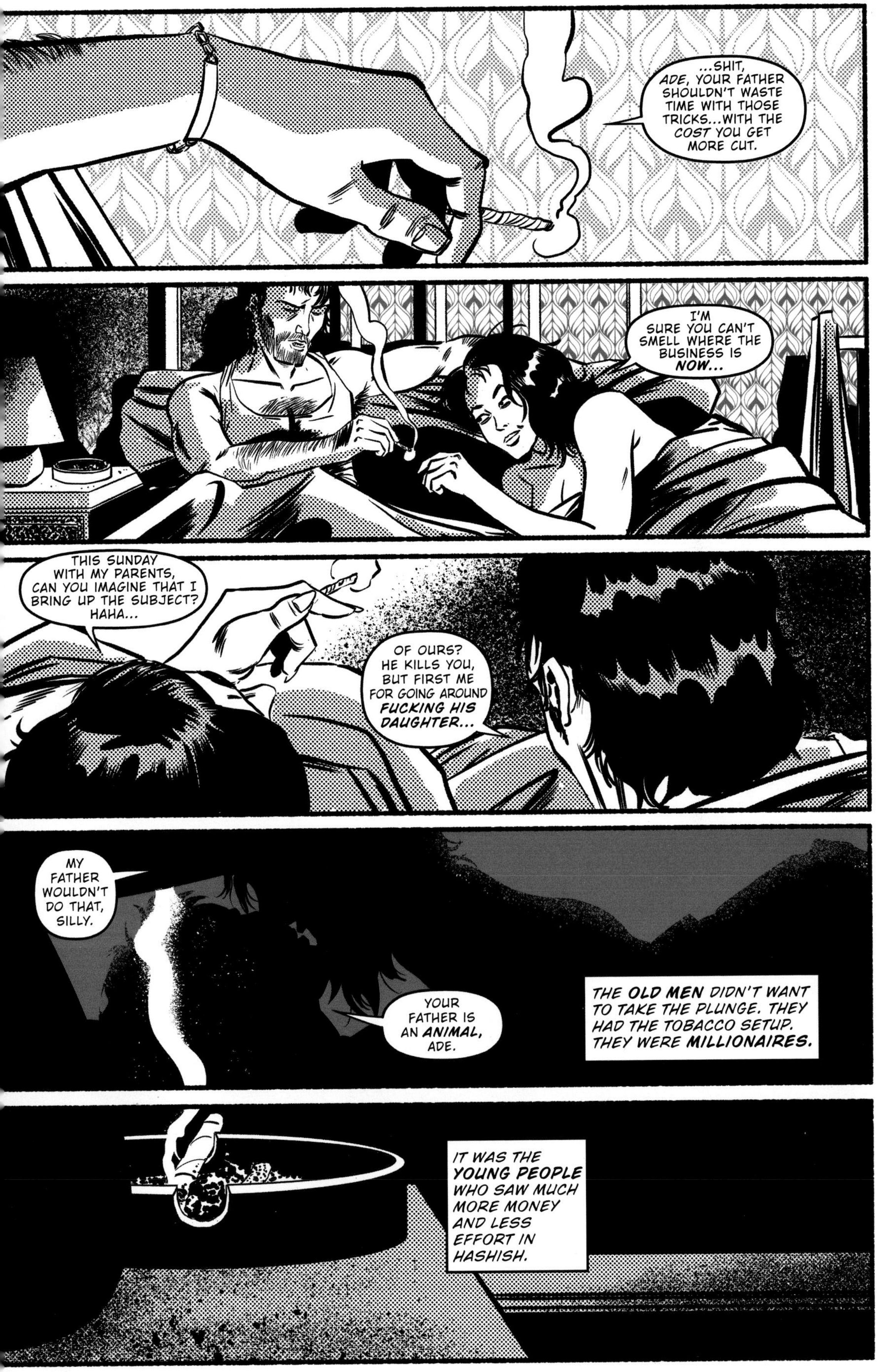
...SHIT, ADE, YOUR FATHER SHOULDN'T WASTE TIME WITH THOSE TRICKS...WITH THE COST YOU GET MORE CUT.
I'M SURE YOU CAN'T SMELL WHERE THE BUSINESS IS NOW...
THIS SUNDAY WITH MY PARENTS, CAN YOU IMAGINE THAT I BRING UP THE SUBJECT? HAHA...
OF OURS? HE KILLS YOU, BUT FIRST ME FOR GOING AROUND FUCKING HIS DAUGHTER...
MY FATHER WOULDN'T DO THAT, SILLY.
YOUR FATHER IS AN ANIMAL, ADE.
THE OLD MEN DIDN'T WANT TO TAKE THE PLUNGE. THEY HAD THE TOBACCO SETUP. THEY WERE MILLIONAIRES.
IT WAS THE YOUNG PEOPLE WHO SAW MUCH MORE MONEY AND LESS EFFORT IN HASHISH.

**LESS WORK, SAME RISK AND MUCH MORE MONEY.**

WITH THESE SLOGANS IT WAS NOT DIFFICULT FOR ADE AND HER BROTHERS TO CONVINCE THEIR FATHER, **MANUEL CHARLIN GAMA,** TO START TRAFFICKING HASHISH...

*...RECEIVING THE DUBIOUS HONOR OF BEING THE **FIRST** GALICIAN SMUGGLER TO SNEAK A DRUG CACHE INTO THE ESTUARY.*

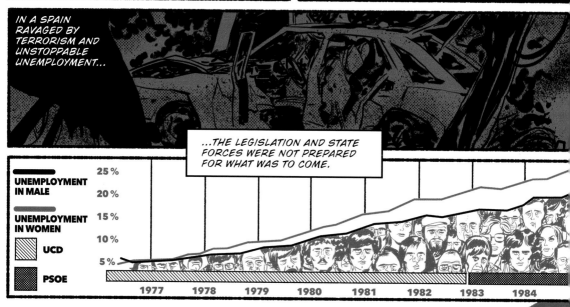

*IN A SPAIN RAVAGED BY TERRORISM AND UNSTOPPABLE UNEMPLOYMENT...*

*...THE LEGISLATION AND STATE FORCES WERE NOT PREPARED FOR WHAT WAS TO COME.*

| | | |
|---|---|---|
| ▬ **UNEMPLOYMENT IN MALE** | 25% | |
| | 20% | |
| ▬ **UNEMPLOYMENT IN WOMEN** | 15% | |
| ▧ **UCD** | 10% | |
| ■ **PSOE** | 5% | |

1977　1978　1979　1980　1981　1982　1983　1984

OUBIÑA, HARDENED BY SMUGGLING SCRAP METAL, DIESEL AND TOBACCO, AND WHO WOULD ALSO END UP MAKING THE LEAP, FELT JUSTIFIED...

IF I TRAFFICKED IN HASHISH, IT WAS BECAUSE I THOUGHT IT WOULD END UP BEING LEGALIZED.

TO MY KNOWLEDGE, NO ONE HAS DIED FROM CONSUMING IT.

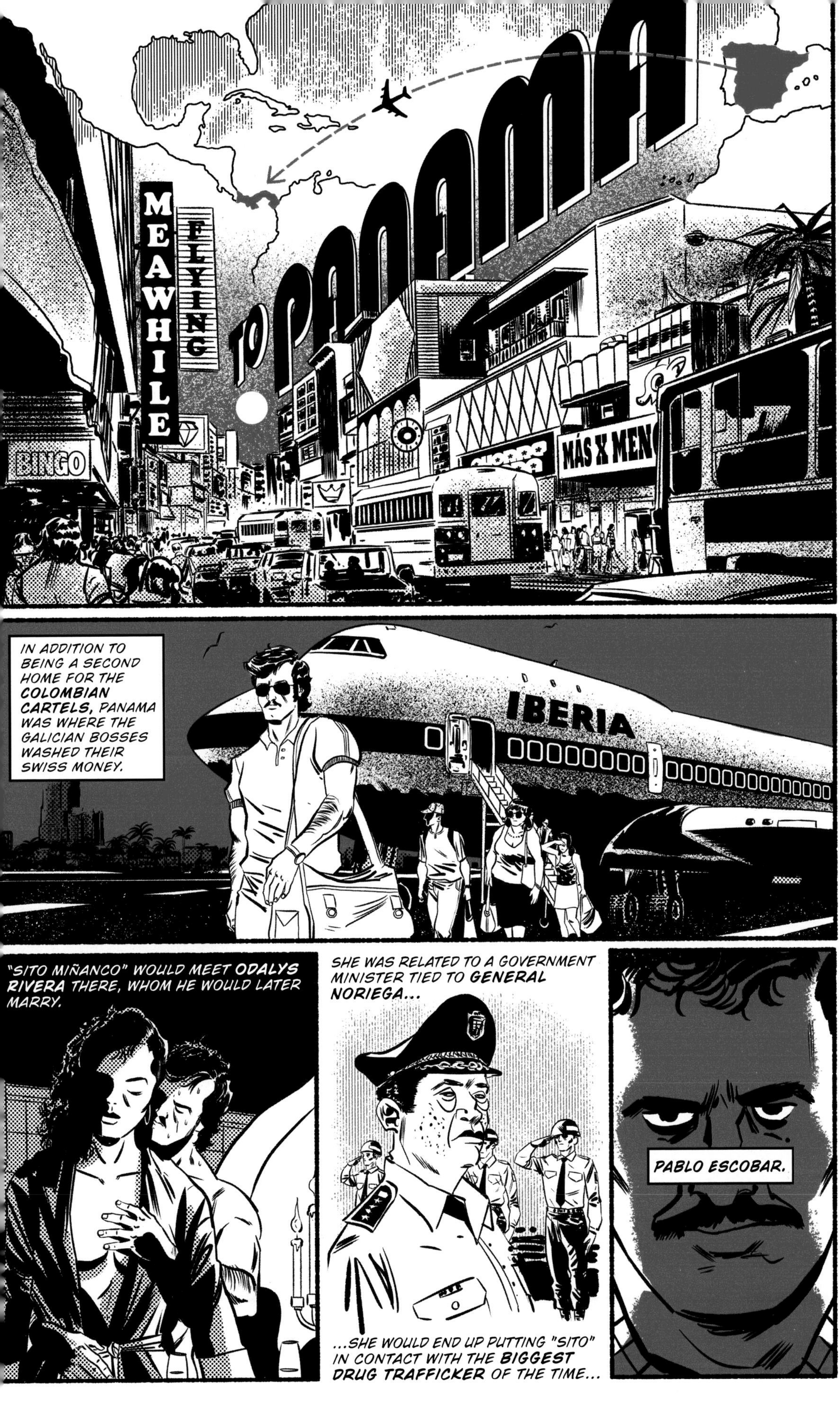
MEANWHILE
FLYING
TO PANAMA
BINGO
MÁS X MEN
IN ADDITION TO BEING A SECOND HOME FOR THE COLOMBIAN CARTELS, PANAMA WAS WHERE THE GALICIAN BOSSES WASHED THEIR SWISS MONEY.
IBERIA
"SITO MIÑANCO" WOULD MEET ODALYS RIVERA THERE, WHOM HE WOULD LATER MARRY.
SHE WAS RELATED TO A GOVERNMENT MINISTER TIED TO GENERAL NORIEGA...
...SHE WOULD END UP PUTTING "SITO" IN CONTACT WITH THE BIGGEST DRUG TRAFFICKER OF THE TIME...
PABLO ESCOBAR.

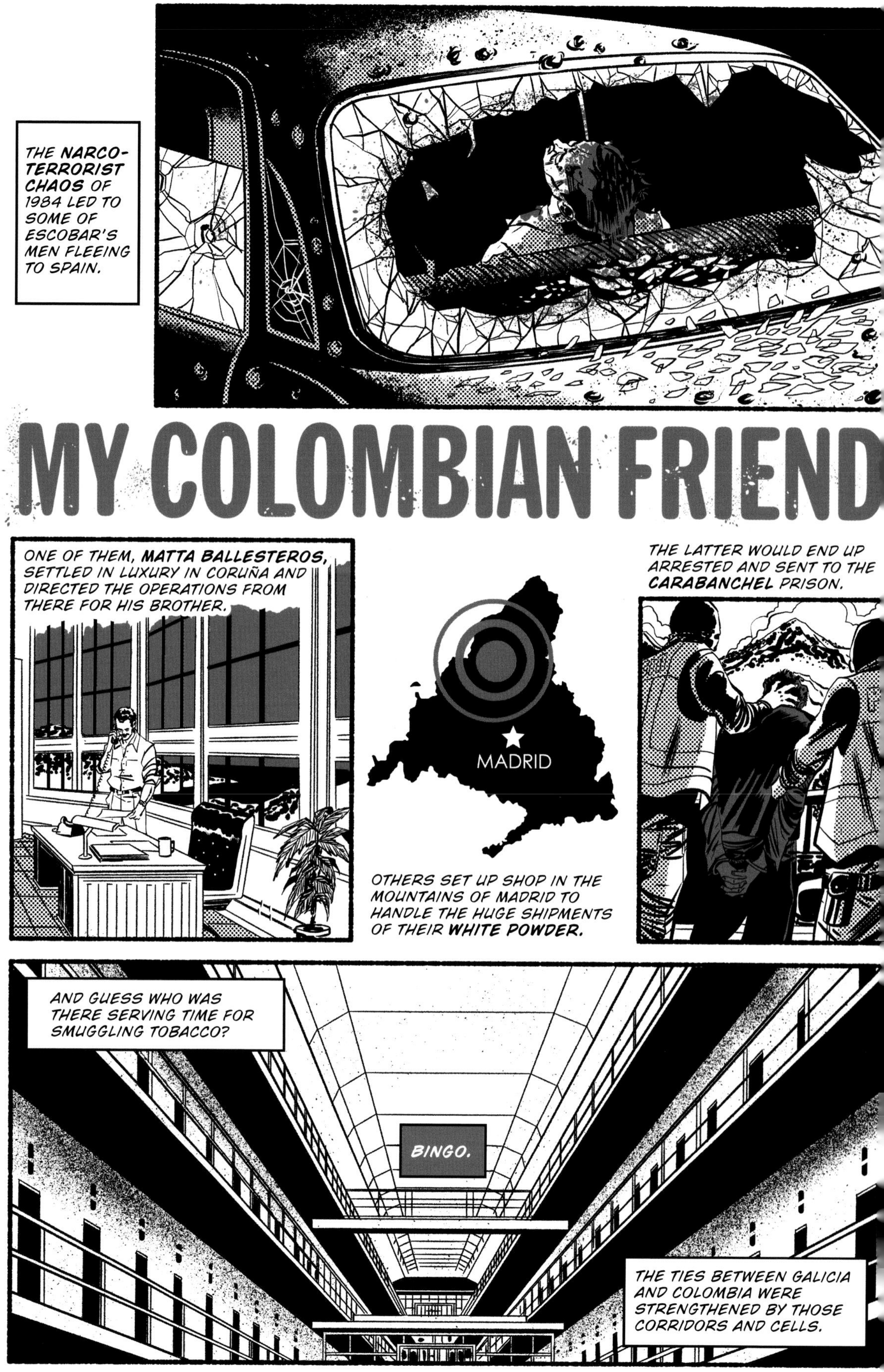
THE NARCO-TERRORIST CHAOS OF 1984 LED TO SOME OF ESCOBAR'S MEN FLEEING TO SPAIN.
MY COLOMBIAN FRIEND
ONE OF THEM, MATTA BALLESTEROS, SETTLED IN LUXURY IN CORUÑA AND DIRECTED THE OPERATIONS FROM THERE FOR HIS BROTHER.
MADRID
OTHERS SET UP SHOP IN THE MOUNTAINS OF MADRID TO HANDLE THE HUGE SHIPMENTS OF THEIR WHITE POWDER.
THE LATTER WOULD END UP ARRESTED AND SENT TO THE CARABANCHEL PRISON.
AND GUESS WHO WAS THERE SERVING TIME FOR SMUGGLING TOBACCO?
BINGO.
THE TIES BETWEEN GALICIA AND COLOMBIA WERE STRENGTHENED BY THOSE CORRIDORS AND CELLS.

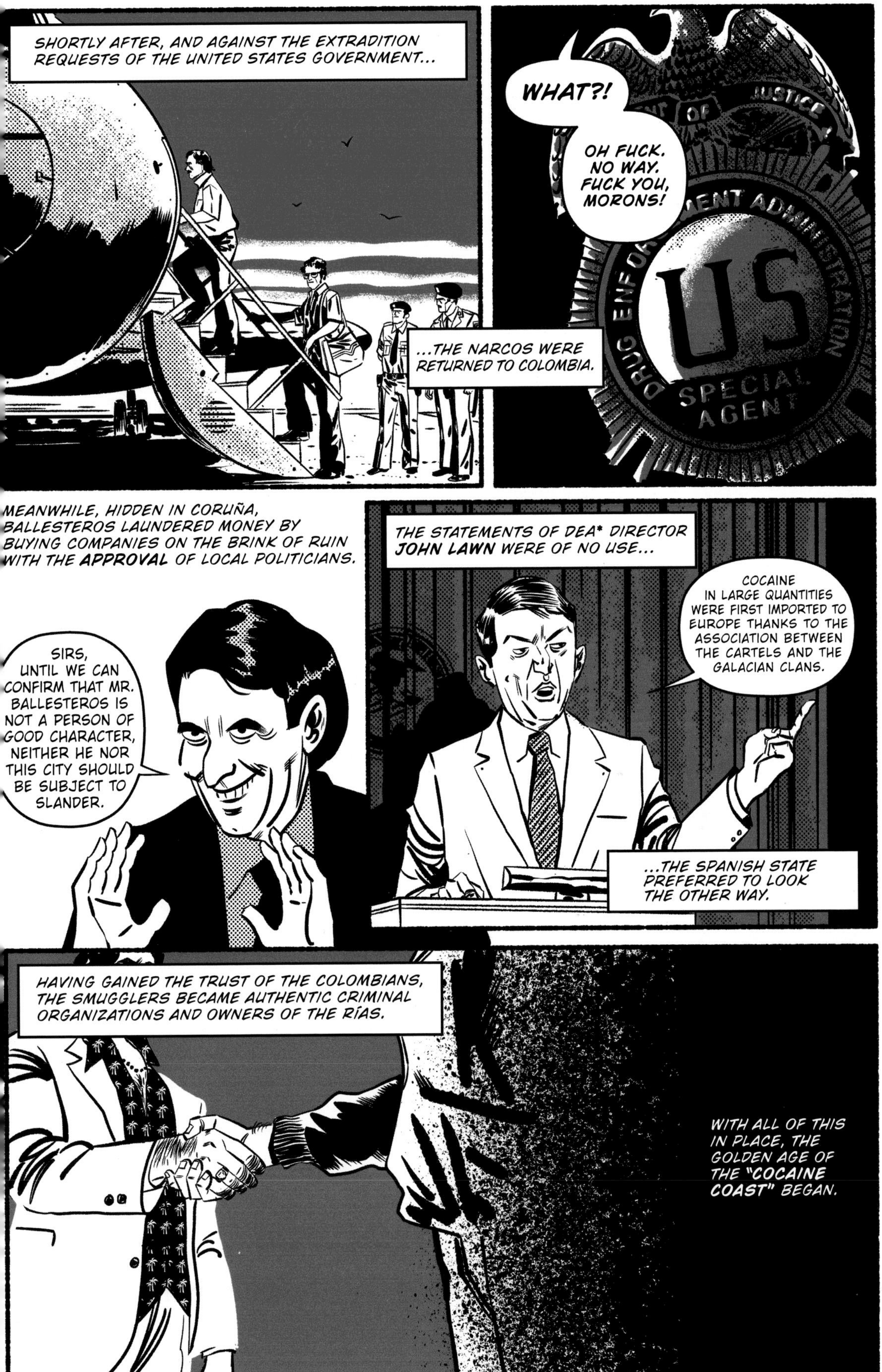
SHORTLY AFTER, AND AGAINST THE EXTRADITION REQUESTS OF THE UNITED STATES GOVERNMENT...
...THE NARCOS WERE RETURNED TO COLOMBIA.
WHAT?!
OH FUCK. NO WAY. FUCK YOU, MORONS!
JUSTICE
DRUG ENFORCEMENT ADMINISTRATION
US
SPECIAL AGENT
MEANWHILE, HIDDEN IN CORUÑA, BALLESTEROS LAUNDERED MONEY BY BUYING COMPANIES ON THE BRINK OF RUIN WITH THE APPROVAL OF LOCAL POLITICIANS.
SIRS, UNTIL WE CAN CONFIRM THAT MR. BALLESTEROS IS NOT A PERSON OF GOOD CHARACTER, NEITHER HE NOR THIS CITY SHOULD BE SUBJECT TO SLANDER.
THE STATEMENTS OF DEA* DIRECTOR JOHN LAWN WERE OF NO USE...
COCAINE IN LARGE QUANTITIES WERE FIRST IMPORTED TO EUROPE THANKS TO THE ASSOCIATION BETWEEN THE CARTELS AND THE GALACIAN CLANS.
...THE SPANISH STATE PREFERRED TO LOOK THE OTHER WAY.
HAVING GAINED THE TRUST OF THE COLOMBIANS, THE SMUGGLERS BECAME AUTHENTIC CRIMINAL ORGANIZATIONS AND OWNERS OF THE RÍAS.
WITH ALL OF THIS IN PLACE, THE GOLDEN AGE OF THE "COCAINE COAST" BEGAN.

*DRUG ENFORCEMENT ADMINISTRATION

THE **CALI CARTEL** WOULD BE THE PREFERRED PARTNER OF THE LARGER CLANS.

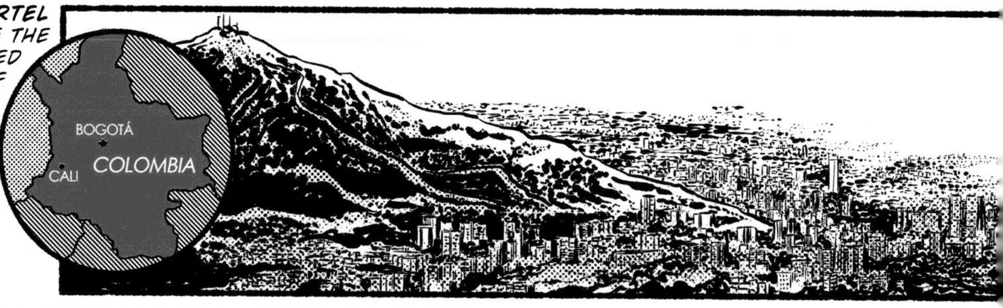
BOGOTÁ
CALI
COLOMBIA

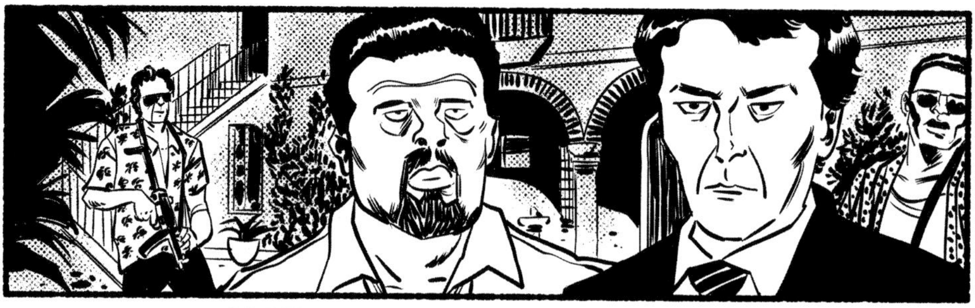

THE BROTHERS GILBERTO AND MIGUEL RODRÍGUE OREJUELA RAN IT WITH AN IRON FIS

THEY WERE RIVALS OF THE **MEDELLÍN CARTEL** AND OPERATED FROM 1975 TO 1996.

THEY WERE PYRAMIDAL IN NATURE, CLOSED OFF TO OTHERS, AND CENTERED ON FAMILY FOR SUPPORT.

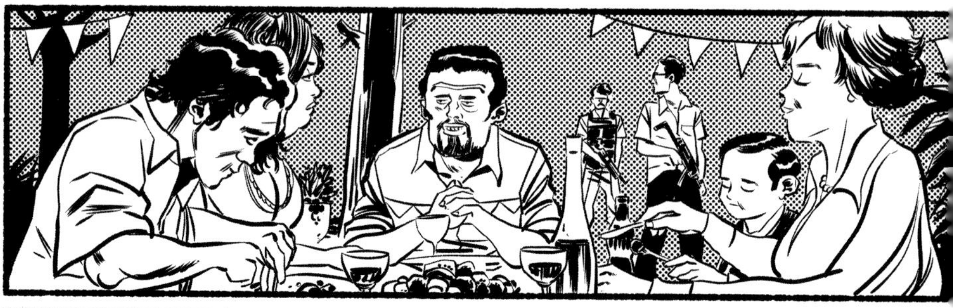

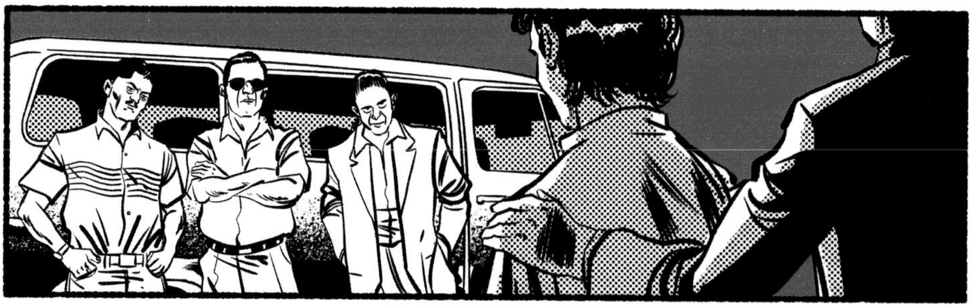

BUSINESS IS BUSINESS AND DURING EACH OPERATION THE GALICIANS HAD TO LEAVE A RELATIVE AS **HUMAN COLLATERAL** IN COLOMBIA.

IF ALL WENT WELL, THEY RETURNED ALIVE TO SPAIN.

IF NOT...WELL, THEY ALWAYS SENT THE WEAKEST LINK IN THE ORGANIZATION...

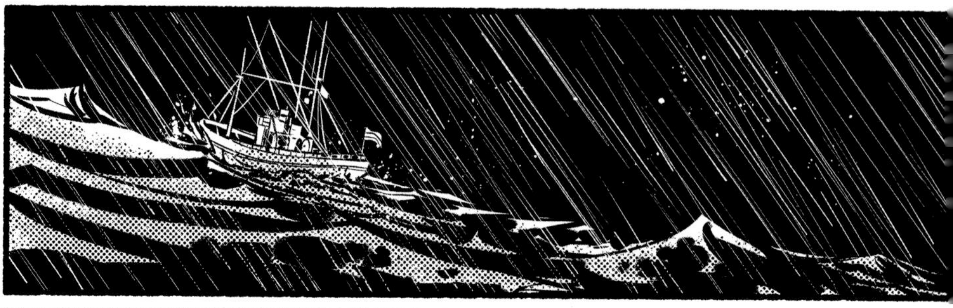

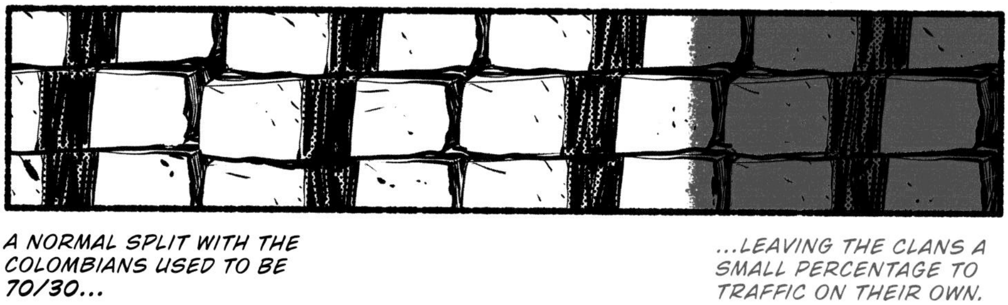

A NORMAL SPLIT WITH THE COLOMBIANS USED TO BE **70/30...**

...LEAVING THE CLANS A SMALL PERCENTAGE TO TRAFFIC ON THEIR OWN.

WHOEVER WANTED TO **RUN DRUGS** HAD TO GO TO AROUSA.

OVER TIME, THEY WOULD FLOOD THE COAST, DRIVING PRICES DOWN.

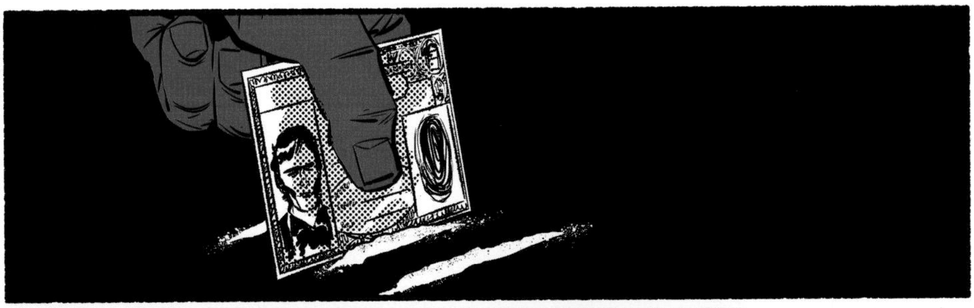

IT WAS **TOO EASY** TO BUY WHITE POWDER.

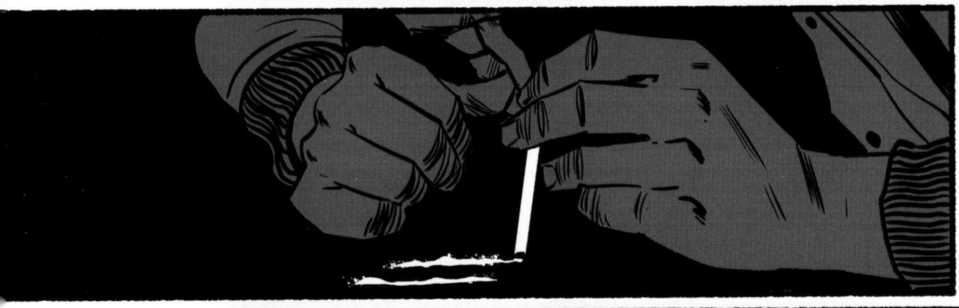

MEANWHILE, A FLEET OF TRUCKS DISTRIBUTED TO THE REST OF THE PENINSULA.

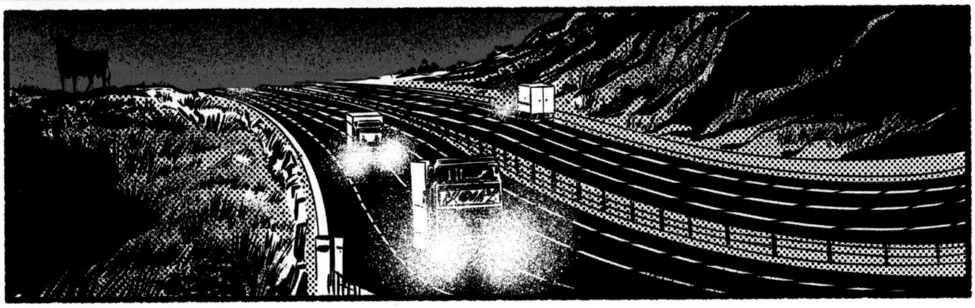

SHIPOWNERS, SAILORS,
GLIDER PILOTS LADS, UNLO
BUNDLES. DELIVERY BOYS..

ALL COLLABORATORS WERE PAID WELL.

AT THAT TIME, A KILO OF COCAINE WAS PRICED AT **10 MILLION PESETAS***.

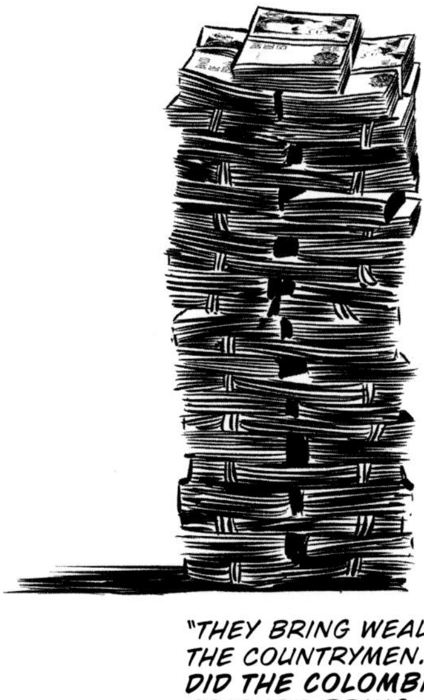

"THEY BRING WEALTH," SAID THE COUNTRYMEN. **AND...BOY, DID THE COLOMBIAN FRIENDS BRING IT!**

*ABOUT $73.000 USD

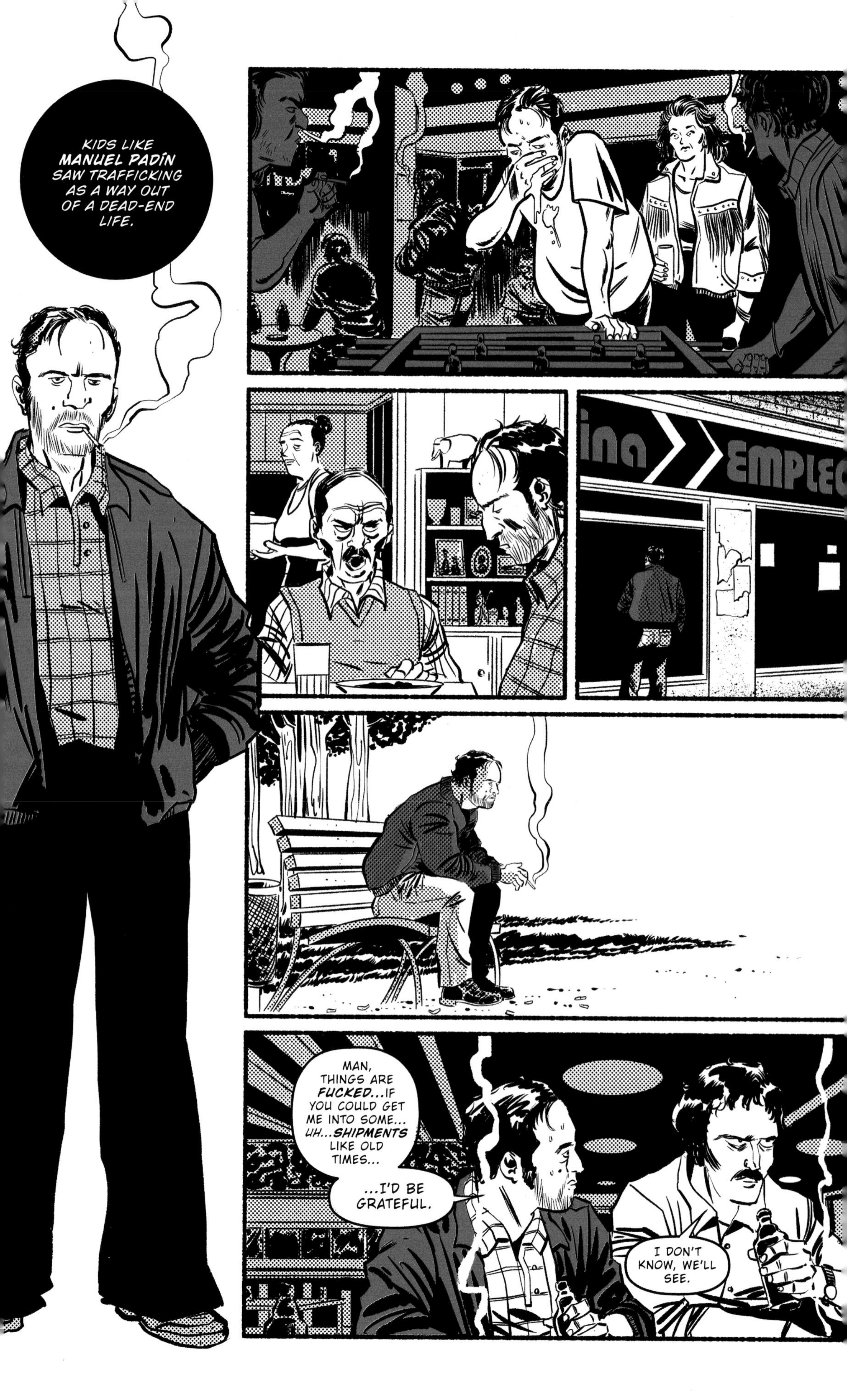

KIDS LIKE MANUEL PADÍN SAW TRAFFICKING AS A WAY OUT OF A DEAD-END LIFE.
ina EMPLEO
MAN, THINGS ARE FUCKED... IF YOU COULD GET ME INTO SOME... UH... SHIPMENTS LIKE OLD TIMES...
...I'D BE GRATEFUL.
I DON'T KNOW, WE'LL SEE.

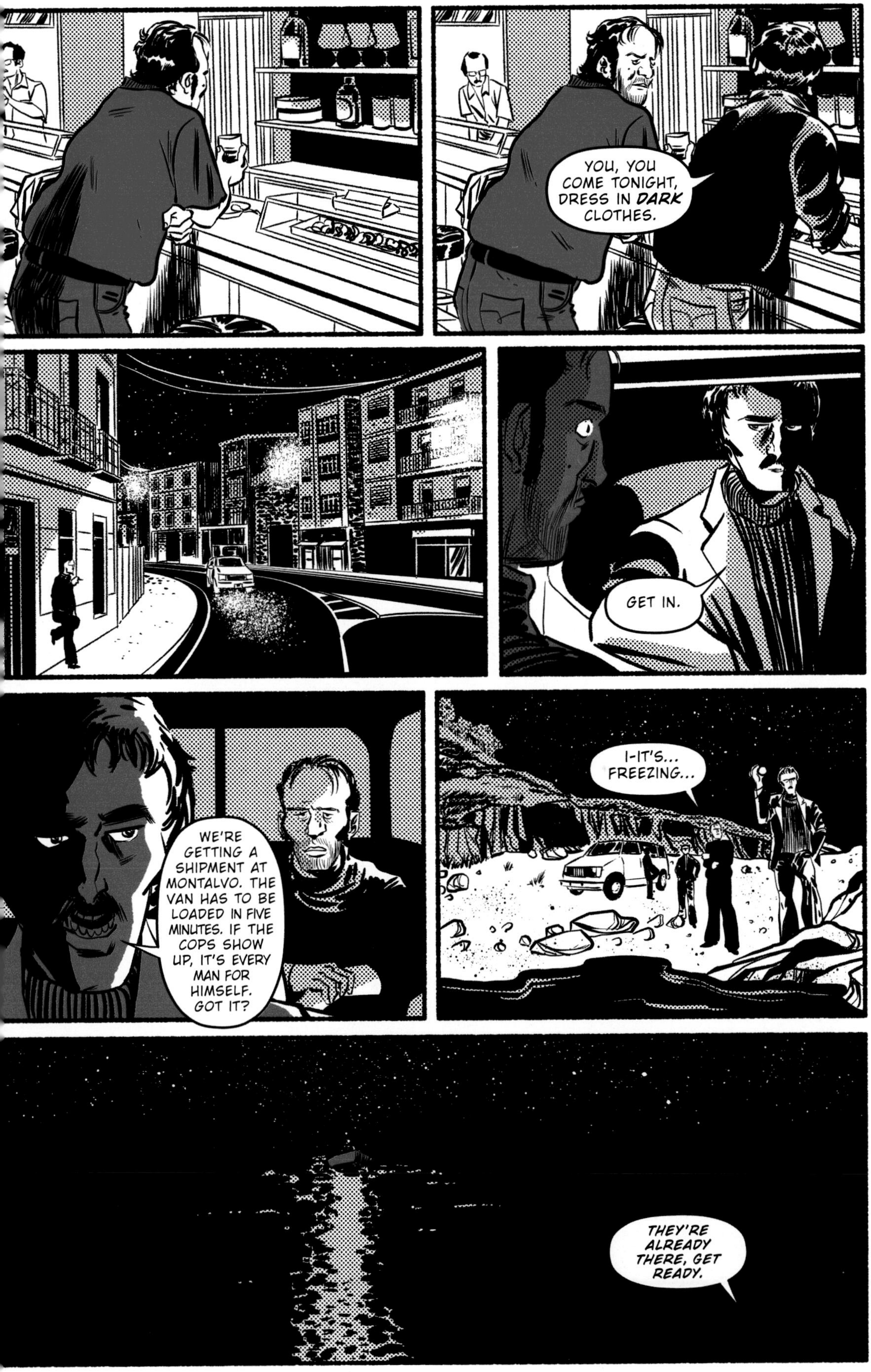
YOU, YOU COME TONIGHT, DRESS IN *DARK* CLOTHES.
GET IN.
WE'RE GETTING A SHIPMENT AT MONTALVO. THE VAN HAS TO BE LOADED IN FIVE MINUTES. IF THE COPS SHOW UP, IT'S EVERY MAN FOR HIMSELF. GOT IT?
I-IT'S... FREEZING...
*THEY'RE ALREADY THERE, GET READY.*

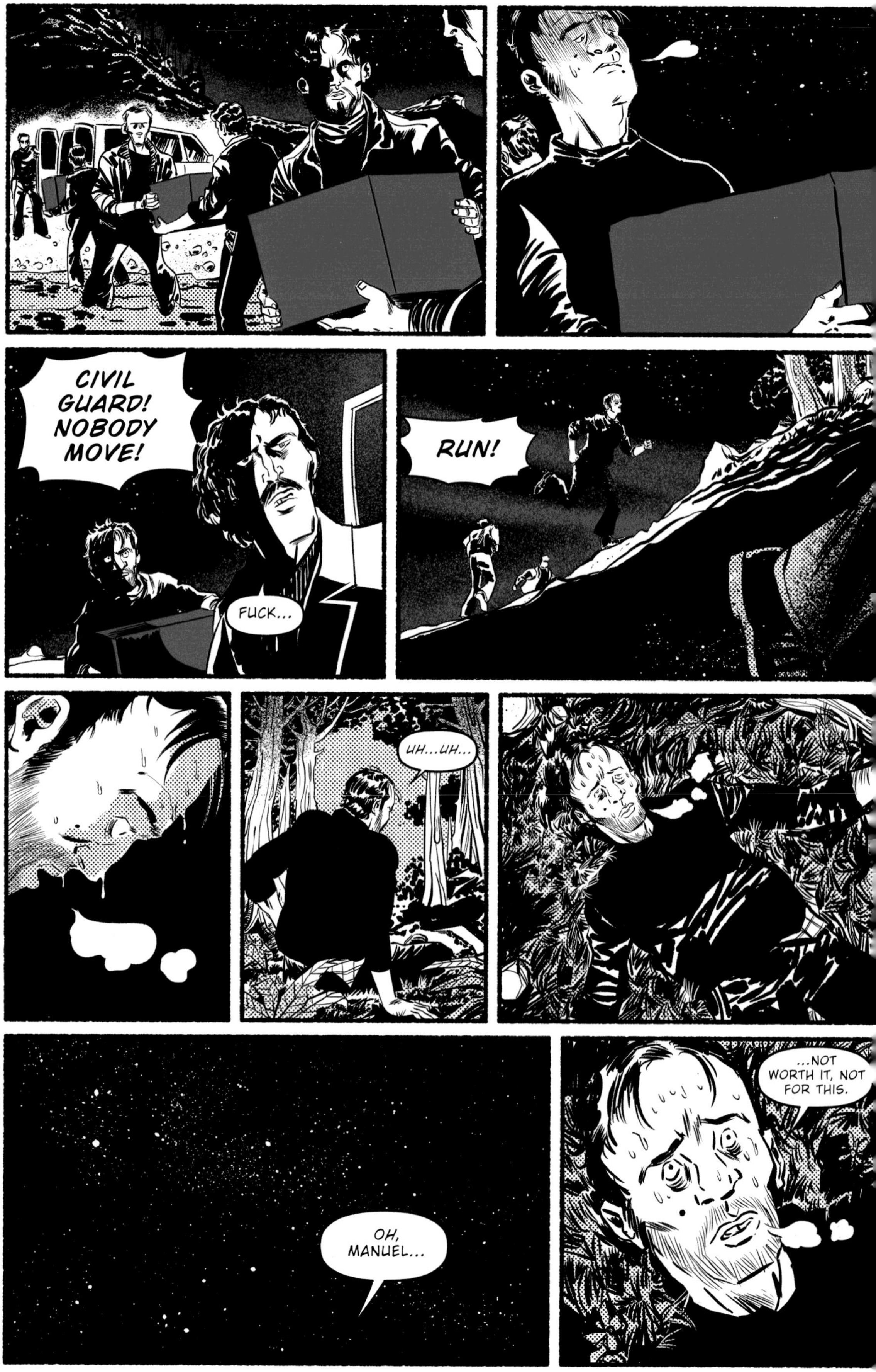
CIVIL GUARD! NOBODY MOVE!
FUCK...
RUN!
UH...UH...
OH, MANUEL...
...NOT WORTH IT, NOT FOR THIS.

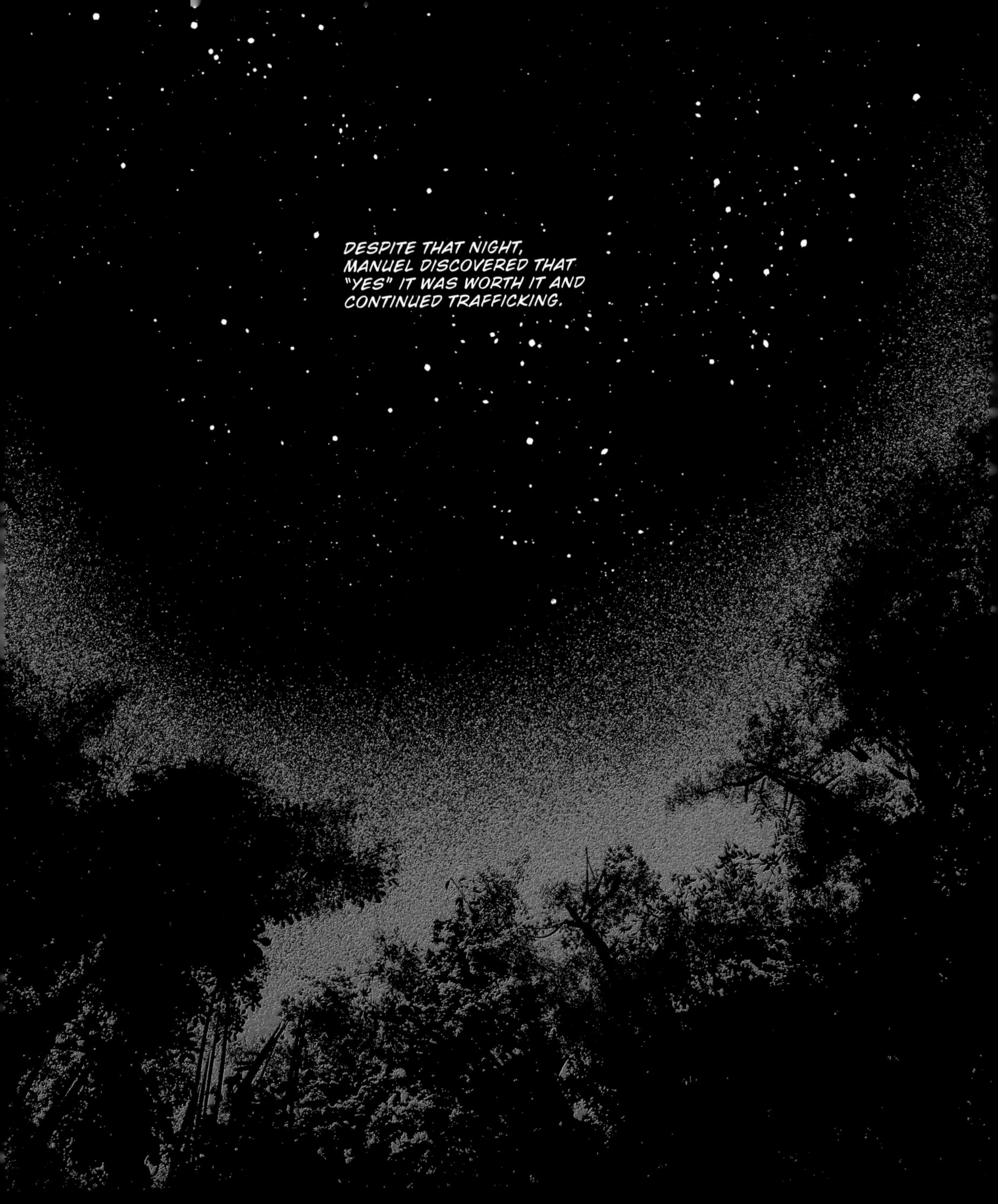
DESPITE THAT NIGHT, MANUEL DISCOVERED THAT "YES" IT WAS WORTH IT AND CONTINUED TRAFFICKING.

PADÍN WOULD GO ON TO MAKE A CAREER WITH "LOS CHARLINES" UNTIL HIS ARREST AND REPENTANCE.

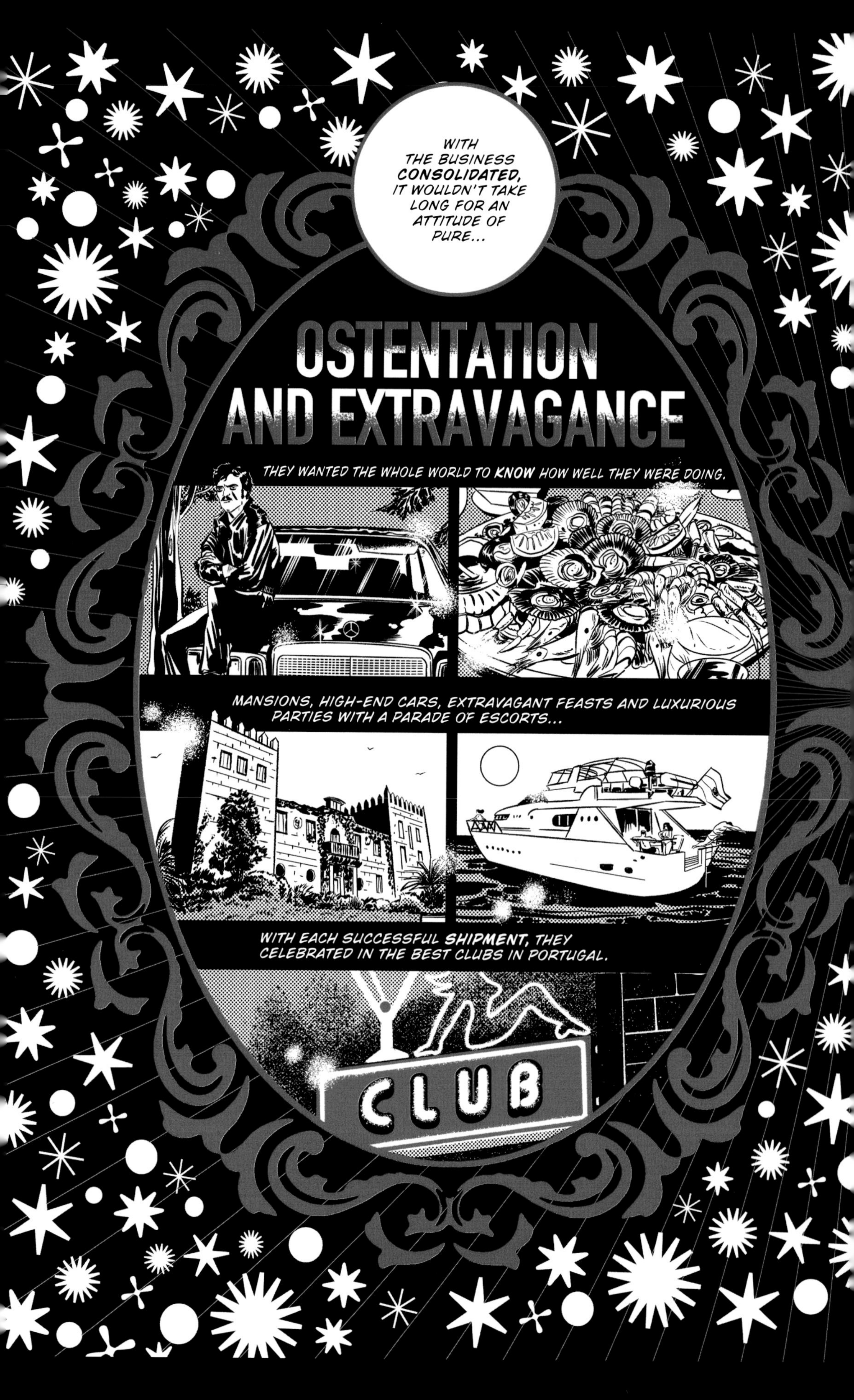
WITH THE BUSINESS CONSOLIDATED, IT WOULDN'T TAKE LONG FOR AN ATTITUDE OF PURE...
OSTENTATION AND EXTRAVAGANCE
THEY WANTED THE WHOLE WORLD TO KNOW HOW WELL THEY WERE DOING.
MANSIONS, HIGH-END CARS, EXTRAVAGANT FEASTS AND LUXURIOUS PARTIES WITH A PARADE OF ESCORTS...
WITH EACH SUCCESSFUL SHIPMENT, THEY CELEBRATED IN THE BEST CLUBS IN PORTUGAL.
CLUB

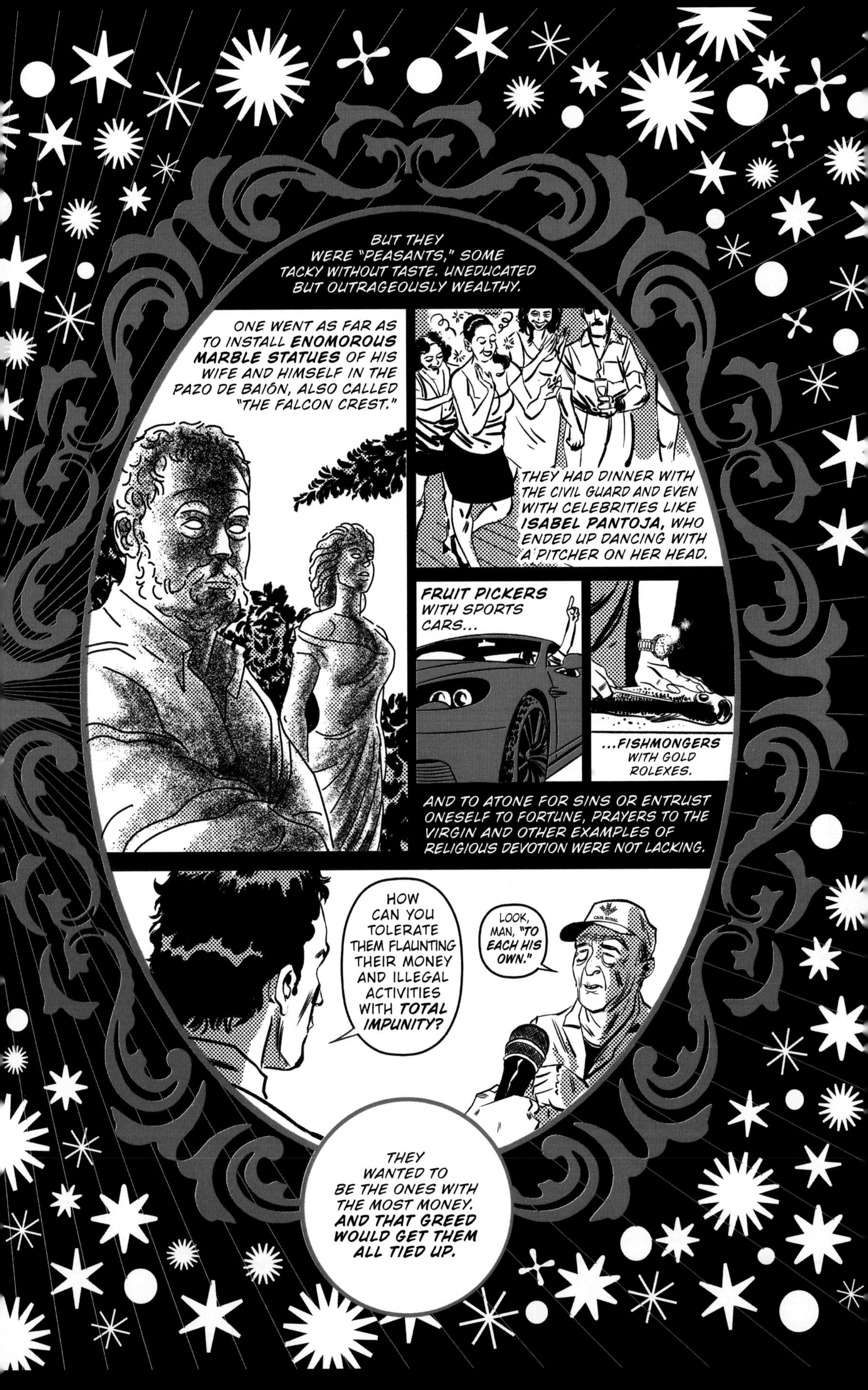
BUT THEY WERE "PEASANTS," SOME TACKY WITHOUT TASTE. UNEDUCATED BUT OUTRAGEOUSLY WEALTHY.
ONE WENT AS FAR AS TO INSTALL **ENOMOROUS MARBLE STATUES** OF HIS WIFE AND HIMSELF IN THE PAZO DE BAIÓN, ALSO CALLED "THE FALCON CREST."
THEY HAD DINNER WITH THE CIVIL GUARD AND EVEN WITH CELEBRITIES LIKE **ISABEL PANTOJA,** WHO ENDED UP DANCING WITH A PITCHER ON HER HEAD.
**FRUIT PICKERS** WITH SPORTS CARS...
...**FISHMONGERS** WITH GOLD ROLEXES.
AND TO ATONE FOR SINS OR ENTRUST ONESELF TO FORTUNE, PRAYERS TO THE VIRGIN AND OTHER EXAMPLES OF RELIGIOUS DEVOTION WERE NOT LACKING.
HOW CAN YOU TOLERATE THEM FLAUNTING THEIR MONEY AND ILLEGAL ACTIVITIES WITH **TOTAL IMPUNITY?**
LOOK, MAN, **"TO EACH HIS OWN."**
THEY WANTED TO BE THE ONES WITH THE MOST MONEY. **AND THAT GREED WOULD GET THEM ALL TIED UP.**

THE **MOST POWERFUL CAPOS OF GALICIA** WERE CONCENTRATED IN THE RÍA DE AROUSA.

# THE CAPOS OF AROUSA

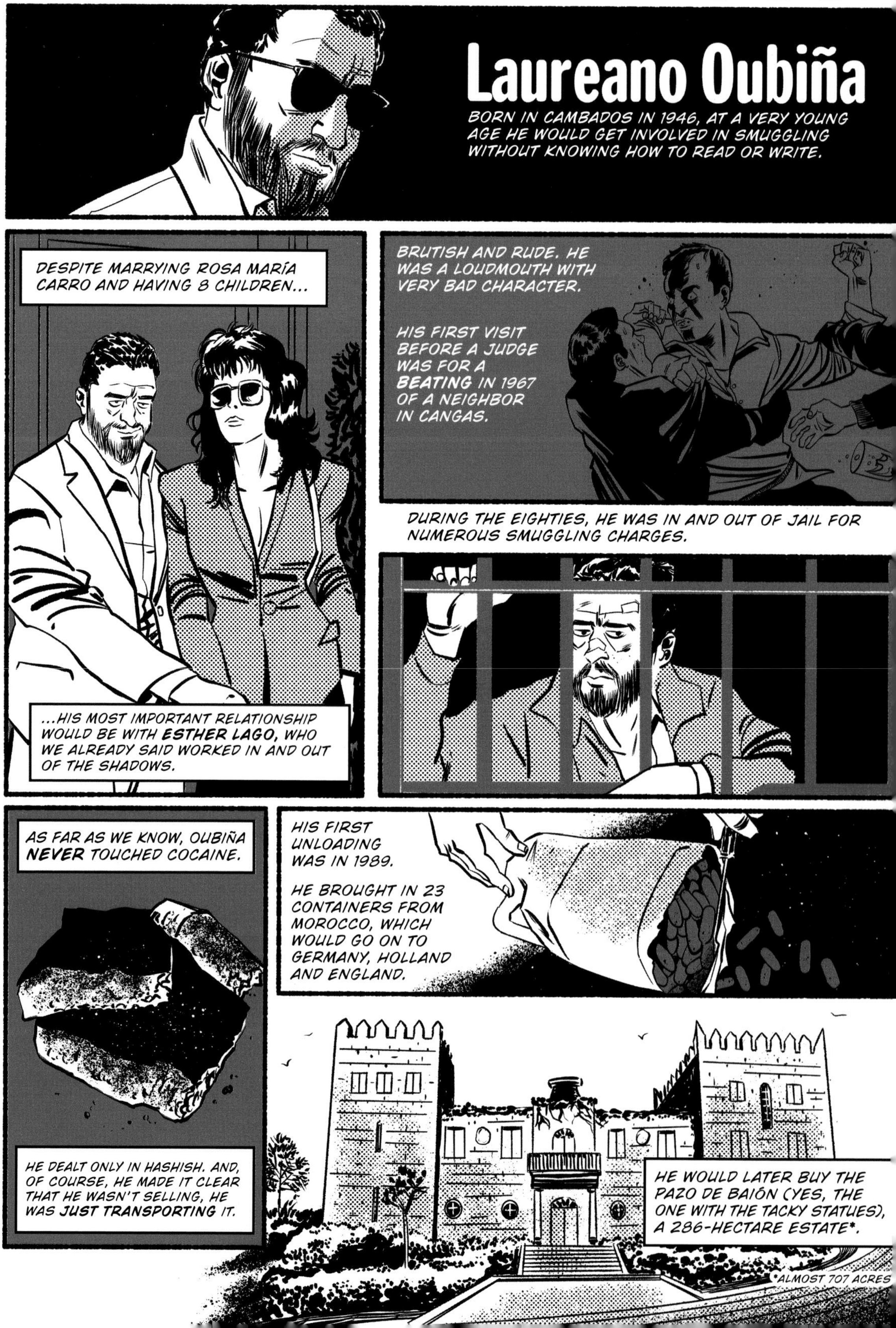
Laureano Oubiña
BORN IN CAMBADOS IN 1946, AT A VERY YOUNG AGE HE WOULD GET INVOLVED IN SMUGGLING WITHOUT KNOWING HOW TO READ OR WRITE.
DESPITE MARRYING ROSA MARÍA CARRO AND HAVING 8 CHILDREN...
...HIS MOST IMPORTANT RELATIONSHIP WOULD BE WITH **ESTHER LAGO**, WHO WE ALREADY SAID WORKED IN AND OUT OF THE SHADOWS.
BRUTISH AND RUDE. HE WAS A LOUDMOUTH WITH VERY BAD CHARACTER.
HIS FIRST VISIT BEFORE A JUDGE WAS FOR A **BEATING** IN 1967 OF A NEIGHBOR IN CANGAS.
DURING THE EIGHTIES, HE WAS IN AND OUT OF JAIL FOR NUMEROUS SMUGGLING CHARGES.
AS FAR AS WE KNOW, OUBIÑA **NEVER** TOUCHED COCAINE.
HE DEALT ONLY IN HASHISH. AND, OF COURSE, HE MADE IT CLEAR THAT HE WASN'T SELLING, HE WAS **JUST TRANSPORTING** IT.
HIS FIRST UNLOADING WAS IN 1989.
HE BROUGHT IN 23 CONTAINERS FROM MOROCCO, WHICH WOULD GO ON TO GERMANY, HOLLAND AND ENGLAND.
HE WOULD LATER BUY THE PAZO DE BAIÓN (YES, THE ONE WITH THE TACKY STATUES), A 286-HECTARE ESTATE*.
*ALMOST 707 ACRES

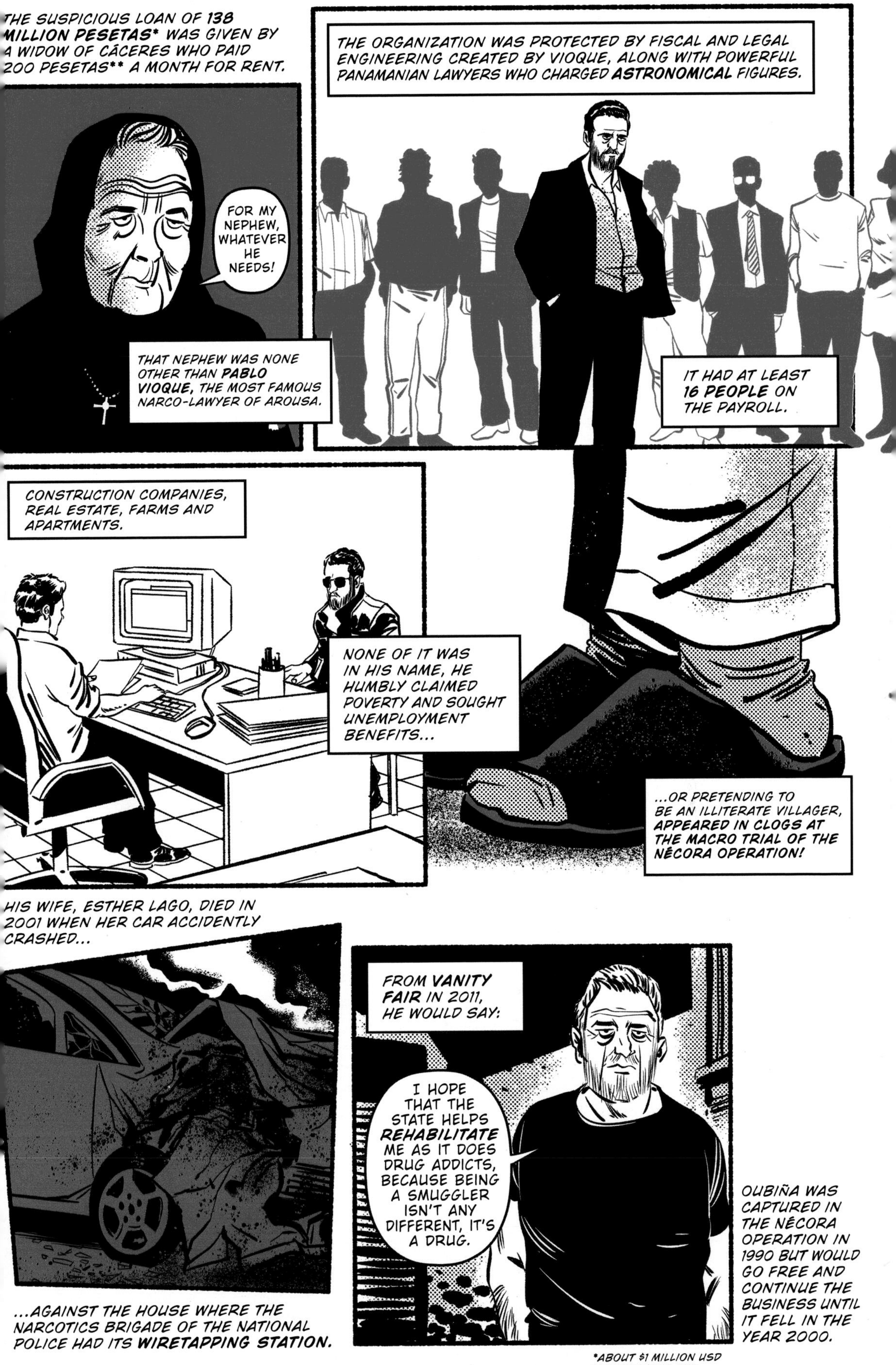
THE SUSPICIOUS LOAN OF 138 MILLION PESETAS* WAS GIVEN BY A WIDOW OF CÁCERES WHO PAID 200 PESETAS** A MONTH FOR RENT.
FOR MY NEPHEW, WHATEVER HE NEEDS!
THAT NEPHEW WAS NONE OTHER THAN PABLO VIOQUE, THE MOST FAMOUS NARCO-LAWYER OF AROUSA.
THE ORGANIZATION WAS PROTECTED BY FISCAL AND LEGAL ENGINEERING CREATED BY VIOQUE, ALONG WITH POWERFUL PANAMANIAN LAWYERS WHO CHARGED ASTRONOMICAL FIGURES.
IT HAD AT LEAST 16 PEOPLE ON THE PAYROLL.
CONSTRUCTION COMPANIES, REAL ESTATE, FARMS AND APARTMENTS.
NONE OF IT WAS IN HIS NAME, HE HUMBLY CLAIMED POVERTY AND SOUGHT UNEMPLOYMENT BENEFITS...
...OR PRETENDING TO BE AN ILLITERATE VILLAGER, APPEARED IN CLOGS AT THE MACRO TRIAL OF THE NÉCORA OPERATION!
HIS WIFE, ESTHER LAGO, DIED IN 2001 WHEN HER CAR ACCIDENTLY CRASHED...
...AGAINST THE HOUSE WHERE THE NARCOTICS BRIGADE OF THE NATIONAL POLICE HAD ITS WIRETAPPING STATION.
FROM VANITY FAIR IN 2011, HE WOULD SAY:
I HOPE THAT THE STATE HELPS REHABILITATE ME AS IT DOES DRUG ADDICTS, BECAUSE BEING A SMUGGLER ISN'T ANY DIFFERENT, IT'S A DRUG.
OUBIÑA WAS CAPTURED IN THE NÉCORA OPERATION IN 1990 BUT WOULD GO FREE AND CONTINUE THE BUSINESS UNTIL IT FELL IN THE YEAR 2000.

*ABOUT $1 MILLION USD
**ABOUT $1.50 USD

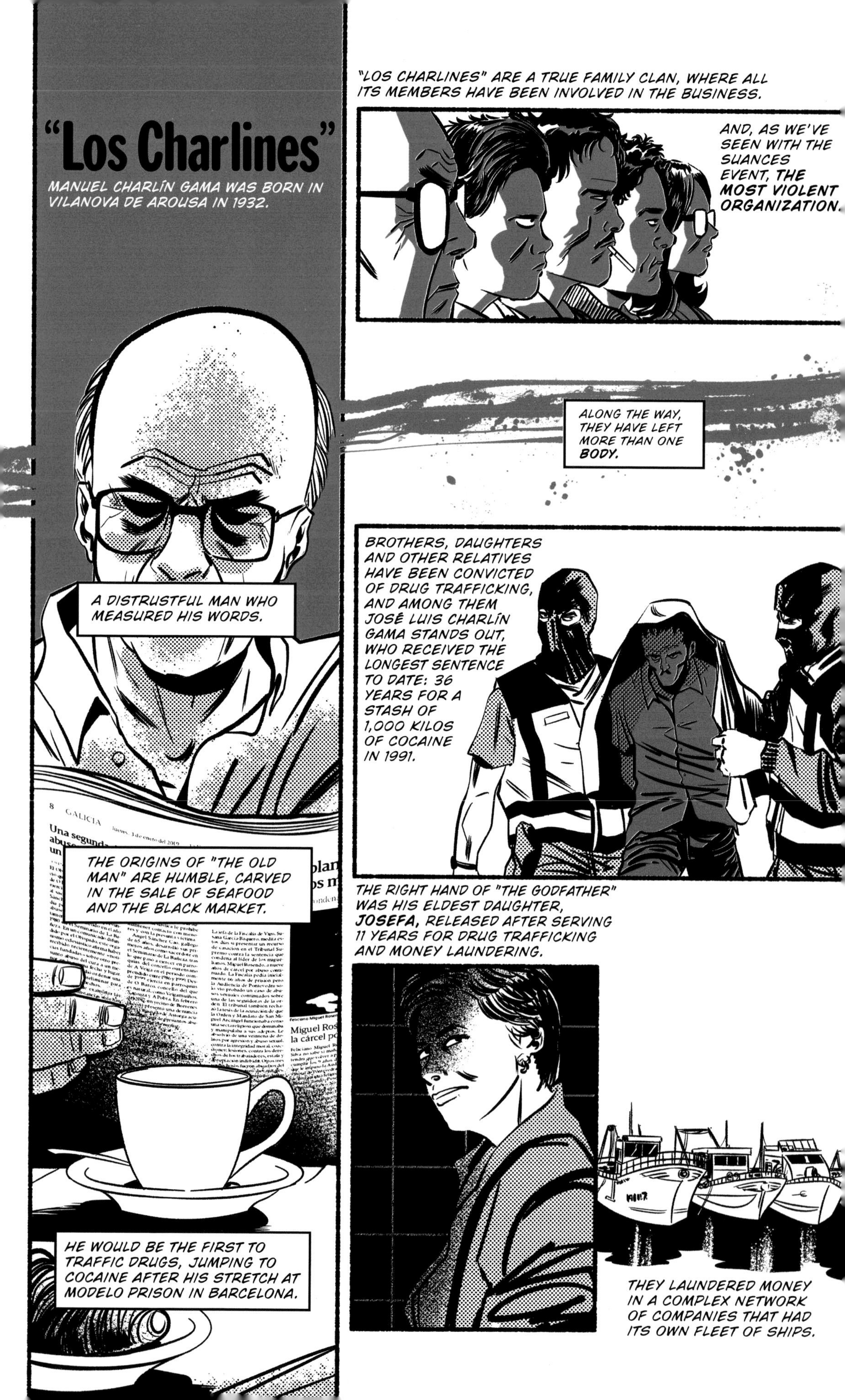
"Los Charlines"
MANUEL CHARLÍN GAMA WAS BORN IN VILANOVA DE AROUSA IN 1932.
A DISTRUSTFUL MAN WHO MEASURED HIS WORDS.
THE ORIGINS OF "THE OLD MAN" ARE HUMBLE, CARVED IN THE SALE OF SEAFOOD AND THE BLACK MARKET.
HE WOULD BE THE FIRST TO TRAFFIC DRUGS, JUMPING TO COCAINE AFTER HIS STRETCH AT MODELO PRISON IN BARCELONA.
"LOS CHARLINES" ARE A TRUE FAMILY CLAN, WHERE ALL ITS MEMBERS HAVE BEEN INVOLVED IN THE BUSINESS.
AND, AS WE'VE SEEN WITH THE SUANCES EVENT, THE MOST VIOLENT ORGANIZATION.
ALONG THE WAY, THEY HAVE LEFT MORE THAN ONE BODY.
BROTHERS, DAUGHTERS AND OTHER RELATIVES HAVE BEEN CONVICTED OF DRUG TRAFFICKING, AND AMONG THEM JOSÉ LUIS CHARLÍN GAMA STANDS OUT, WHO RECEIVED THE LONGEST SENTENCE TO DATE: 36 YEARS FOR A STASH OF 1,000 KILOS OF COCAINE IN 1991.
THE RIGHT HAND OF "THE GODFATHER" WAS HIS ELDEST DAUGHTER, JOSEFA, RELEASED AFTER SERVING 11 YEARS FOR DRUG TRAFFICKING AND MONEY LAUNDERING.
THEY LAUNDERED MONEY IN A COMPLEX NETWORK OF COMPANIES THAT HAD ITS OWN FLEET OF SHIPS.

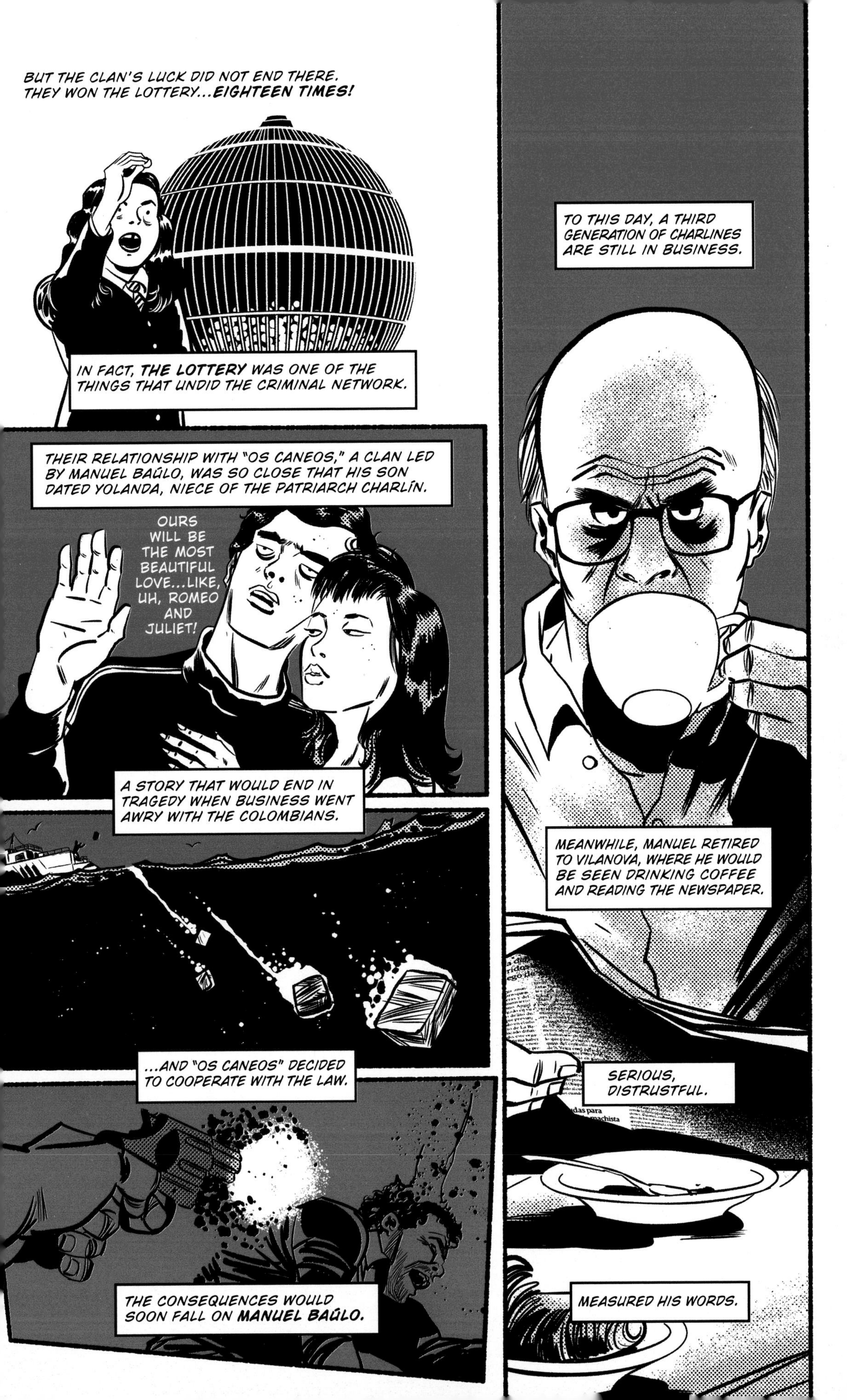
BUT THE CLAN'S LUCK DID NOT END THERE. THEY WON THE LOTTERY...EIGHTEEN TIMES!
IN FACT, THE LOTTERY WAS ONE OF THE THINGS THAT UNDID THE CRIMINAL NETWORK.
THEIR RELATIONSHIP WITH "OS CANEOS," A CLAN LED BY MANUEL BAÚLO, WAS SO CLOSE THAT HIS SON DATED YOLANDA, NIECE OF THE PATRIARCH CHARLÍN.
OURS WILL BE THE MOST BEAUTIFUL LOVE...LIKE, UH, ROMEO AND JULIET!
A STORY THAT WOULD END IN TRAGEDY WHEN BUSINESS WENT AWRY WITH THE COLOMBIANS.
...AND "OS CANEOS" DECIDED TO COOPERATE WITH THE LAW.
THE CONSEQUENCES WOULD SOON FALL ON MANUEL BAÚLO.
TO THIS DAY, A THIRD GENERATION OF CHARLINES ARE STILL IN BUSINESS.
MEANWHILE, MANUEL RETIRED TO VILANOVA, WHERE HE WOULD BE SEEN DRINKING COFFEE AND READING THE NEWSPAPER.
SERIOUS, DISTRUSTFUL.
MEASURED HIS WORDS.

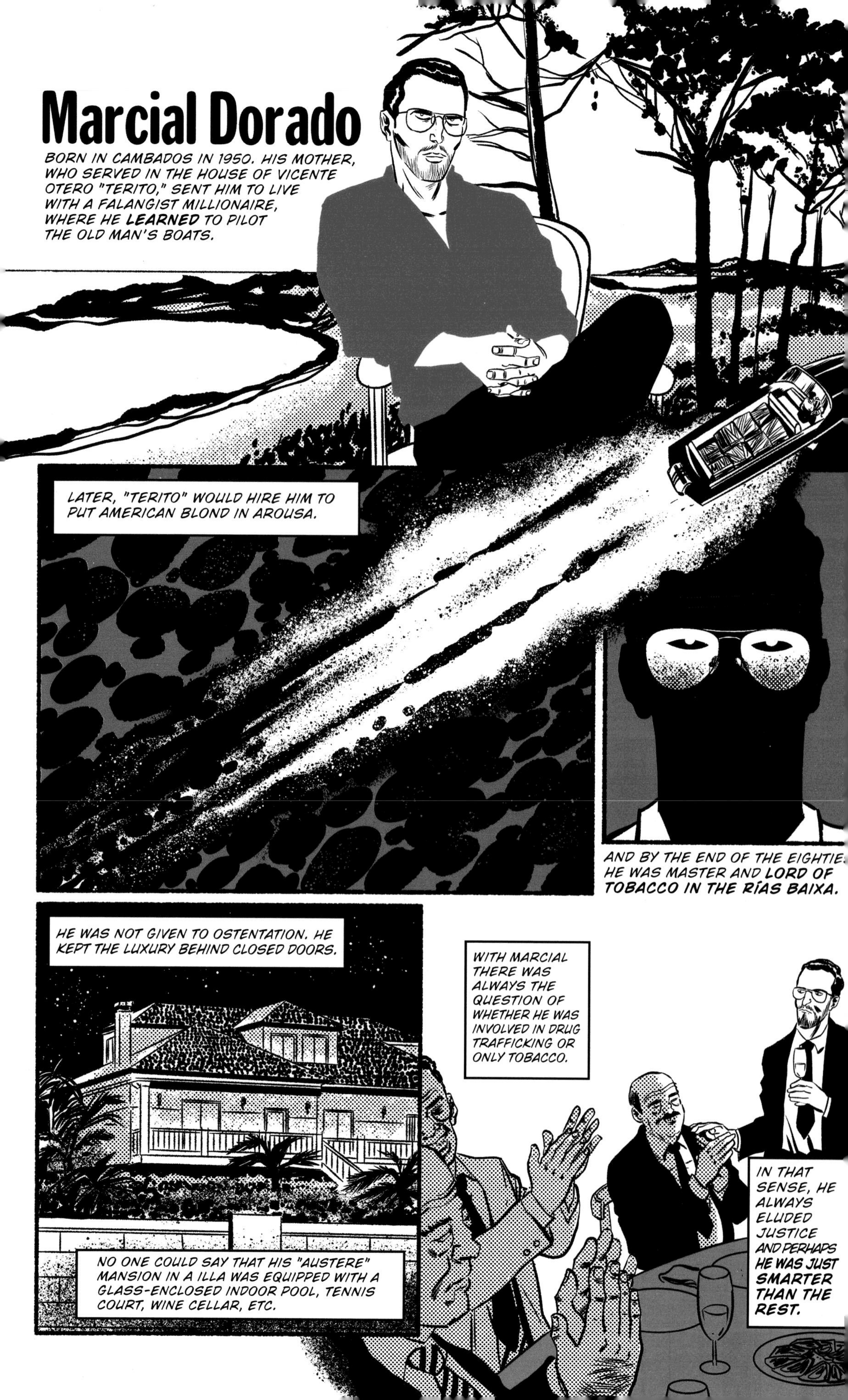
Marcial Dorado
BORN IN CAMBADOS IN 1950. HIS MOTHER, WHO SERVED IN THE HOUSE OF VICENTE OTERO "TERITO," SENT HIM TO LIVE WITH A FALANGIST MILLIONAIRE, WHERE HE **LEARNED** TO PILOT THE OLD MAN'S BOATS.
LATER, "TERITO" WOULD HIRE HIM TO PUT AMERICAN BLOND IN AROUSA.
AND BY THE END OF THE EIGHTIE HE WAS MASTER AND **LORD OF TOBACCO IN THE RÍAS BAIXA.**
HE WAS NOT GIVEN TO OSTENTATION. HE KEPT THE LUXURY BEHIND CLOSED DOORS.
NO ONE COULD SAY THAT HIS "AUSTERE" MANSION IN A ILLA WAS EQUIPPED WITH A GLASS-ENCLOSED INDOOR POOL, TENNIS COURT, WINE CELLAR, ETC.
WITH MARCIAL THERE WAS ALWAYS THE QUESTION OF WHETHER HE WAS INVOLVED IN DRUG TRAFFICKING OR ONLY TOBACCO.
IN THAT SENSE, HE ALWAYS ELUDED JUSTICE AND PERHAPS **HE WAS JUST SMARTER THAN THE REST.**

"MARCIAL DE LA ISLA" WAS WIDELY KNOWN IN GALICIA, AS WAS HIS CLOSE RELATIONSHIP WITH EVENTUAL PRESIDENT OF THE XUNTA DE GALICIA, **ALBERTO NÚÑEZ FEIJÓO**, WHO WAS AT THAT TIME NUMBER TWO AT THE DEPARTMENT OF HEALTH.

ORATUS

COMPROMISING PHOTOS OF THEM ON A YACHT IN THE SUMMER OF '95 WOULD SHAKE THE SPANISH MEDIA IN EARLY 2013.

MY RELATIONSHIP WITH LORD DORADO IS LIMITED TO THE PERSONAL SPHERE, AND I DO NOT KNOW HIS BUSINESS AFFAIRS.

SURPRISING, CONSIDERING HE WAS PARADED BEFORE THE COURTS BOTH FOR THE **MACROSUMMARY 11/84** AND THE **NÉCORA OPERATION**. ALTHOUGH HE WOULD BE FREED OF CHARGES.

PRESIDENT FEIJÓO IS A **GOOD MAN**, A HARD WORKER. I ALWAYS SENSED THAT HE WOULD GO FAR AND I'M SURE YOU KNOW THAT I WAS NOT, NOR AM I, NOR WILL I EVER BE A DRUG DEALER.

HIS REAL ESTATE ASSETS WITH THE PURCHASE OF 200 FARMS IN THE ILLA DE AROUSA WERE THE LEGAL FACE OF HIS DARK FINANCES...

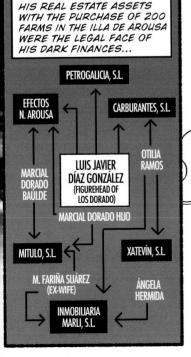

PETROGALICIA, S.L.

EFECTOS N. AROUSA

CARBURANTES, S.L.

MARCIAL DORADO BAÚLDE

LUIS JAVIER DÍAZ GONZÁLEZ (FIGUREHEAD OF LOS DORADO)

OTILIA RAMOS

MARCIAL DORADO HIJO

MITULO, S.L.

XATEVÍN, S.L.

M. FARIÑA SUÁREZ (EX-WIFE)

ÁNGELA HERMIDA

INMOBILIARIA MARLI, S.L.

FINALLY, IN 2015 HE WAS SENTENCED TO 6 YEARS FOR MONEY LAUNDERING.

HE MOVED AN OBSCENE AMOUNT OF MONEY TO SWITZERLAND, PORTUGAL AND THE BAHAMAS THAT COULDN'T BE ACCOUNTED FOR THROUGH ONLY THE SALE OF TOBACCO.

FOR WHAT THEY HAVE NOT JUDGED ME, THEY WILL NO LONGER JUDGE ME. I AM OUT OF EVERYTHING.

HE IS CURRENTLY IN PRISON.

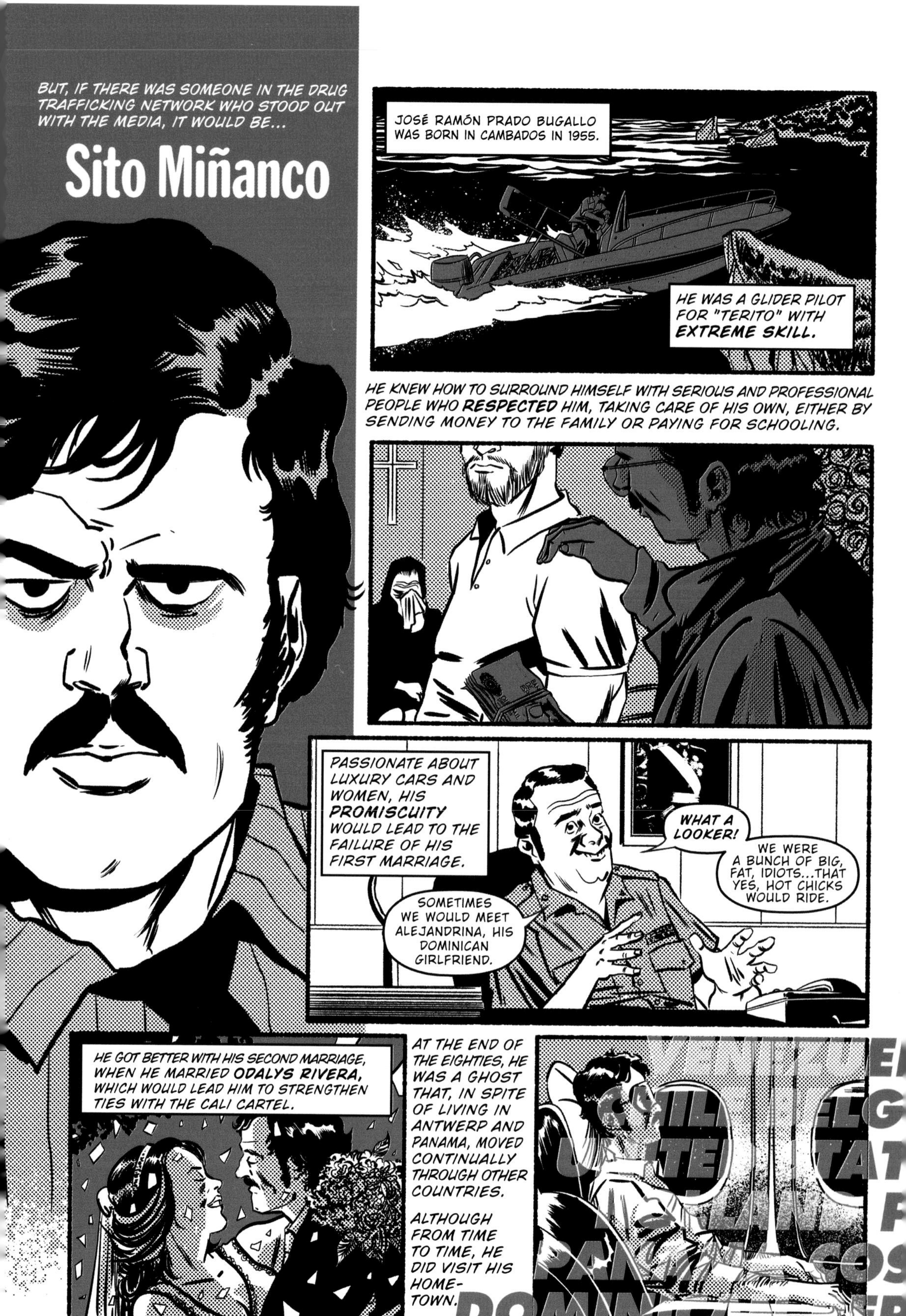

BUT, IF THERE WAS SOMEONE IN THE DRUG TRAFFICKING NETWORK WHO STOOD OUT WITH THE MEDIA, IT WOULD BE...
Sito Miñanco
JOSÉ RAMÓN PRADO BUGALLO WAS BORN IN CAMBADOS IN 1955.
HE WAS A GLIDER PILOT FOR "TERITO" WITH EXTREME SKILL.
HE KNEW HOW TO SURROUND HIMSELF WITH SERIOUS AND PROFESSIONAL PEOPLE WHO RESPECTED HIM, TAKING CARE OF HIS OWN, EITHER BY SENDING MONEY TO THE FAMILY OR PAYING FOR SCHOOLING.
PASSIONATE ABOUT LUXURY CARS AND WOMEN, HIS PROMISCUITY WOULD LEAD TO THE FAILURE OF HIS FIRST MARRIAGE.
WHAT A LOOKER!
WE WERE A BUNCH OF BIG, FAT, IDIOTS...THAT YES, HOT CHICKS WOULD RIDE.
SOMETIMES WE WOULD MEET ALEJANDRINA, HIS DOMINICAN GIRLFRIEND.
HE GOT BETTER WITH HIS SECOND MARRIAGE, WHEN HE MARRIED ODALYS RIVERA, WHICH WOULD LEAD HIM TO STRENGTHEN TIES WITH THE CALI CARTEL.
AT THE END OF THE EIGHTIES, HE WAS A GHOST THAT, IN SPITE OF LIVING IN ANTWERP AND PANAMA, MOVED CONTINUALLY THROUGH OTHER COUNTRIES.
ALTHOUGH FROM TIME TO TIME, HE DID VISIT HIS HOME-TOWN.

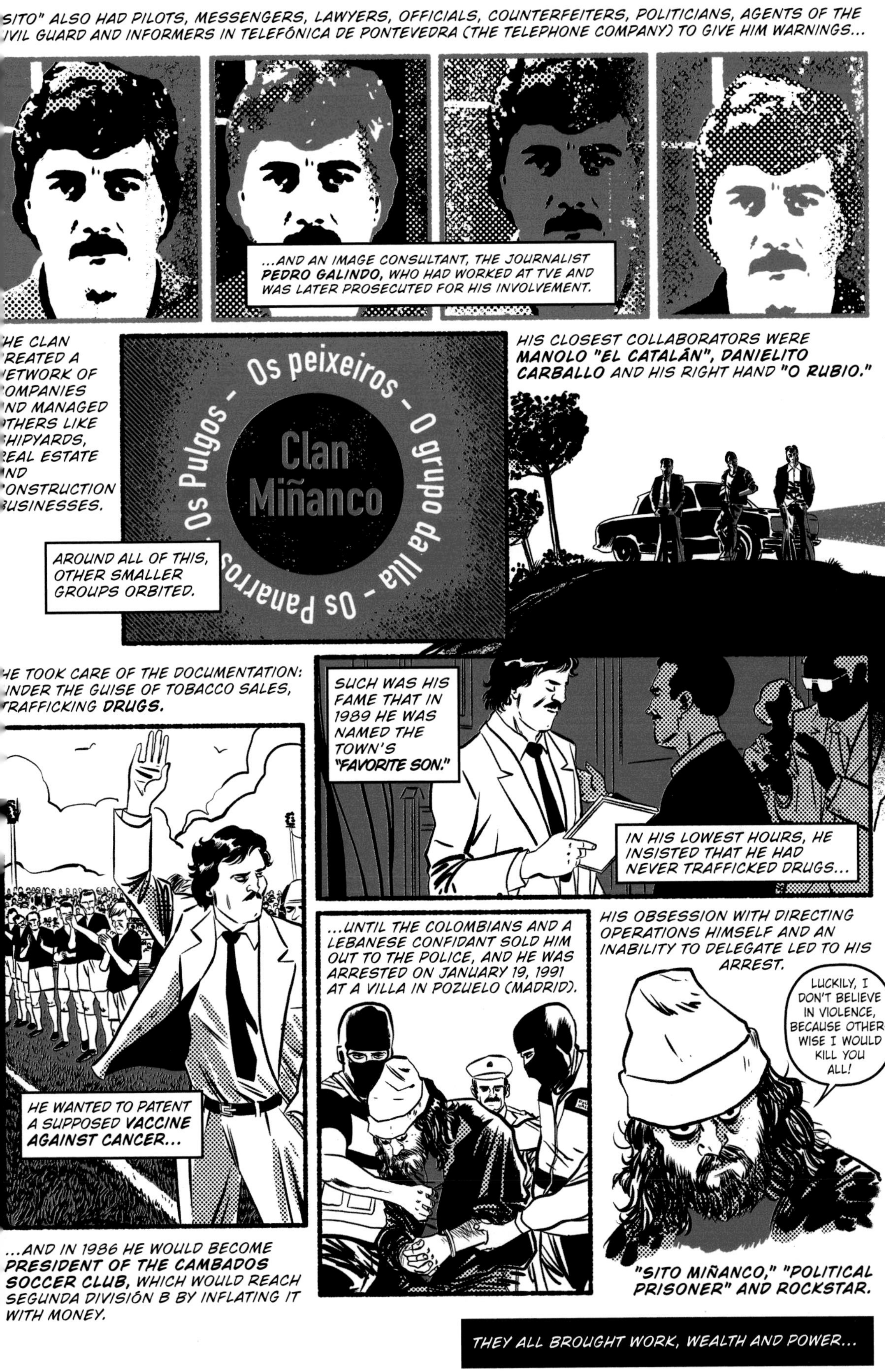

SITO" ALSO HAD PILOTS, MESSENGERS, LAWYERS, OFFICIALS, COUNTERFEITERS, POLITICIANS, AGENTS OF THE IVIL GUARD AND INFORMERS IN TELEFÓNICA DE PONTEVEDRA (THE TELEPHONE COMPANY) TO GIVE HIM WARNINGS...
...AND AN IMAGE CONSULTANT, THE JOURNALIST PEDRO GALINDO, WHO HAD WORKED AT TVE AND WAS LATER PROSECUTED FOR HIS INVOLVEMENT.
HE CLAN REATED A ETWORK OF OMPANIES ND MANAGED THERS LIKE HIPYARDS, EAL ESTATE ND ONSTRUCTION USINESSES.
Clan Miñanco
Os peixeiros – O grupo da Illa – Os Panarros – Os Pulgos –
AROUND ALL OF THIS, OTHER SMALLER GROUPS ORBITED.
HIS CLOSEST COLLABORATORS WERE MANOLO "EL CATALÁN", DANIELITO CARBALLO AND HIS RIGHT HAND "O RUBIO."
HE TOOK CARE OF THE DOCUMENTATION: NDER THE GUISE OF TOBACCO SALES, RAFFICKING DRUGS.
HE WANTED TO PATENT A SUPPOSED VACCINE AGAINST CANCER...
...AND IN 1986 HE WOULD BECOME PRESIDENT OF THE CAMBADOS SOCCER CLUB, WHICH WOULD REACH SEGUNDA DIVISIÓN B BY INFLATING IT WITH MONEY.
SUCH WAS HIS FAME THAT IN 1989 HE WAS NAMED THE TOWN'S "FAVORITE SON."
IN HIS LOWEST HOURS, HE INSISTED THAT HE HAD NEVER TRAFFICKED DRUGS...
...UNTIL THE COLOMBIANS AND A LEBANESE CONFIDANT SOLD HIM OUT TO THE POLICE, AND HE WAS ARRESTED ON JANUARY 19, 1991 AT A VILLA IN POZUELO (MADRID).
HIS OBSESSION WITH DIRECTING OPERATIONS HIMSELF AND AN INABILITY TO DELEGATE LED TO HIS ARREST.
LUCKILY, I DON'T BELIEVE IN VIOLENCE, BECAUSE OTHERWISE I WOULD KILL YOU ALL!
"SITO MIÑANCO," "POLITICAL PRISONER" AND ROCKSTAR.
THEY ALL BROUGHT WORK, WEALTH AND POWER...

...BUT ALSO CORRUPTION AND DEATH.

Part Three

# WHITE TIDE

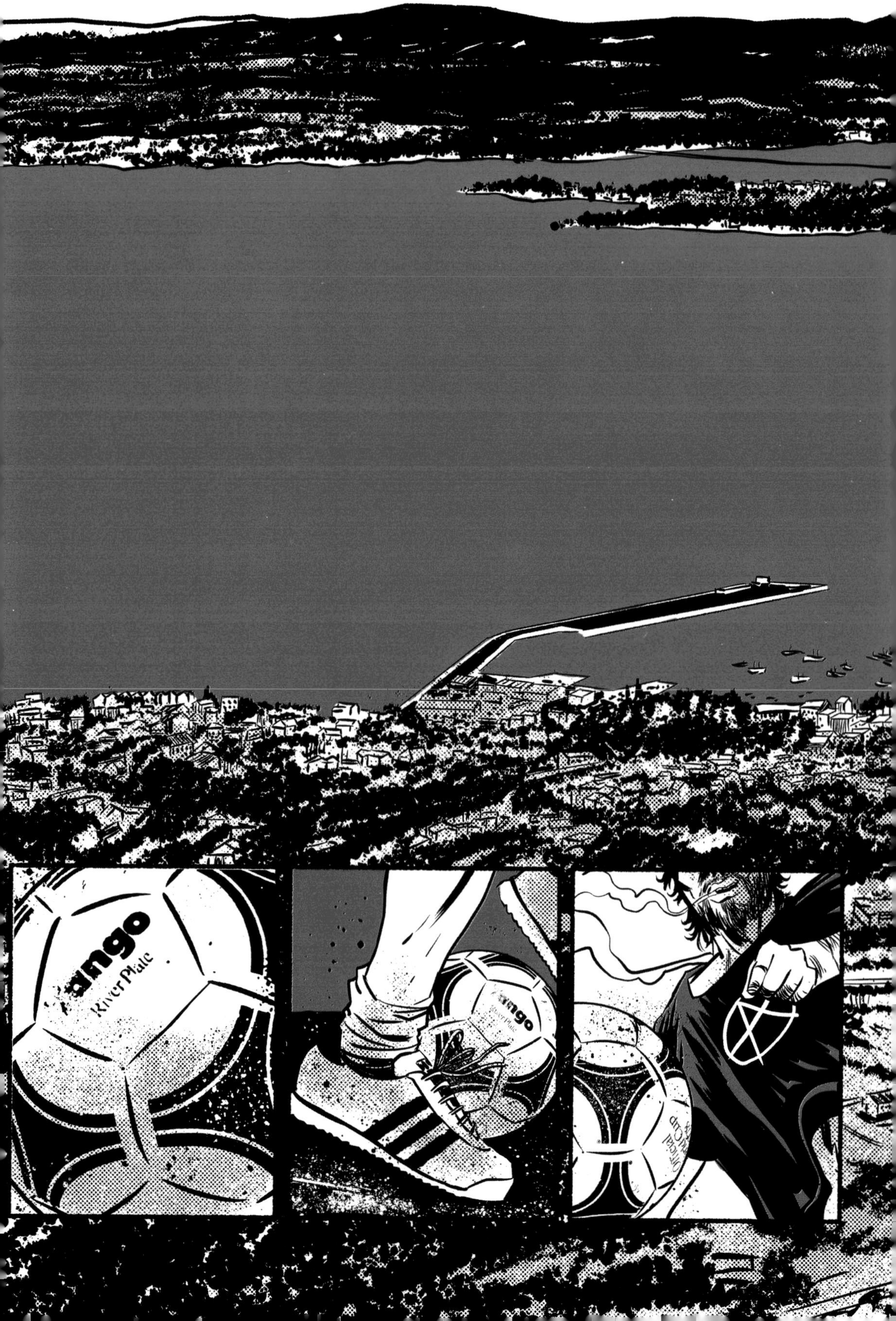
ango
River Plate

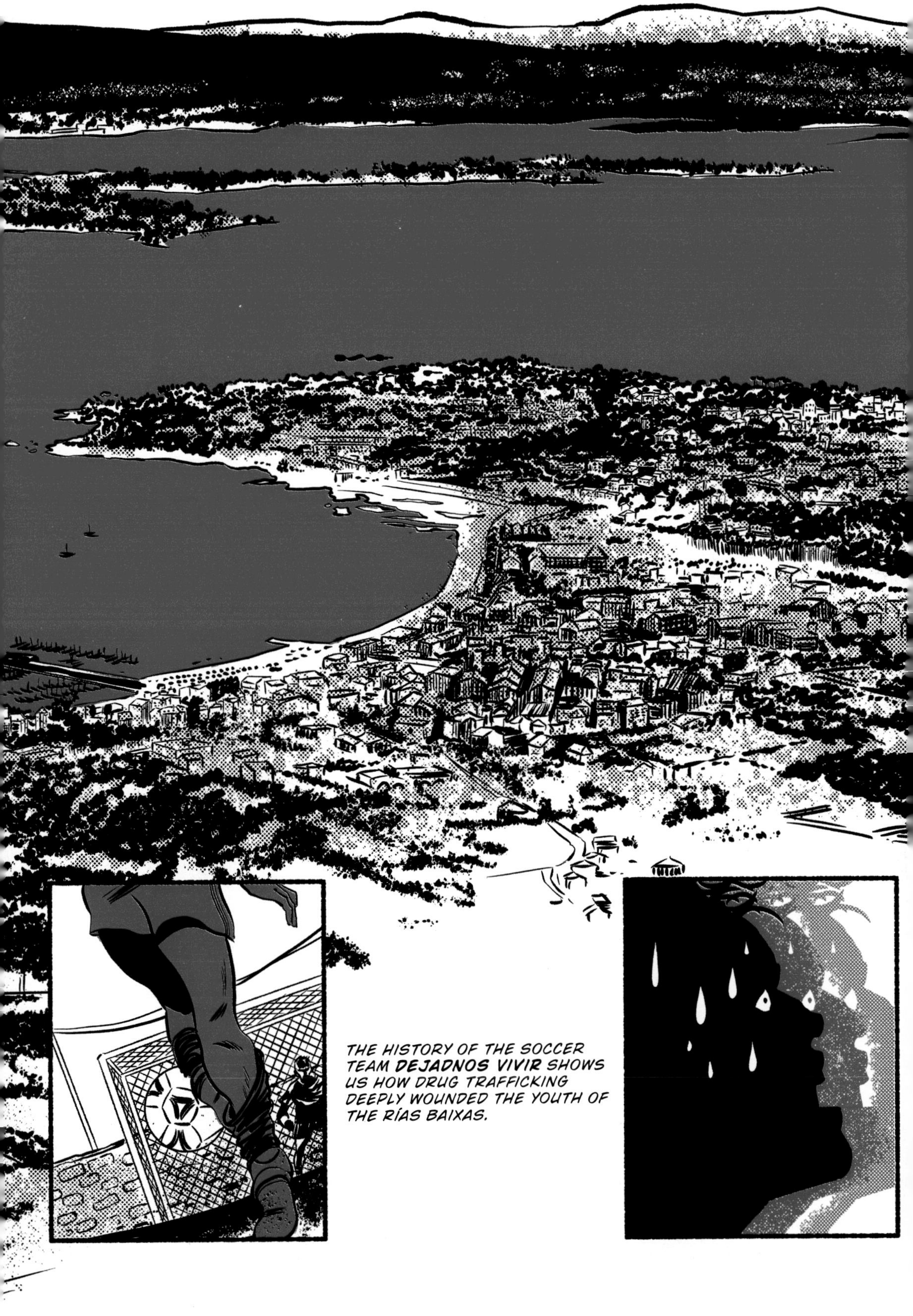
THE HISTORY OF THE SOCCER TEAM **DEJADNOS VIVIR** SHOWS US HOW DRUG TRAFFICKING DEEPLY WOUNDED THE YOUTH OF THE RÍAS BAIXAS.

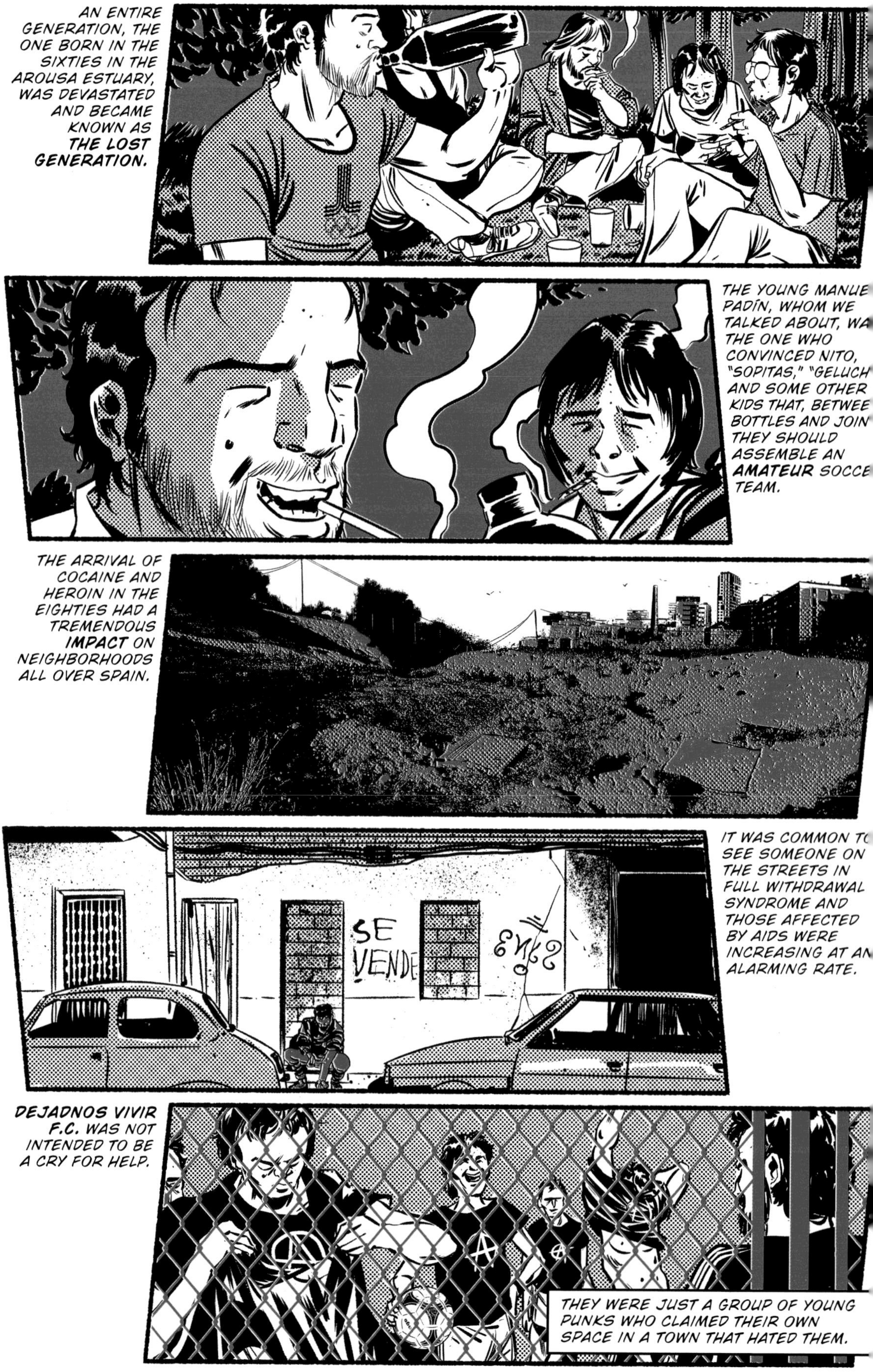

AN ENTIRE GENERATION, THE ONE BORN IN THE SIXTIES IN THE AROUSA ESTUARY, WAS DEVASTATED AND BECAME KNOWN AS **THE LOST GENERATION.**
THE YOUNG MANUE PADÍN, WHOM WE TALKED ABOUT, WA THE ONE WHO CONVINCED NITO, "SOPITAS," "GELUCH AND SOME OTHER KIDS THAT, BETWEE BOTTLES AND JOIN THEY SHOULD ASSEMBLE AN **AMATEUR** SOCCE TEAM.
THE ARRIVAL OF COCAINE AND HEROIN IN THE EIGHTIES HAD A TREMENDOUS **IMPACT** ON NEIGHBORHOODS ALL OVER SPAIN.
SE VENDE
IT WAS COMMON TO SEE SOMEONE ON THE STREETS IN FULL WITHDRAWAL SYNDROME AND THOSE AFFECTED BY AIDS WERE INCREASING AT AN ALARMING RATE.
**DEJADNOS VIVIR F.C.** WAS NOT INTENDED TO BE A CRY FOR HELP.
THEY WERE JUST A GROUP OF YOUNG PUNKS WHO CLAIMED THEIR OWN SPACE IN A TOWN THAT HATED THEM.

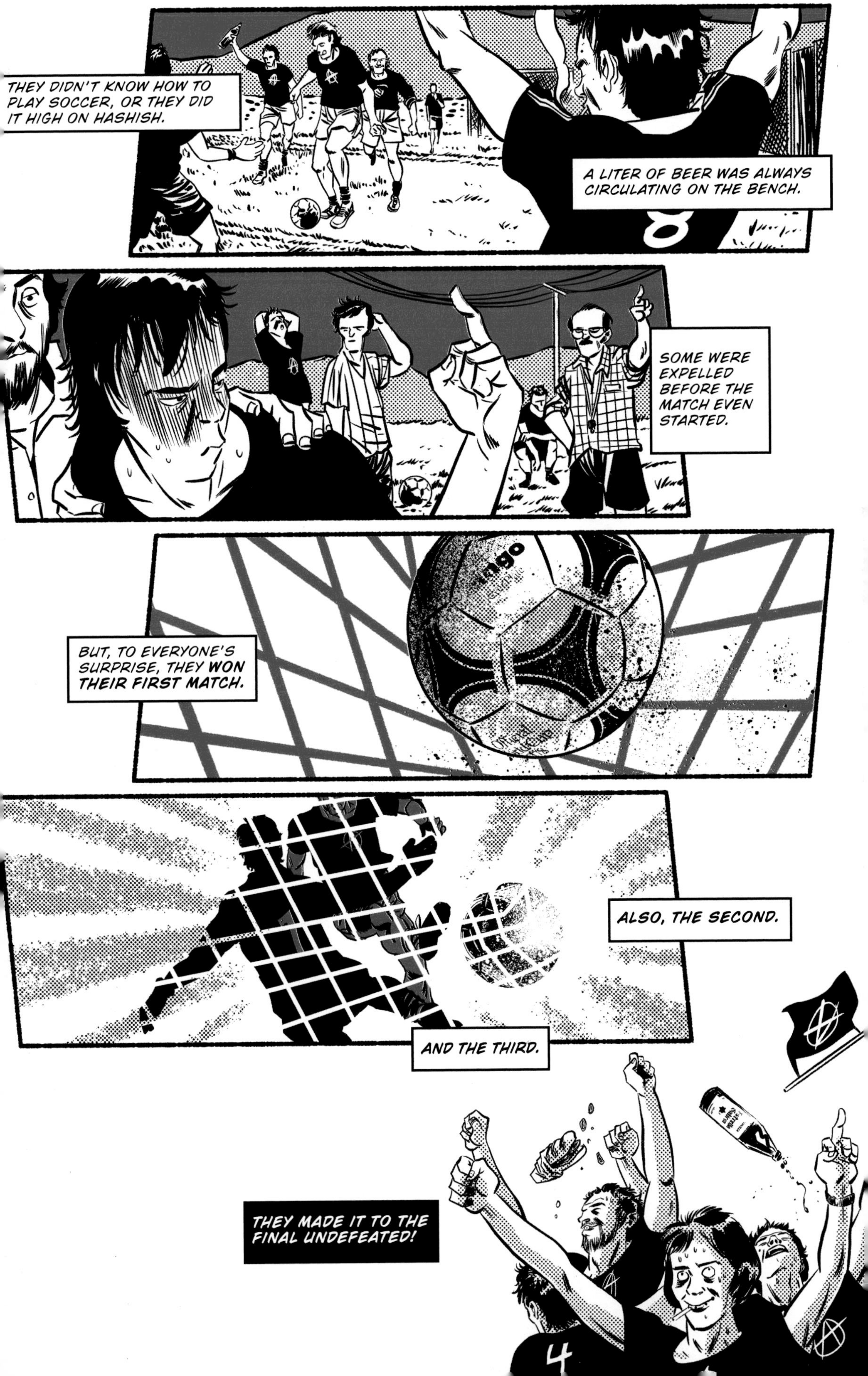
THEY DIDN'T KNOW HOW TO PLAY SOCCER, OR THEY DID IT HIGH ON HASHISH.
A LITER OF BEER WAS ALWAYS CIRCULATING ON THE BENCH.
SOME WERE EXPELLED BEFORE THE MATCH EVEN STARTED.
BUT, TO EVERYONE'S SURPRISE, THEY WON THEIR FIRST MATCH.
ALSO, THE SECOND.
AND THE THIRD.
THEY MADE IT TO THE FINAL UNDEFEATED!

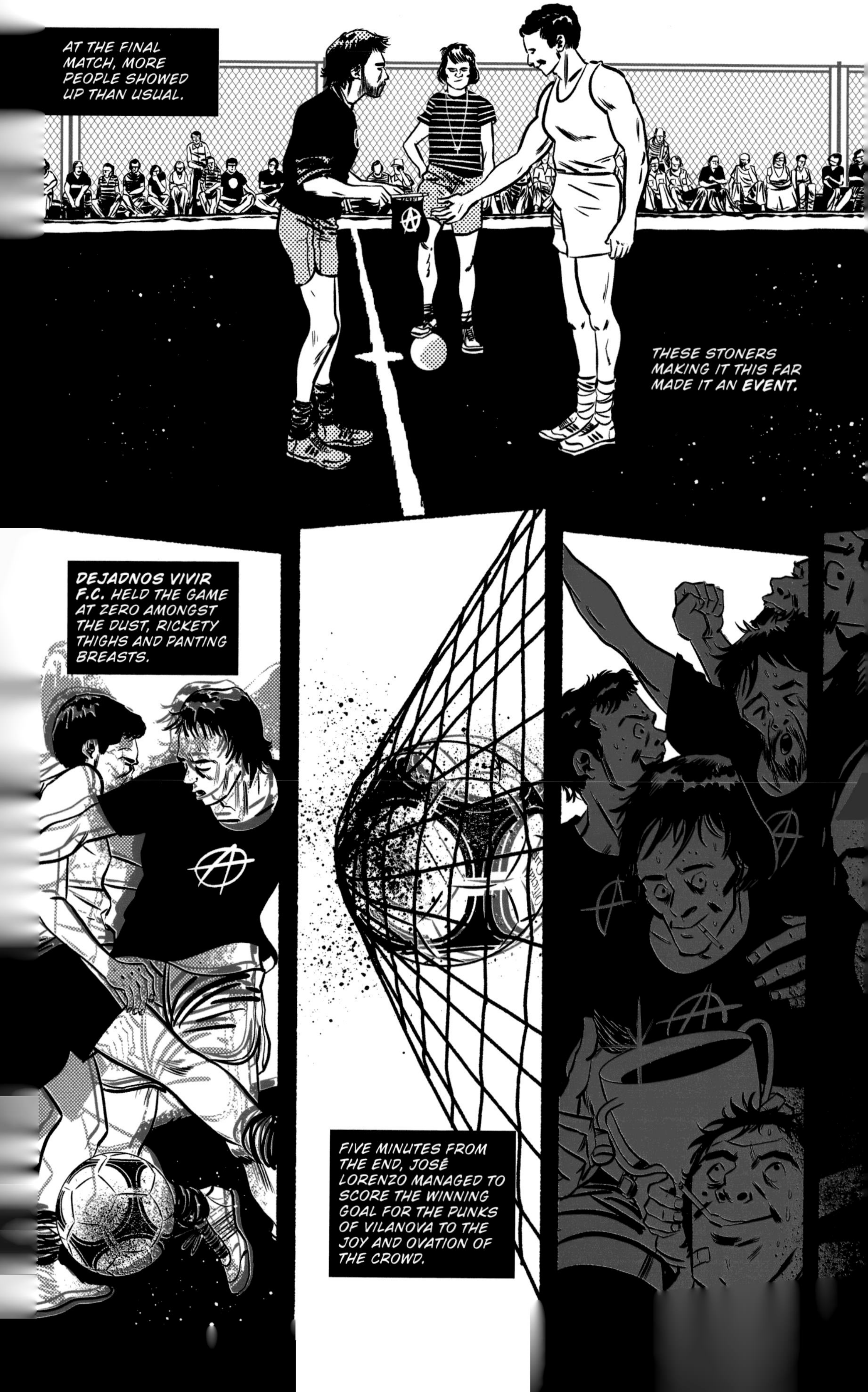
AT THE FINAL MATCH, MORE PEOPLE SHOWED UP THAN USUAL.
THESE STONERS MAKING IT THIS FAR MADE IT AN **EVENT.**
**DEJADNOS VIVIR F.C.** HELD THE GAME AT ZERO AMONGST THE DUST, RICKETY THIGHS AND PANTING BREASTS.
FIVE MINUTES FROM THE END, JOSÉ LORENZO MANAGED TO SCORE THE WINNING GOAL FOR THE PUNKS OF VILANOVA TO THE JOY AND OVATION OF THE CROWD.

SHORTLY AFTER, JOSÉ LORENZO DIED ON THE BEACH OF AN EPILEPTIC SEIZURE.

MANOLO PANADERO, OF A HEROIN OVER-DOSE.

PACHECO, THE GOALKEEPER, WOULD DIE IN A FIRE CAUSED BY HIS OWN CIGARETTE AFTER YEARS OF ALCOHOLISM.

REIGOSA AND BARETA FROM AIDS.

OUT OF THE WHOLE TEAM, ONLY THREE ARE STILL ALIVE TODAY.

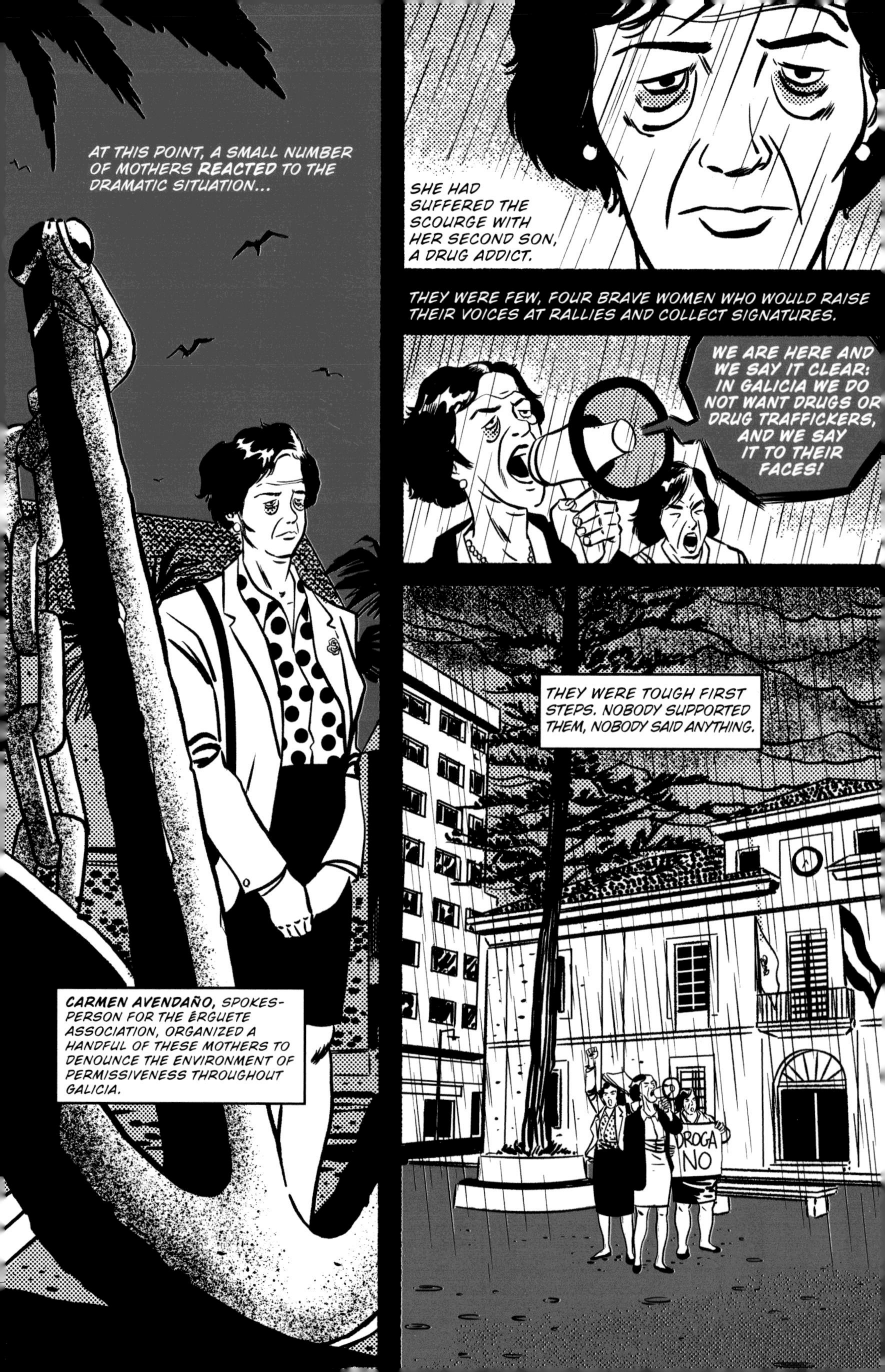
AT THIS POINT, A SMALL NUMBER OF MOTHERS **REACTED** TO THE DRAMATIC SITUATION...
**CARMEN AVENDAÑO,** SPOKESPERSON FOR THE ÉRGUETE ASSOCIATION, ORGANIZED A HANDFUL OF THESE MOTHERS TO DENOUNCE THE ENVIRONMENT OF PERMISSIVENESS THROUGHOUT GALICIA.
SHE HAD SUFFERED THE SCOURGE WITH HER SECOND SON, A DRUG ADDICT.
THEY WERE FEW, FOUR BRAVE WOMEN WHO WOULD RAISE THEIR VOICES AT RALLIES AND COLLECT SIGNATURES.
WE ARE HERE AND WE SAY IT CLEAR: IN GALICIA WE DO NOT WANT DRUGS OR DRUG TRAFFICKERS, AND WE SAY IT TO THEIR FACES!
THEY WERE TOUGH FIRST STEPS. NOBODY SUPPORTED THEM, NOBODY SAID ANYTHING.
DROGA NO

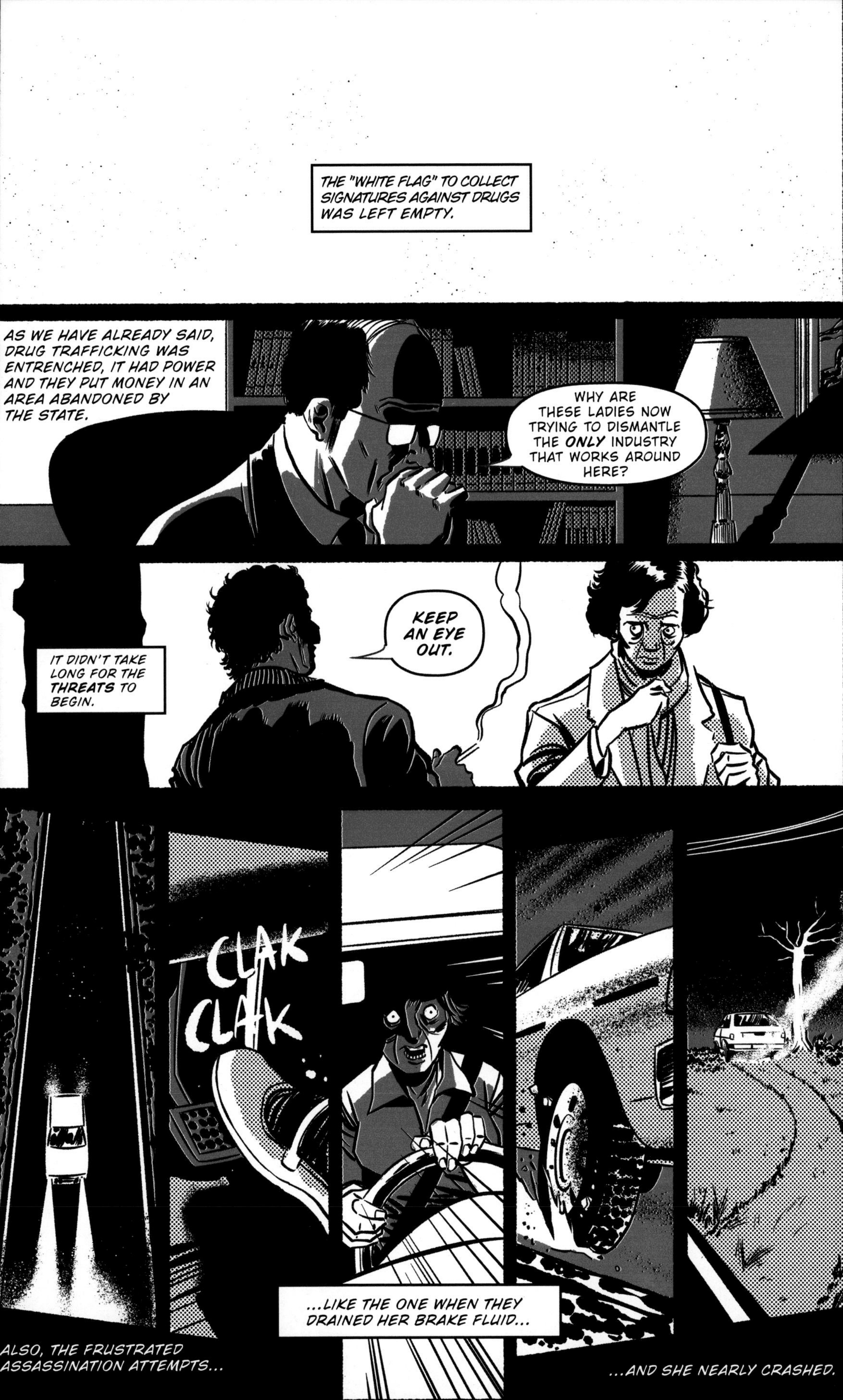

THE "WHITE FLAG" TO COLLECT SIGNATURES AGAINST DRUGS WAS LEFT EMPTY.
AS WE HAVE ALREADY SAID, DRUG TRAFFICKING WAS ENTRENCHED, IT HAD POWER AND THEY PUT MONEY IN AN AREA ABANDONED BY THE STATE.
WHY ARE THESE LADIES NOW TRYING TO DISMANTLE THE ONLY INDUSTRY THAT WORKS AROUND HERE?
IT DIDN'T TAKE LONG FOR THE THREATS TO BEGIN.
KEEP AN EYE OUT.
ALSO, THE FRUSTRATED ASSASSINATION ATTEMPTS...
CLAK
CLAK
...LIKE THE ONE WHEN THEY DRAINED HER BRAKE FLUID...
...AND SHE NEARLY CRASHED.

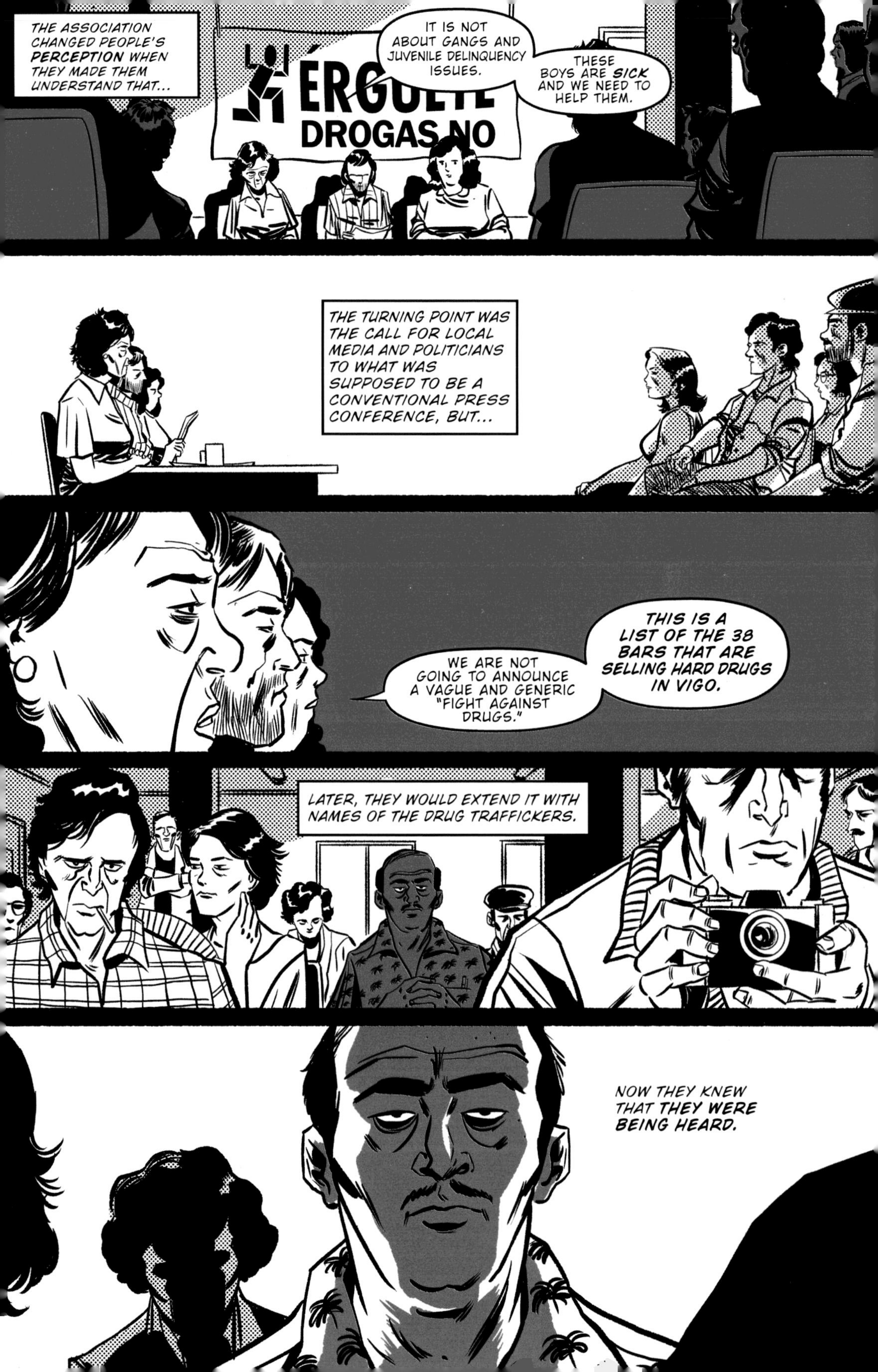

THE ASSOCIATION CHANGED PEOPLE'S **PERCEPTION** WHEN THEY MADE THEM UNDERSTAND THAT...
IT IS NOT ABOUT GANGS AND JUVENILE DELINQUENCY ISSUES.
THESE BOYS ARE **SICK** AND WE NEED TO HELP THEM.
DROGAS NO
THE TURNING POINT WAS THE CALL FOR LOCAL MEDIA AND POLITICIANS TO WHAT WAS SUPPOSED TO BE A CONVENTIONAL PRESS CONFERENCE, BUT...
WE ARE NOT GOING TO ANNOUNCE A VAGUE AND GENERIC "FIGHT AGAINST DRUGS."
**THIS IS A LIST OF THE 38 BARS THAT ARE SELLING HARD DRUGS IN VIGO.**
LATER, THEY WOULD EXTEND IT WITH NAMES OF THE DRUG TRAFFICKERS.
NOW THEY KNEW THAT **THEY WERE BEING HEARD.**

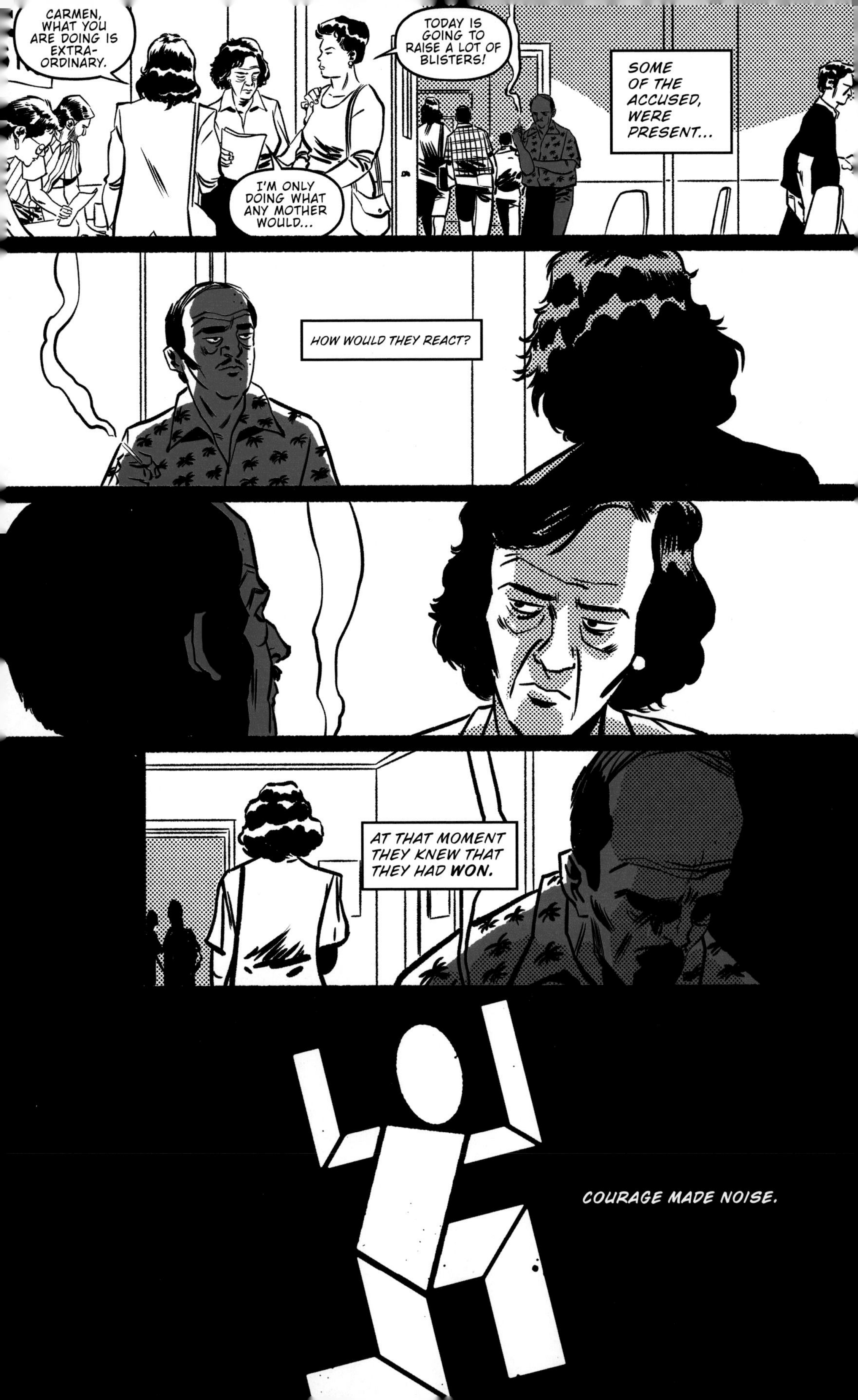

CARMEN, WHAT YOU ARE DOING IS EXTRA-ORDINARY.
TODAY IS GOING TO RAISE A LOT OF BLISTERS!
I'M ONLY DOING WHAT ANY MOTHER WOULD...
SOME OF THE ACCUSED, WERE PRESENT...
HOW WOULD THEY REACT?
AT THAT MOMENT THEY KNEW THAT THEY HAD WON.
COURAGE MADE NOISE.

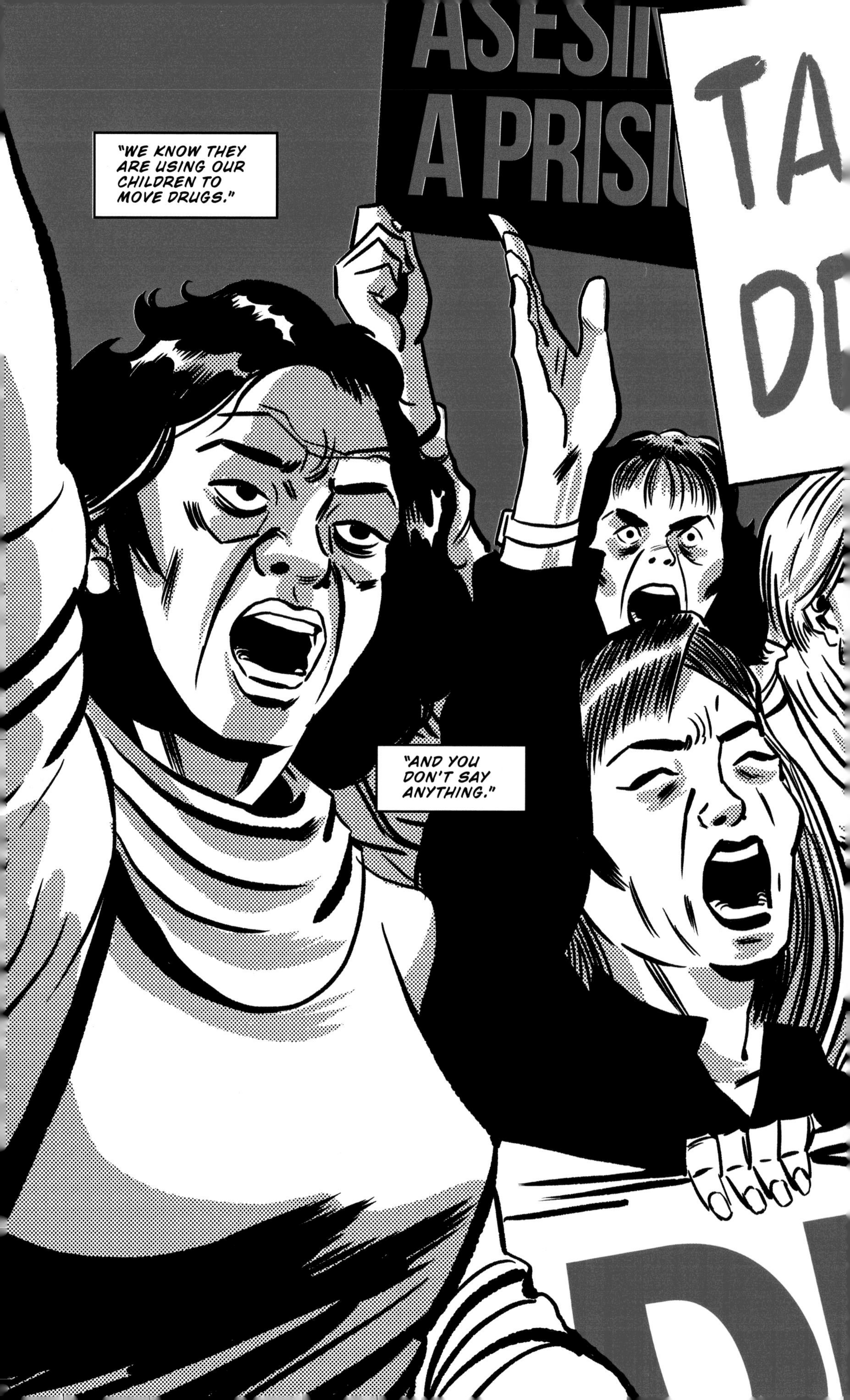
ASESIN
A PRISIO
TA
DE
"WE KNOW THEY ARE USING OUR CHILDREN TO MOVE DRUGS."
"AND YOU DON'T SAY ANYTHING."

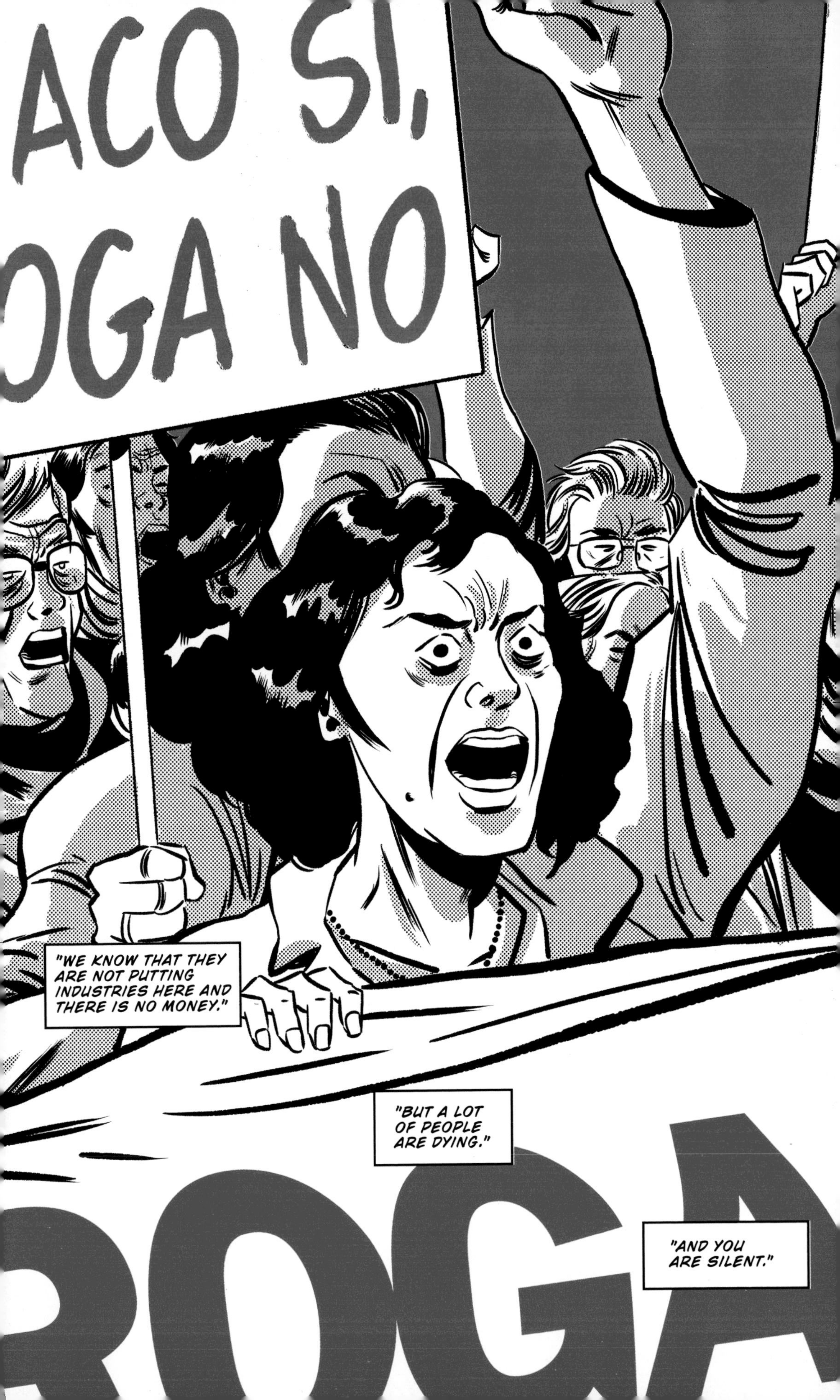
ACO SI,
OGA NO
"WE KNOW THAT THEY ARE NOT PUTTING INDUSTRIES HERE AND THERE IS NO MONEY."
"BUT A LOT OF PEOPLE ARE DYING."
ROGA
"AND YOU ARE SILENT."

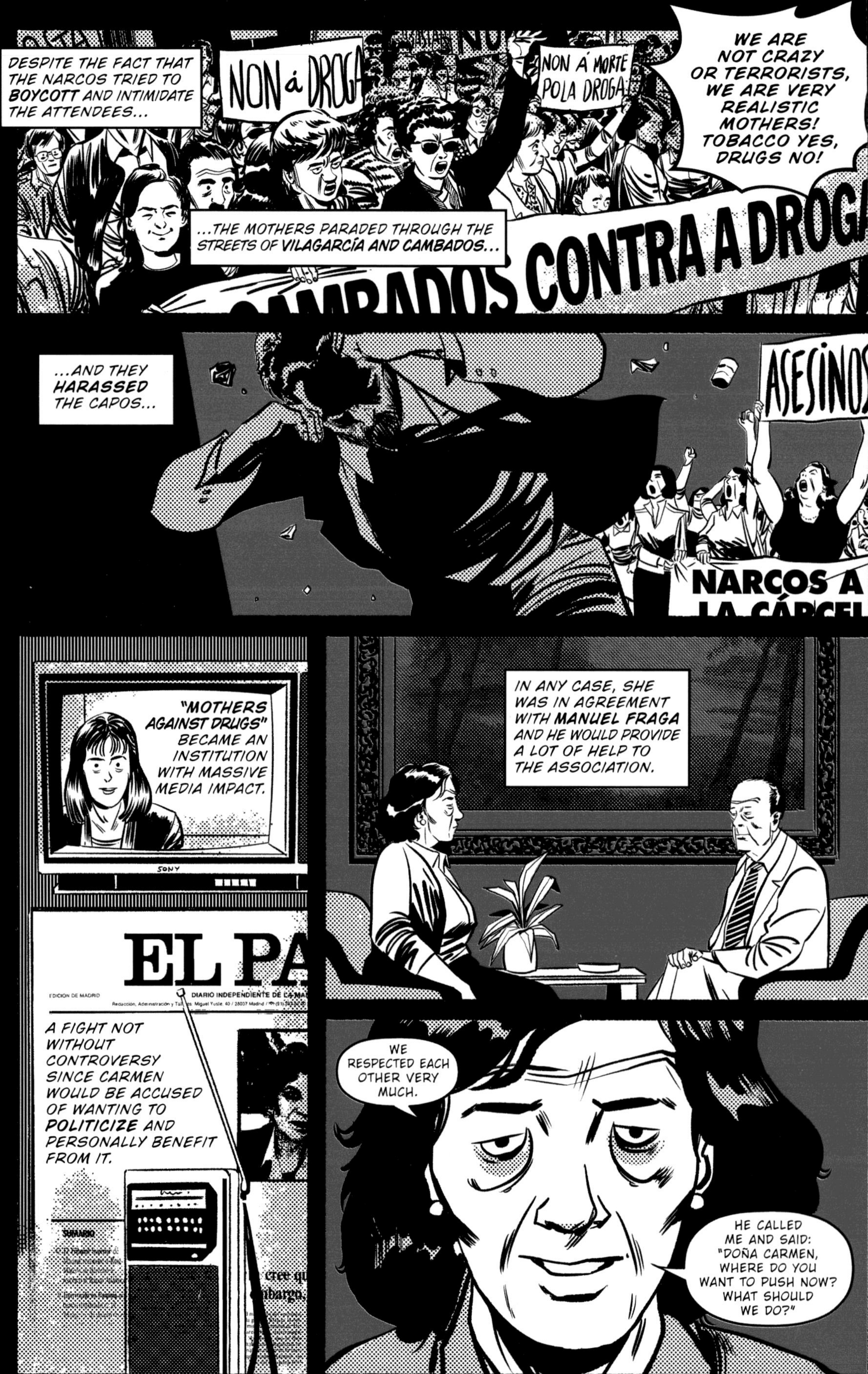
DESPITE THE FACT THAT THE NARCOS TRIED TO BOYCOTT AND INTIMIDATE THE ATTENDEES...
NON á DROGA
NON Á MORTE POLA DROGA
WE ARE NOT CRAZY OR TERRORISTS, WE ARE VERY REALISTIC MOTHERS! TOBACCO YES, DRUGS NO!
...THE MOTHERS PARADED THROUGH THE STREETS OF VILAGARCÍA AND CAMBADOS...
CONTRA A DROGA
...AND THEY HARASSED THE CAPOS...
ASESINOS
NARCOS A
"MOTHERS AGAINST DRUGS" BECAME AN INSTITUTION WITH MASSIVE MEDIA IMPACT.
SONY
EL PA
EDICION DE MADRID
A FIGHT NOT WITHOUT CONTROVERSY SINCE CARMEN WOULD BE ACCUSED OF WANTING TO POLITICIZE AND PERSONALLY BENEFIT FROM IT.
IN ANY CASE, SHE WAS IN AGREEMENT WITH MANUEL FRAGA AND HE WOULD PROVIDE A LOT OF HELP TO THE ASSOCIATION.
WE RESPECTED EACH OTHER VERY MUCH.
HE CALLED ME AND SAID: "DOÑA CARMEN, WHERE DO YOU WANT TO PUSH NOW? WHAT SHOULD WE DO?"

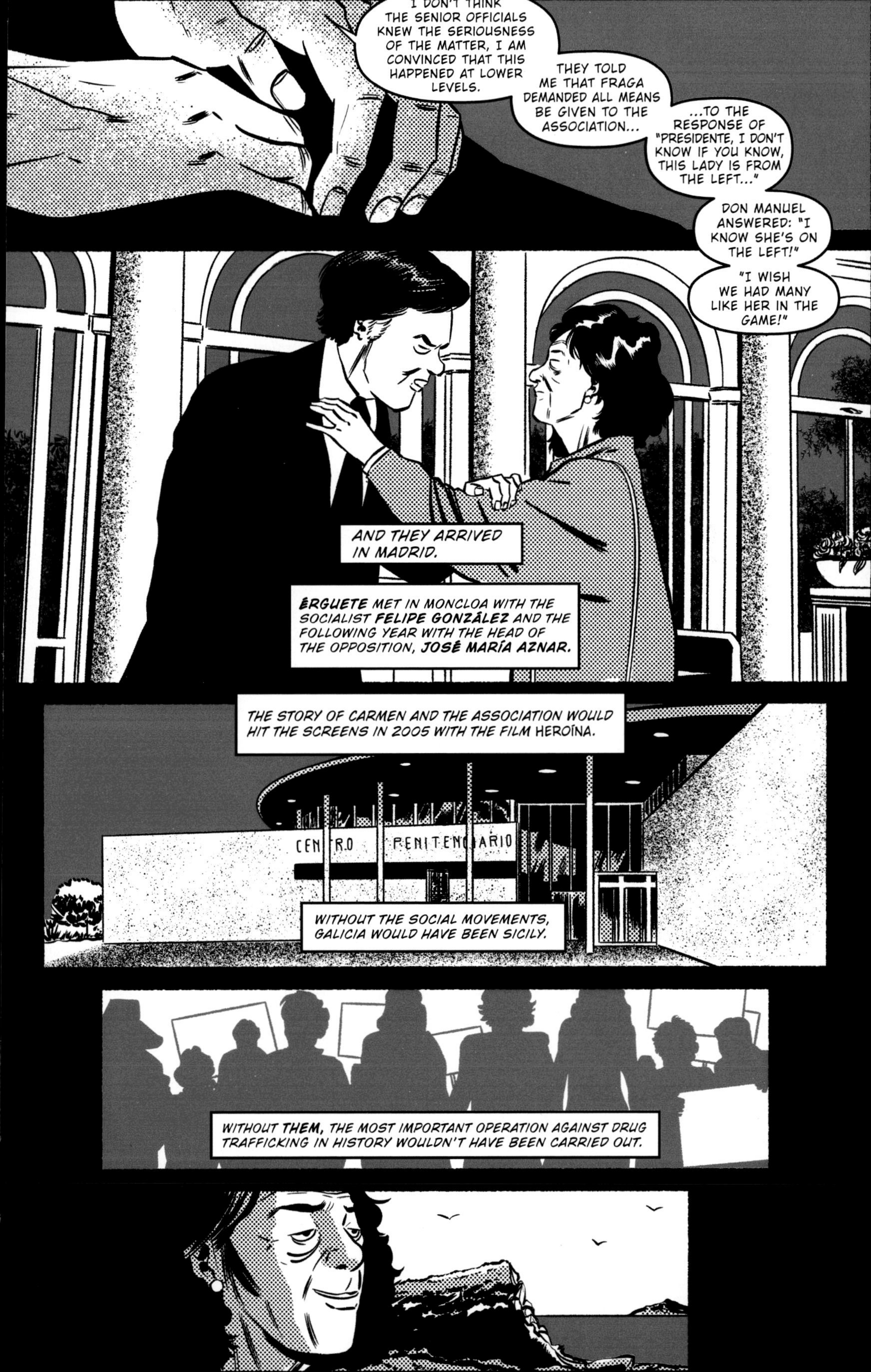
I DON'T THINK THE SENIOR OFFICIALS KNEW THE SERIOUSNESS OF THE MATTER, I AM CONVINCED THAT THIS HAPPENED AT LOWER LEVELS.
THEY TOLD ME THAT FRAGA DEMANDED ALL MEANS BE GIVEN TO THE ASSOCIATION...
...TO THE RESPONSE OF "PRESIDENTE, I DON'T KNOW IF YOU KNOW, THIS LADY IS FROM THE LEFT..."
DON MANUEL ANSWERED: "I KNOW SHE'S ON THE LEFT!"
"I WISH WE HAD MANY LIKE HER IN THE GAME!"
AND THEY ARRIVED IN MADRID.
ÉRGUETE MET IN MONCLOA WITH THE SOCIALIST FELIPE GONZÁLEZ AND THE FOLLOWING YEAR WITH THE HEAD OF THE OPPOSITION, JOSÉ MARÍA AZNAR.
THE STORY OF CARMEN AND THE ASSOCIATION WOULD HIT THE SCREENS IN 2005 WITH THE FILM HEROÍNA.
CENTRO PENITENCIARIO
WITHOUT THE SOCIAL MOVEMENTS, GALICIA WOULD HAVE BEEN SICILY.
WITHOUT THEM, THE MOST IMPORTANT OPERATION AGAINST DRUG TRAFFICKING IN HISTORY WOULDN'T HAVE BEEN CARRIED OUT.

# LA OPERACIÓN NÉCORA

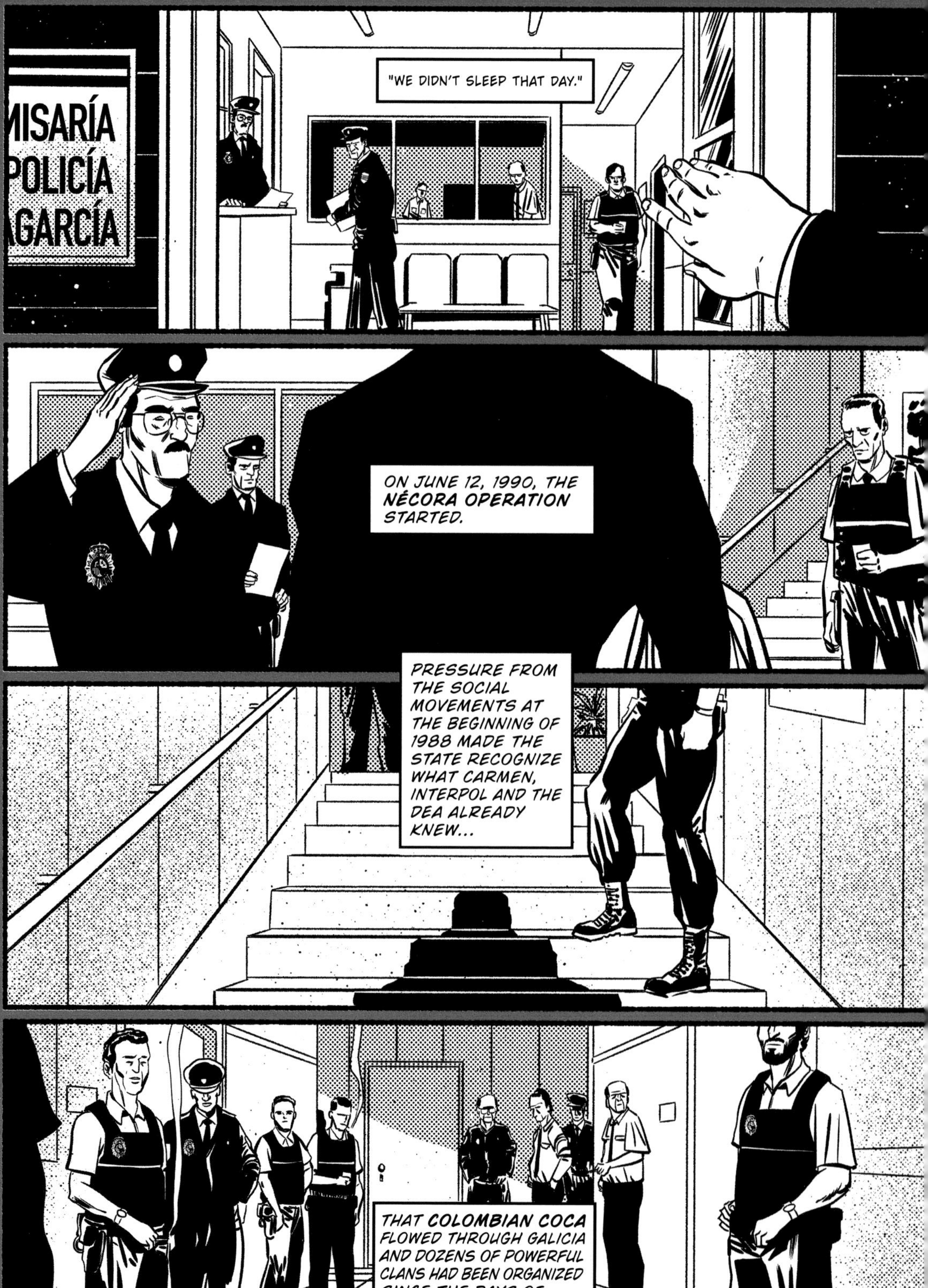
"WE DIDN'T SLEEP THAT DAY."
ON JUNE 12, 1990, THE **NÉCORA OPERATION** STARTED.
PRESSURE FROM THE SOCIAL MOVEMENTS AT THE BEGINNING OF 1988 MADE THE STATE RECOGNIZE WHAT CARMEN, INTERPOL AND THE DEA ALREADY KNEW...
THAT **COLOMBIAN COCA** FLOWED THROUGH GALICIA AND DOZENS OF POWERFUL CLANS HAD BEEN ORGANIZED SINCE THE DAYS OF TOBACCO SMUGGLING.

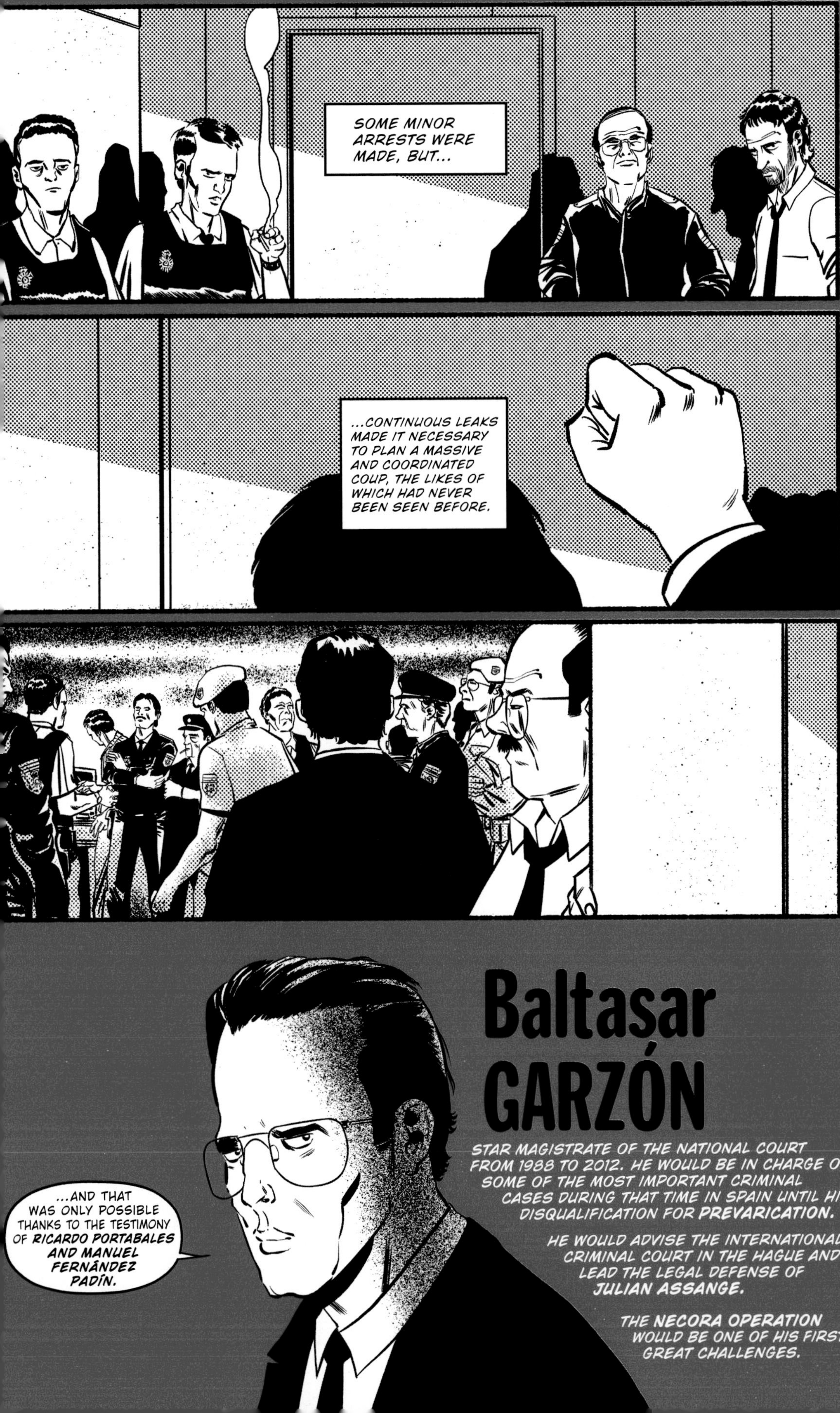
SOME MINOR ARRESTS WERE MADE, BUT...
...CONTINUOUS LEAKS MADE IT NECESSARY TO PLAN A MASSIVE AND COORDINATED COUP, THE LIKES OF WHICH HAD NEVER BEEN SEEN BEFORE.
...AND THAT WAS ONLY POSSIBLE THANKS TO THE TESTIMONY OF RICARDO PORTABALES AND MANUEL FERNÁNDEZ PADÍN.
Baltasar GARZÓN
STAR MAGISTRATE OF THE NATIONAL COURT FROM 1988 TO 2012. HE WOULD BE IN CHARGE OF SOME OF THE MOST IMPORTANT CRIMINAL CASES DURING THAT TIME IN SPAIN UNTIL HIS DISQUALIFICATION FOR PREVARICATION.
HE WOULD ADVISE THE INTERNATIONAL CRIMINAL COURT IN THE HAGUE AND LEAD THE LEGAL DEFENSE OF JULIAN ASSANGE.
THE NECORA OPERATION WOULD BE ONE OF HIS FIRST GREAT CHALLENGES.

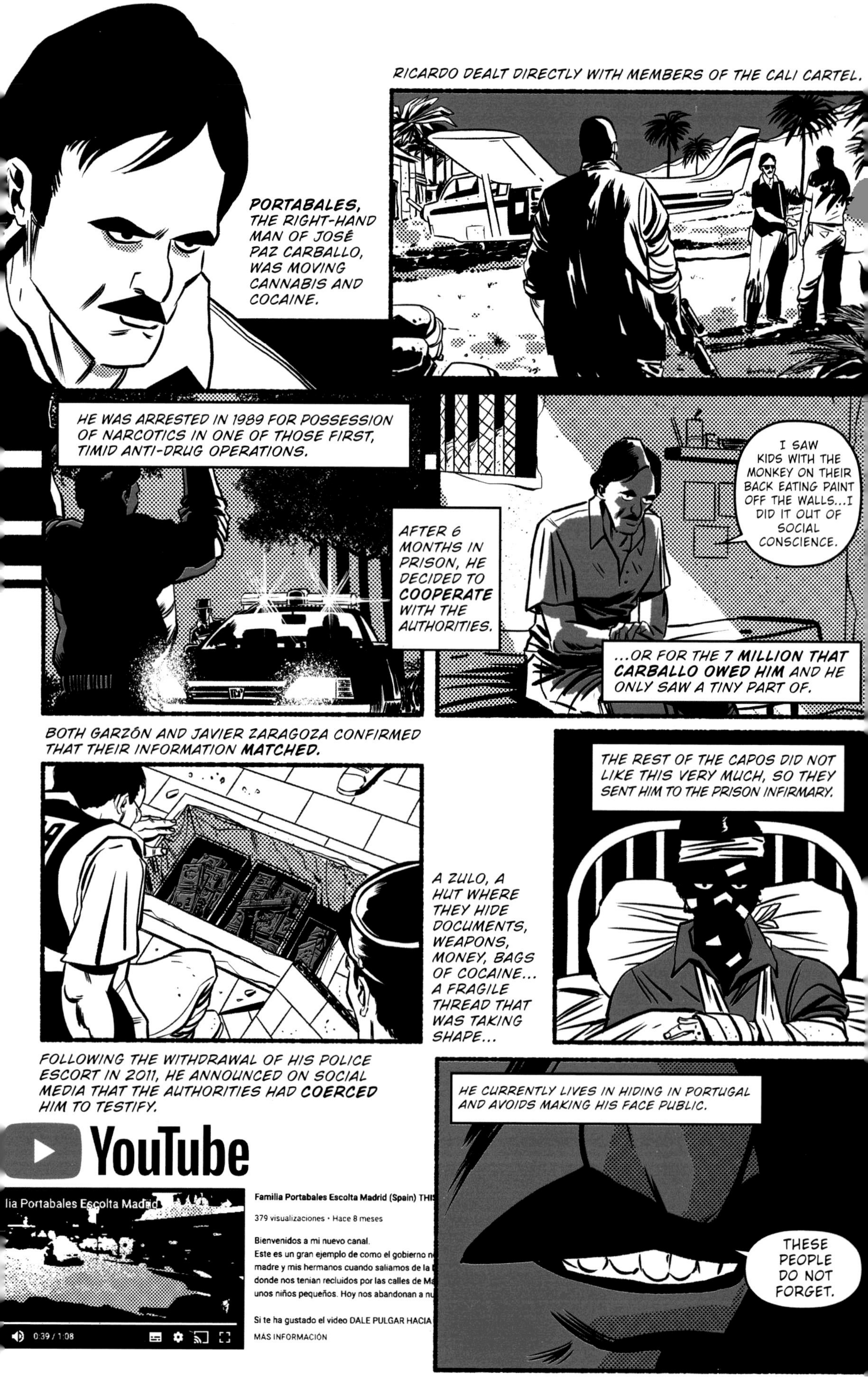
PORTABALES, THE RIGHT-HAND MAN OF JOSÉ PAZ CARBALLO, WAS MOVING CANNABIS AND COCAINE.
RICARDO DEALT DIRECTLY WITH MEMBERS OF THE CALI CARTEL.
HE WAS ARRESTED IN 1989 FOR POSSESSION OF NARCOTICS IN ONE OF THOSE FIRST, TIMID ANTI-DRUG OPERATIONS.
AFTER 6 MONTHS IN PRISON, HE DECIDED TO COOPERATE WITH THE AUTHORITIES.
I SAW KIDS WITH THE MONKEY ON THEIR BACK EATING PAINT OFF THE WALLS...I DID IT OUT OF SOCIAL CONSCIENCE.
...OR FOR THE 7 MILLION THAT CARBALLO OWED HIM AND HE ONLY SAW A TINY PART OF.
BOTH GARZÓN AND JAVIER ZARAGOZA CONFIRMED THAT THEIR INFORMATION MATCHED.
A ZULO, A HUT WHERE THEY HIDE DOCUMENTS, WEAPONS, MONEY, BAGS OF COCAINE... A FRAGILE THREAD THAT WAS TAKING SHAPE...
THE REST OF THE CAPOS DID NOT LIKE THIS VERY MUCH, SO THEY SENT HIM TO THE PRISON INFIRMARY.
FOLLOWING THE WITHDRAWAL OF HIS POLICE ESCORT IN 2011, HE ANNOUNCED ON SOCIAL MEDIA THAT THE AUTHORITIES HAD COERCED HIM TO TESTIFY.
YouTube
lia Portabales Escolta Madrid
0:39 / 1:08
Familia Portabales Escolta Madrid (Spain) THIS
379 visualizaciones • Hace 8 meses
Bienvenidos a mi nuevo canal.
Este es un gran ejemplo de como el gobierno n
madre y mis hermanos cuando salíamos de la
donde nos tenían recluidos por las calles de M
unos niños pequeños. Hoy nos abandonan a nu
Si te ha gustado el video DALE PULGAR HACIA
MÁS INFORMACIÓN
HE CURRENTLY LIVES IN HIDING IN PORTUGAL AND AVOIDS MAKING HIS FACE PUBLIC.
THESE PEOPLE DO NOT FORGET.

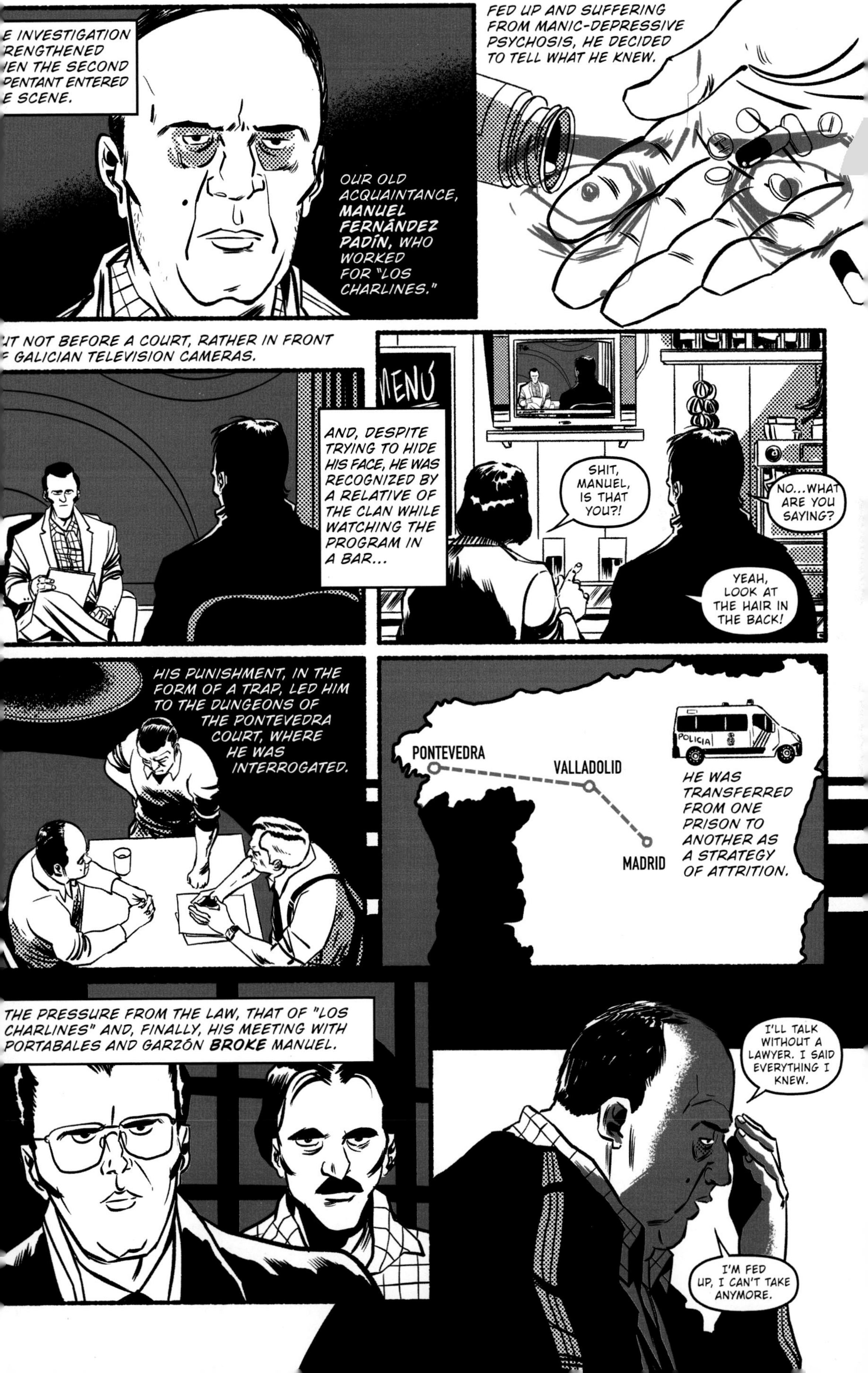
E INVESTIGATION
RENGTHENED
IEN THE SECOND
PENTANT ENTERED
E SCENE.
OUR OLD ACQUAINTANCE, MANUEL FERNÁNDEZ PADÍN, WHO WORKED FOR "LOS CHARLINES."
FED UP AND SUFFERING FROM MANIC-DEPRESSIVE PSYCHOSIS, HE DECIDED TO TELL WHAT HE KNEW.
IT NOT BEFORE A COURT, RATHER IN FRONT
F GALICIAN TELEVISION CAMERAS.
AND, DESPITE TRYING TO HIDE HIS FACE, HE WAS RECOGNIZED BY A RELATIVE OF THE CLAN WHILE WATCHING THE PROGRAM IN A BAR...
MENU
SHIT, MANUEL, IS THAT YOU?!
NO...WHAT ARE YOU SAYING?
YEAH, LOOK AT THE HAIR IN THE BACK!
HIS PUNISHMENT, IN THE FORM OF A TRAP, LED HIM TO THE DUNGEONS OF THE PONTEVEDRA COURT, WHERE HE WAS INTERROGATED.
POLICIA
PONTEVEDRA
VALLADOLID
MADRID
HE WAS TRANSFERRED FROM ONE PRISON TO ANOTHER AS A STRATEGY OF ATTRITION.
THE PRESSURE FROM THE LAW, THAT OF "LOS CHARLINES" AND, FINALLY, HIS MEETING WITH PORTABALES AND GARZÓN BROKE MANUEL.
I'LL TALK WITHOUT A LAWYER. I SAID EVERYTHING I KNEW.
I'M FED UP, I CAN'T TAKE ANYMORE.

IN 1990, JUDGES GARZÓN AND ZARAGOZA MET WITH VARIOUS POLICE OFFICERS.

NONE FROM GALICIA.

THE PROPOSED PLAN WAS HUGE AND **THE LARGEST IN THE HISTORY OF THE DEMOCRACY.**

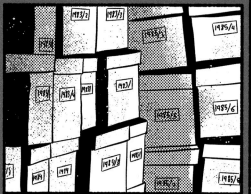

A SIMULTANEOUS RAID AGAINST MORE THAN 50 DEFENDANTS.

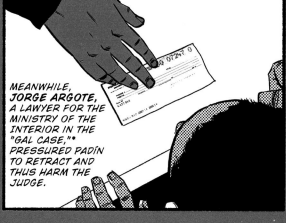

MEANWHILE, JORGE ARGOTE, A LAWYER FOR THE MINISTRY OF THE INTERIOR IN THE "GAL CASE,"* PRESSURED PADÍN TO RETRACT AND THUS HARM THE JUDGE.

ARE YOU WILLING TO COOPERATE? YOU JUST HAVE TO TELL THE **TRUTH.**

NAME YOUR PRICE.

SOMETHING THAT, FORTUNATELY, DID NOT HAPPEN THANKS TO THE PROSECUTION OF POLICE OFFICERS **AMEDO AND DOMÍNGUEZ.**

CONTINUE READING...

# THE BIG RAID

*STATE TERRORISM FINANCED WITH FUNDS RESERVED DURING THE LEGISLATURE OF THE PSOE.

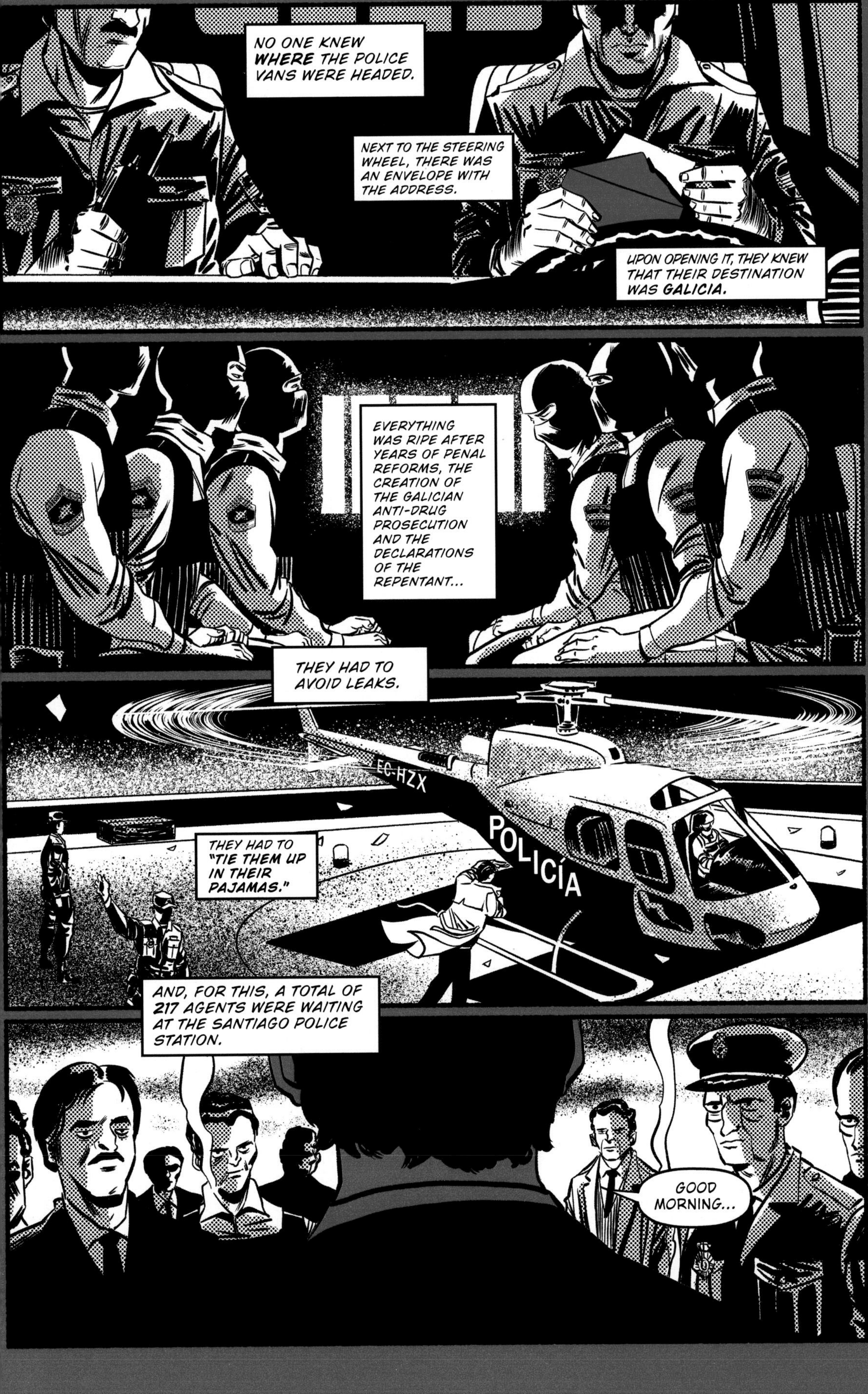
NO ONE KNEW WHERE THE POLICE VANS WERE HEADED.
NEXT TO THE STEERING WHEEL, THERE WAS AN ENVELOPE WITH THE ADDRESS.
UPON OPENING IT, THEY KNEW THAT THEIR DESTINATION WAS GALICIA.
EVERYTHING WAS RIPE AFTER YEARS OF PENAL REFORMS, THE CREATION OF THE GALICIAN ANTI-DRUG PROSECUTION AND THE DECLARATIONS OF THE REPENTANT...
THEY HAD TO AVOID LEAKS.
EC-HZX
POLICÍA
THEY HAD TO "TIE THEM UP IN THEIR PAJAMAS."
AND, FOR THIS, A TOTAL OF 217 AGENTS WERE WAITING AT THE SANTIAGO POLICE STATION.
GOOD MORNING...

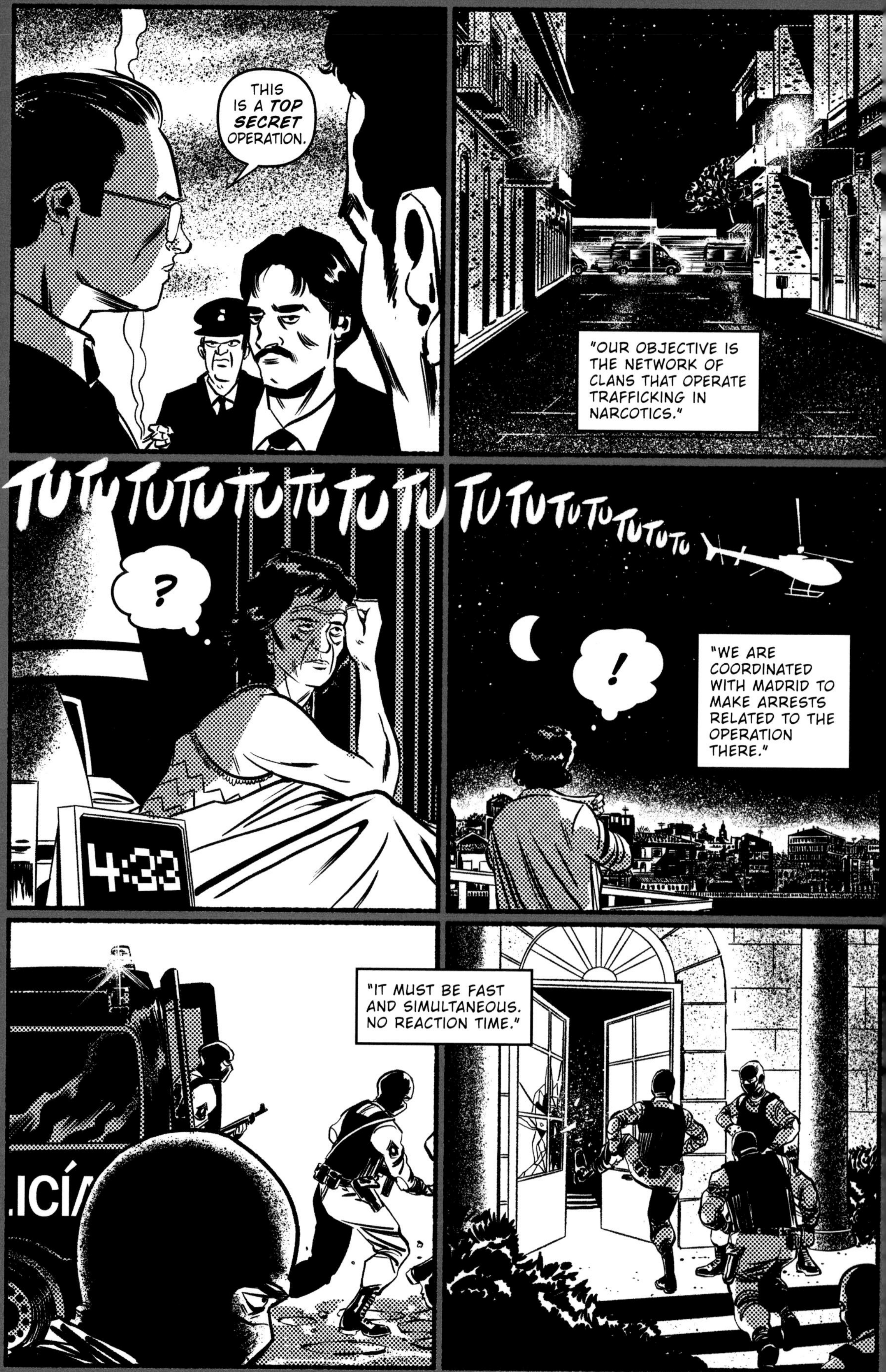
THIS IS A TOP SECRET OPERATION.
"OUR OBJECTIVE IS THE NETWORK OF CLANS THAT OPERATE TRAFFICKING IN NARCOTICS."
TUTUTUTUTUTUTUTUTUTUTUTUTUTUTUTUTUTUTUTU
?
4:33
!
"WE ARE COORDINATED WITH MADRID TO MAKE ARRESTS RELATED TO THE OPERATION THERE."
"IT MUST BE FAST AND SIMULTANEOUS. NO REACTION TIME."

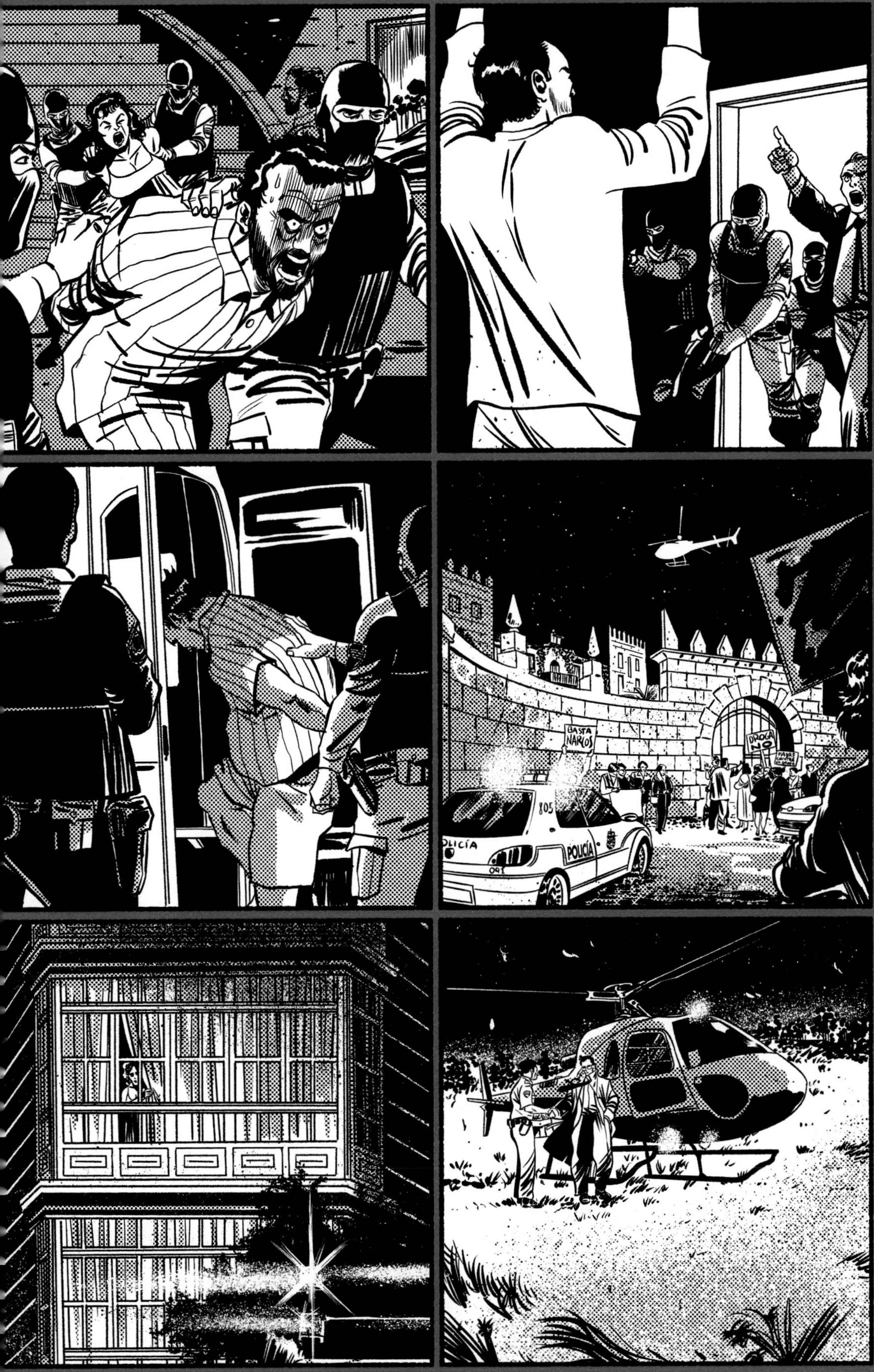
BASTA NARCOS
DROGA NO
805
POLICÍA
091

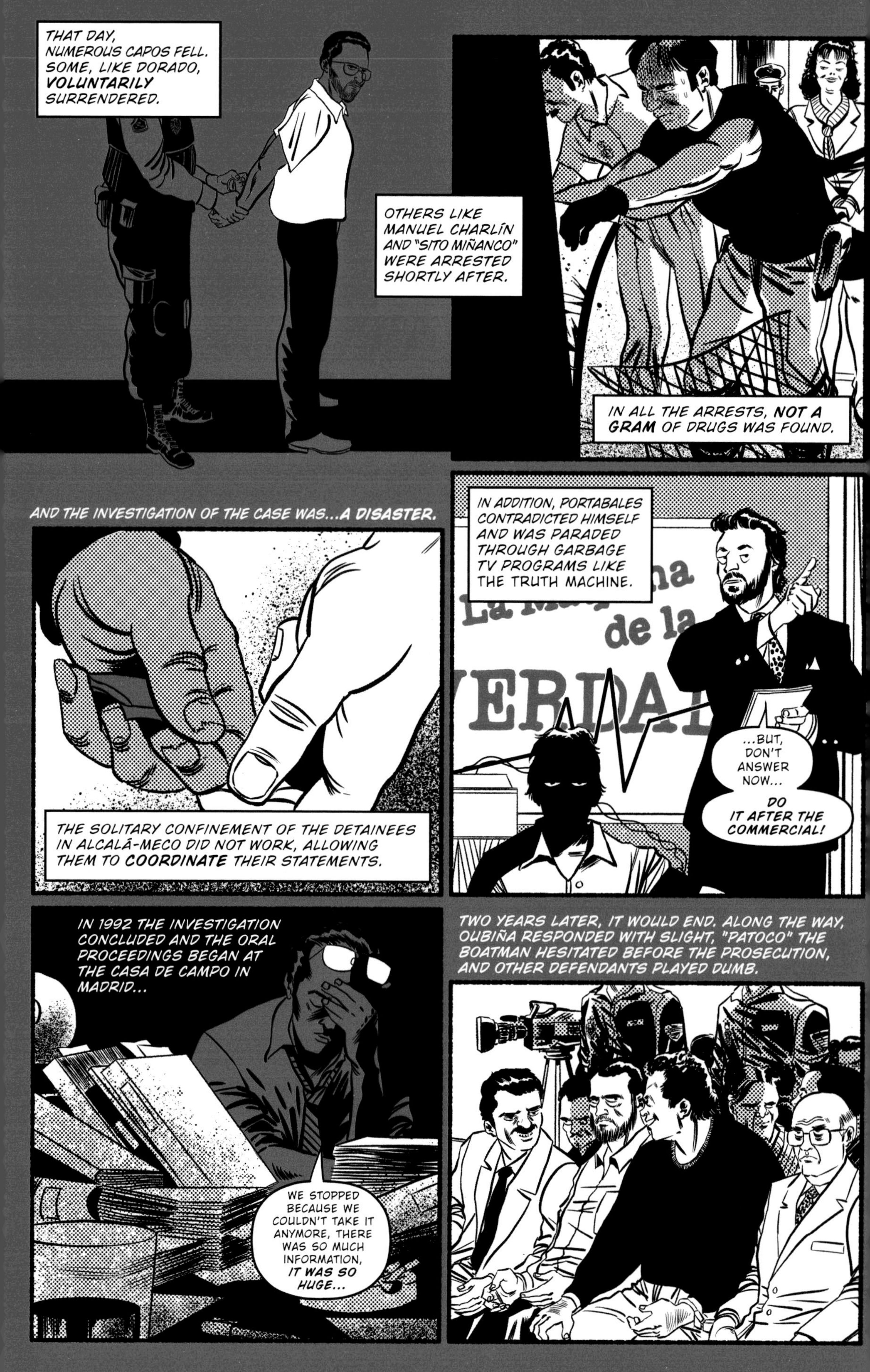
THAT DAY, NUMEROUS CAPOS FELL. SOME, LIKE DORADO, VOLUNTARILY SURRENDERED.
OTHERS LIKE MANUEL CHARLÍN AND "SITO MIÑANCO" WERE ARRESTED SHORTLY AFTER.
IN ALL THE ARRESTS, NOT A GRAM OF DRUGS WAS FOUND.
AND THE INVESTIGATION OF THE CASE WAS...A DISASTER.
THE SOLITARY CONFINEMENT OF THE DETAINEES IN ALCALÁ-MECO DID NOT WORK, ALLOWING THEM TO COORDINATE THEIR STATEMENTS.
IN ADDITION, PORTABALES CONTRADICTED HIMSELF AND WAS PARADED THROUGH GARBAGE TV PROGRAMS LIKE THE TRUTH MACHINE.
de la
...BUT, DON'T ANSWER NOW...
DO IT AFTER THE COMMERCIAL!
IN 1992 THE INVESTIGATION CONCLUDED AND THE ORAL PROCEEDINGS BEGAN AT THE CASA DE CAMPO IN MADRID...
WE STOPPED BECAUSE WE COULDN'T TAKE IT ANYMORE, THERE WAS SO MUCH INFORMATION, IT WAS SO HUGE...
TWO YEARS LATER, IT WOULD END. ALONG THE WAY, OUBIÑA RESPONDED WITH SLIGHT, "PATOCO" THE BOATMAN HESITATED BEFORE THE PROSECUTION, AND OTHER DEFENDANTS PLAYED DUMB.

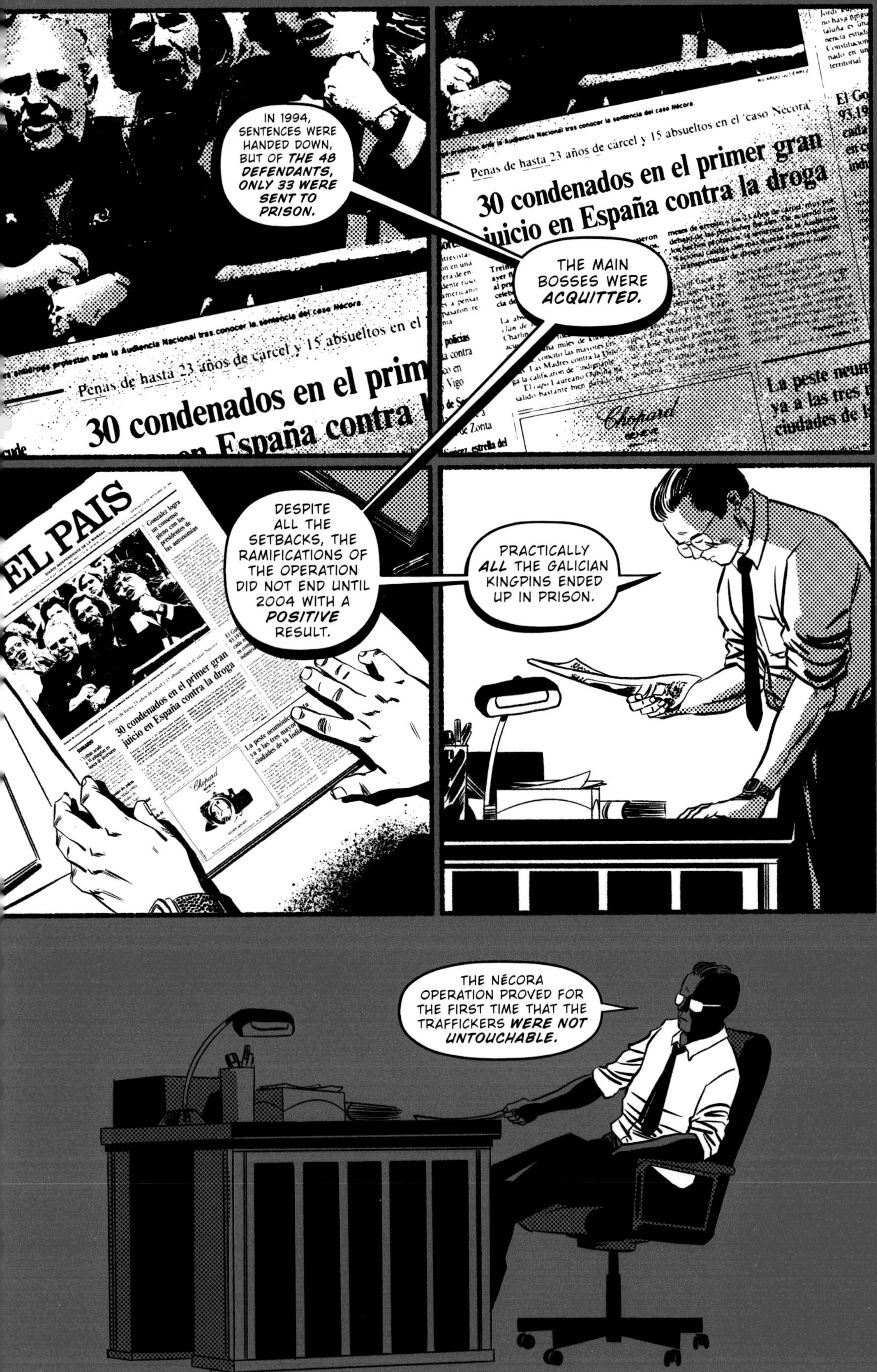
IN 1994, SENTENCES WERE HANDED DOWN, BUT OF THE 48 DEFENDANTS, ONLY 33 WERE SENT TO PRISON.
Penas de hasta 23 años de cárcel y 15 absueltos en el 'caso Nécora'
30 condenados en el primer gran juicio en España contra la droga
THE MAIN BOSSES WERE ACQUITTED.
EL PAIS
DESPITE ALL THE SETBACKS, THE RAMIFICATIONS OF THE OPERATION DID NOT END UNTIL 2004 WITH A POSITIVE RESULT.
PRACTICALLY ALL THE GALICIAN KINGPINS ENDED UP IN PRISON.
THE NÉCORA OPERATION PROVED FOR THE FIRST TIME THAT THE TRAFFICKERS WERE NOT UNTOUCHABLE.

Chapter Four

# AT FULL SPEED

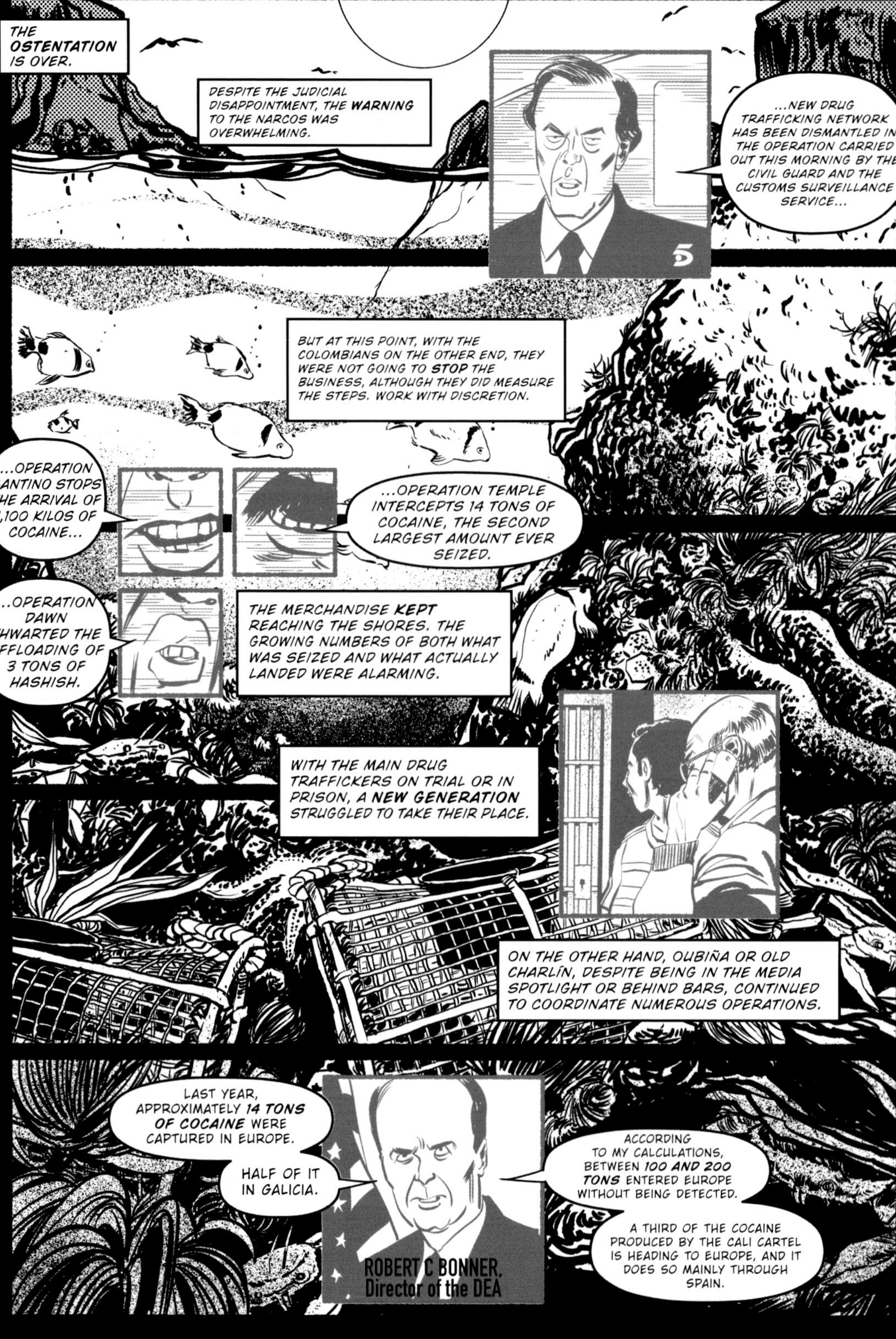
THE OSTENTATION IS OVER.
DESPITE THE JUDICIAL DISAPPOINTMENT, THE WARNING TO THE NARCOS WAS OVERWHELMING.
...NEW DRUG TRAFFICKING NETWORK HAS BEEN DISMANTLED IN THE OPERATION CARRIED OUT THIS MORNING BY THE CIVIL GUARD AND THE CUSTOMS SURVEILLANCE SERVICE...
BUT AT THIS POINT, WITH THE COLOMBIANS ON THE OTHER END, THEY WERE NOT GOING TO STOP THE BUSINESS, ALTHOUGH THEY DID MEASURE THE STEPS. WORK WITH DISCRETION.
...OPERATION SANTINO STOPS THE ARRIVAL OF 1,100 KILOS OF COCAINE...
...OPERATION TEMPLE INTERCEPTS 14 TONS OF COCAINE, THE SECOND LARGEST AMOUNT EVER SEIZED.
...OPERATION DAWN THWARTED THE OFFLOADING OF 3 TONS OF HASHISH.
THE MERCHANDISE KEPT REACHING THE SHORES. THE GROWING NUMBERS OF BOTH WHAT WAS SEIZED AND WHAT ACTUALLY LANDED WERE ALARMING.
WITH THE MAIN DRUG TRAFFICKERS ON TRIAL OR IN PRISON, A NEW GENERATION STRUGGLED TO TAKE THEIR PLACE.
ON THE OTHER HAND, OUBIÑA OR OLD CHARLÍN, DESPITE BEING IN THE MEDIA SPOTLIGHT OR BEHIND BARS, CONTINUED TO COORDINATE NUMEROUS OPERATIONS.
LAST YEAR, APPROXIMATELY 14 TONS OF COCAINE WERE CAPTURED IN EUROPE.
HALF OF IT IN GALICIA.
ROBERT C BONNER, Director of the DEA
ACCORDING TO MY CALCULATIONS, BETWEEN 100 AND 200 TONS ENTERED EUROPE WITHOUT BEING DETECTED.
A THIRD OF THE COCAINE PRODUCED BY THE CALI CARTEL IS HEADING TO EUROPE, AND IT DOES SO MAINLY THROUGH SPAIN.

*LIKE A GREAT PYRAMID OF BLOW, THIS **NARCO ICEBERG** ONLY GAVE A SMALL GLIMPSE OF **EVERYTHING** THAT PASSED THROUGH THE REGION.*

# THE OTHERS

AND, WHILE EVERYONE WAS AWARE OF THE OLD CLANS, GROUPS LIKE "OS LULÚS" WORKED EFFICIENTLY AND DISCREETLY IN COSTA DA MORTE.

HE BOSS, **FERNANDO GARCÍA ESTO**, WOULD REMAIN HIDDEN OR MONTHS IN THE SMALL TOWN F MUXÍA.

ON ANOTHER OCCASION, WE HAD TO ESCORT A GROUP OF REPORTERS TO THE BARRACKS WHO WERE PREPARING A REPORT ABOUT HIM.

THEY LEFT QUICKLY BECAUSE ALL OF "OS LULÚS" WAS WAITING FOR THEM.

DESPITE OUR EFFORTS, SOME FORTY PEOPLE FROM THE VILLAGE PREVENTED US FROM FINDING HIM...

FALCONETTI" WAS ALREADY KNOWN S THE GUY WHO PUT A GUN ON HE TABLE AND THREATENED A COUNCILMAN WITH HIRING A **HITMAN.**

HE WASN'T ARRESTED IN THE NÉCORA OPERATION BECAUSE HE HAD BEEN SEIZED EARLIER IN HONDARRIBIA WITH 1,200 KILOS OF HASHISH.

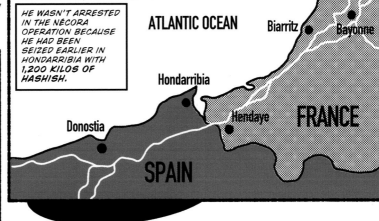

ATLANTIC OCEAN

Biarritz

Bayonne

Hondarribia

FRANCE

Donostia

Hendaye

SPAIN

HE WAS SMART AND, AFTER HIS RELEASE, IT IS RUMORED THAT HE PUT 8,000 KILOS IN LUGO, BUT IT COULD NEVER BE PROVEN.

A PERFECT WAY TO PLAY... **AND TO LIVE.**

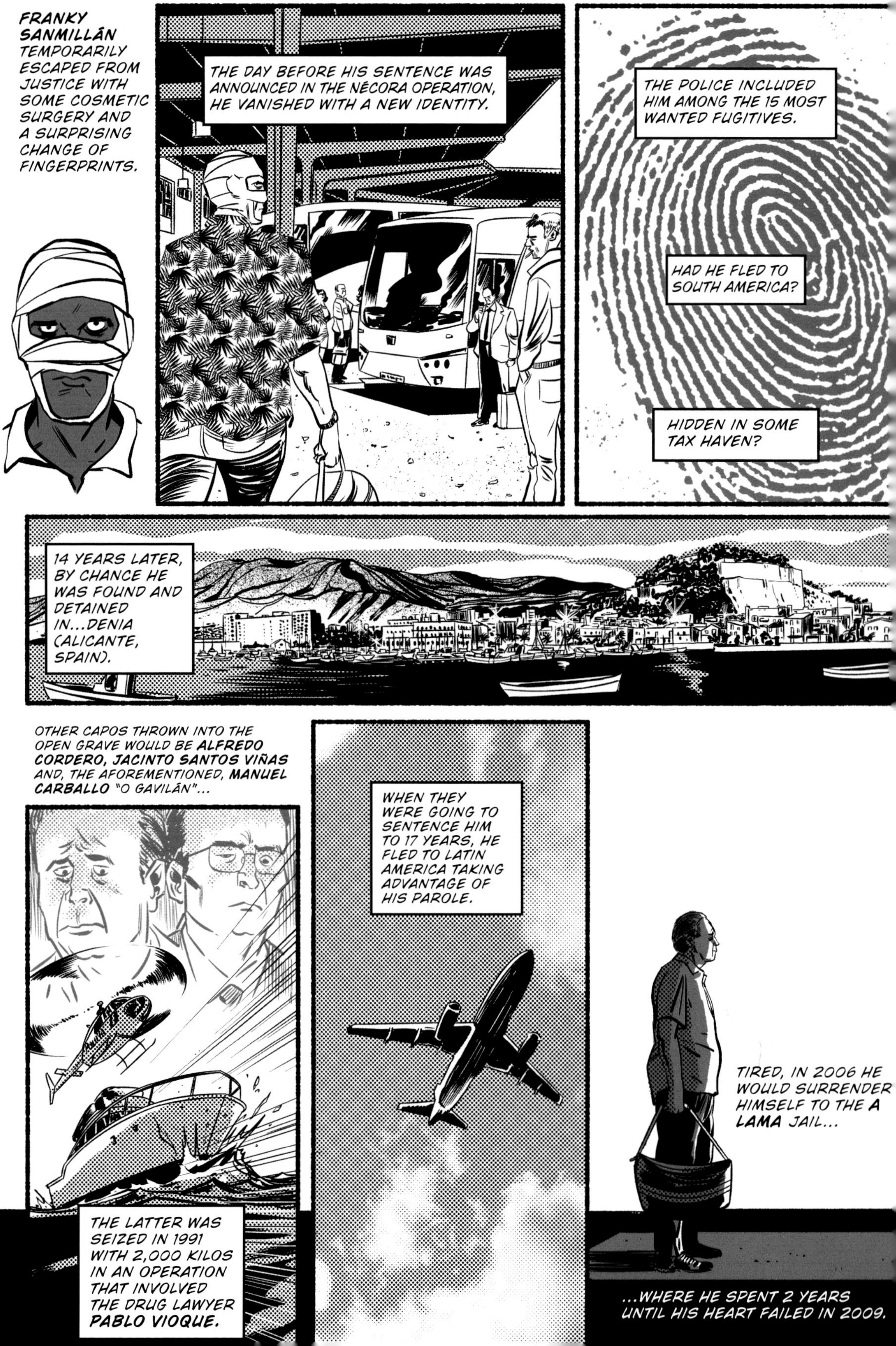
FRANKY SANMILLÁN TEMPORARILY ESCAPED FROM JUSTICE WITH SOME COSMETIC SURGERY AND A SURPRISING CHANGE OF FINGERPRINTS.
THE DAY BEFORE HIS SENTENCE WAS ANNOUNCED IN THE NÉCORA OPERATION, HE VANISHED WITH A NEW IDENTITY.
THE POLICE INCLUDED HIM AMONG THE 15 MOST WANTED FUGITIVES.
HAD HE FLED TO SOUTH AMERICA?
HIDDEN IN SOME TAX HAVEN?
14 YEARS LATER, BY CHANCE HE WAS FOUND AND DETAINED IN...DENIA (ALICANTE, SPAIN).
OTHER CAPOS THROWN INTO THE OPEN GRAVE WOULD BE ALFREDO CORDERO, JACINTO SANTOS VIÑAS AND, THE AFOREMENTIONED, MANUEL CARBALLO "O GAVILÁN"...
THE LATTER WAS SEIZED IN 1991 WITH 2,000 KILOS IN AN OPERATION THAT INVOLVED THE DRUG LAWYER PABLO VIOQUE.
WHEN THEY WERE GOING TO SENTENCE HIM TO 17 YEARS, HE FLED TO LATIN AMERICA TAKING ADVANTAGE OF HIS PAROLE.
TIRED, IN 2006 HE WOULD SURRENDER HIMSELF TO THE A LAMA JAIL...
...WHERE HE SPENT 2 YEARS UNTIL HIS HEART FAILED IN 2009.

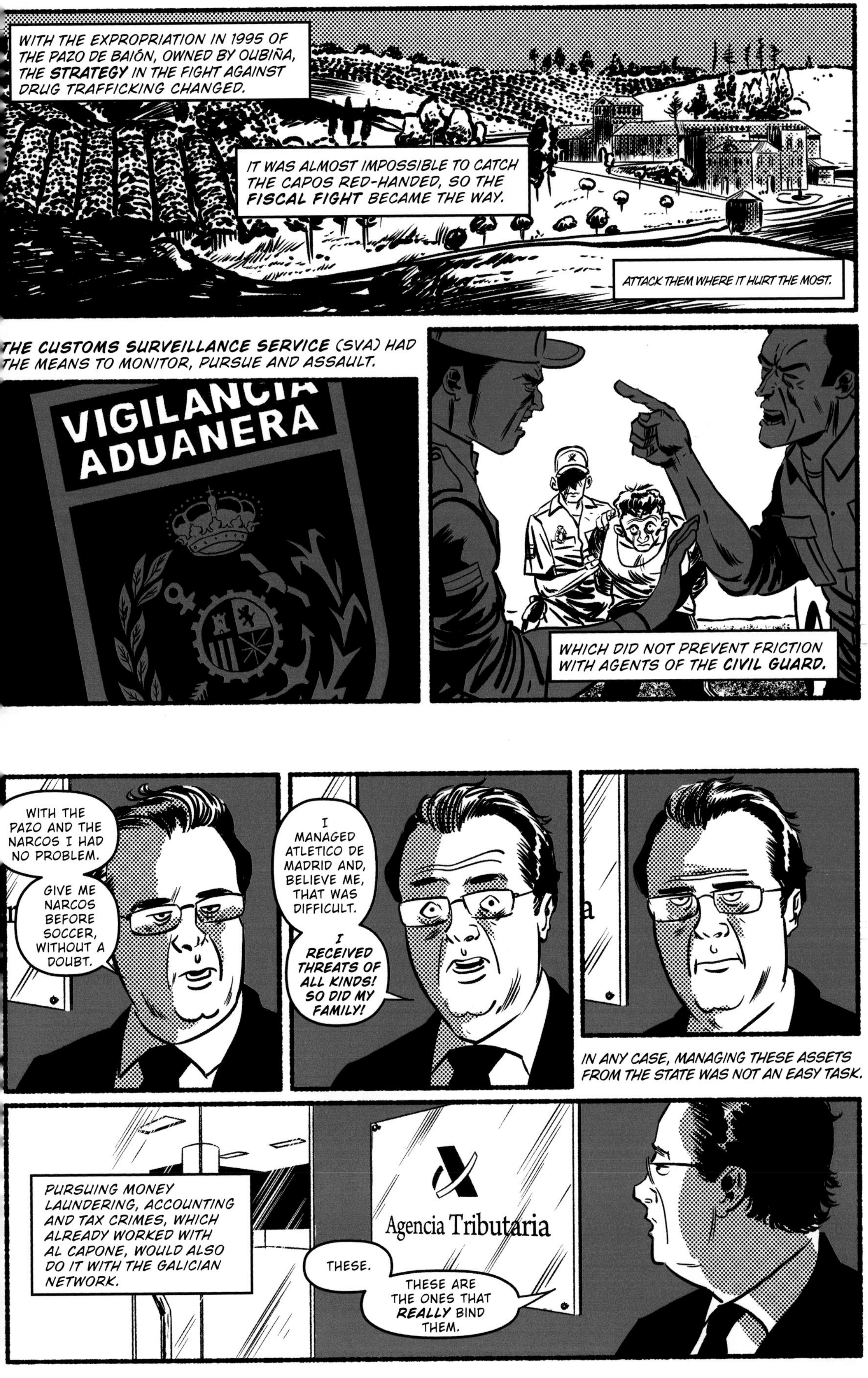

WITH THE EXPROPRIATION IN 1995 OF THE PAZO DE BAIÓN, OWNED BY OUBIÑA, THE STRATEGY IN THE FIGHT AGAINST DRUG TRAFFICKING CHANGED.
IT WAS ALMOST IMPOSSIBLE TO CATCH THE CAPOS RED-HANDED, SO THE FISCAL FIGHT BECAME THE WAY.
ATTACK THEM WHERE IT HURT THE MOST.
THE CUSTOMS SURVEILLANCE SERVICE (SVA) HAD THE MEANS TO MONITOR, PURSUE AND ASSAULT.
VIGILANCIA ADUANERA
WHICH DID NOT PREVENT FRICTION WITH AGENTS OF THE CIVIL GUARD.
WITH THE PAZO AND THE NARCOS I HAD NO PROBLEM.
GIVE ME NARCOS BEFORE SOCCER, WITHOUT A DOUBT.
I MANAGED ATLETICO DE MADRID AND, BELIEVE ME, THAT WAS DIFFICULT.
I RECEIVED THREATS OF ALL KINDS! SO DID MY FAMILY!
IN ANY CASE, MANAGING THESE ASSETS FROM THE STATE WAS NOT AN EASY TASK.
PURSUING MONEY LAUNDERING, ACCOUNTING AND TAX CRIMES, WHICH ALREADY WORKED WITH AL CAPONE, WOULD ALSO DO IT WITH THE GALICIAN NETWORK.
Agencia Tributaria
THESE.
THESE ARE THE ONES THAT REALLY BIND THEM.

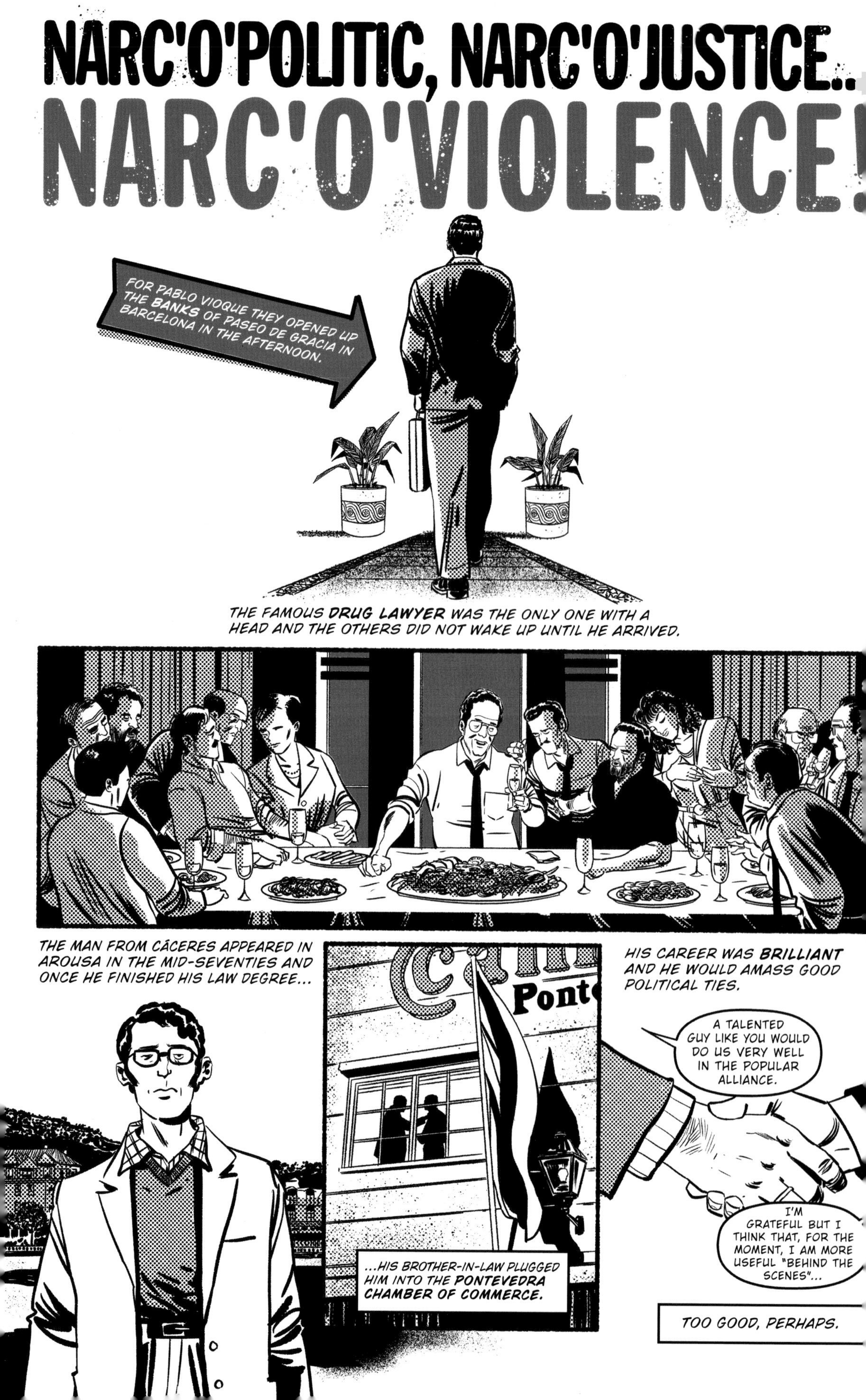
NARC'O'POLITIC, NARC'O'JUSTICE...
NARC'O'VIOLENCE!
FOR PABLO VIOQUE THEY OPENED UP THE BANKS OF PASEO DE GRACIA IN BARCELONA IN THE AFTERNOON.
THE FAMOUS DRUG LAWYER WAS THE ONLY ONE WITH A HEAD AND THE OTHERS DID NOT WAKE UP UNTIL HE ARRIVED.
THE MAN FROM CÁCERES APPEARED IN AROUSA IN THE MID-SEVENTIES AND ONCE HE FINISHED HIS LAW DEGREE...
Pont
...HIS BROTHER-IN-LAW PLUGGED HIM INTO THE PONTEVEDRA CHAMBER OF COMMERCE.
HIS CAREER WAS BRILLIANT AND HE WOULD AMASS GOOD POLITICAL TIES.
A TALENTED GUY LIKE YOU WOULD DO US VERY WELL IN THE POPULAR ALLIANCE.
I'M GRATEFUL BUT I THINK THAT, FOR THE MOMENT, I AM MORE USEFUL "BEHIND THE SCENES"...
TOO GOOD, PERHAPS.

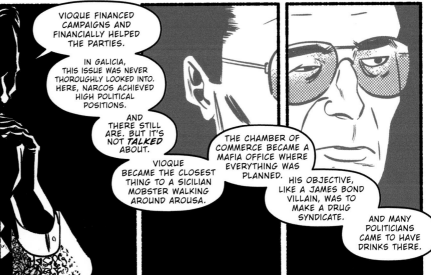

VIOQUE FINANCED CAMPAIGNS AND FINANCIALLY HELPED THE PARTIES.

IN GALICIA, THIS ISSUE WAS NEVER THOROUGHLY LOOKED INTO. HERE, NARCOS ACHIEVED HIGH POLITICAL POSITIONS.

AND THERE STILL ARE. BUT IT'S NOT **TALKED** ABOUT.

VIOQUE BECAME THE CLOSEST THING TO A SICILIAN MOBSTER WALKING AROUND AROUSA.

THE CHAMBER OF COMMERCE BECAME A MAFIA OFFICE WHERE EVERYTHING WAS PLANNED.

HIS OBJECTIVE, LIKE A JAMES BOND VILLAIN, WAS TO MAKE A DRUG SYNDICATE.

AND MANY POLITICIANS CAME TO HAVE DRINKS THERE.

HIS LUCK WOULD START TO RUN OUT, ALONG WITH THAT OF MANUEL CARBALLO, WITH THE FAILED LANDING IN CEDEIRA, WHERE HE LOST ALMOST **2,000 KILOS** FROM THE COLOMBIANS.

THE CALI CARTEL WOULD TAKE **REVENGE** BY ASSASSINATING A CLOSE ASSOCIATE OF VIOQUE.

THE FAMOUS DRUG LAWYER WOULD BE DETAINED BY THE CIVIL GUARD.

DIAGNOSED IN PRISON WITH COLON CANCER, HE WANTED TO LEAVE THROUGH THE FRONT DOOR BY HIRING AN ECUADORIAN TO **TAKE CARE** OF JUDGE ZARAGOZA.

HE TURNED OUT TO BE A POLICE **INFORMANT** AND THE PLOT LED TO AN EXTENSION OF HIS SENTENCE.

VIOQUE DIED OF TERMINAL CANCER AT HIS HOME IN 2009.

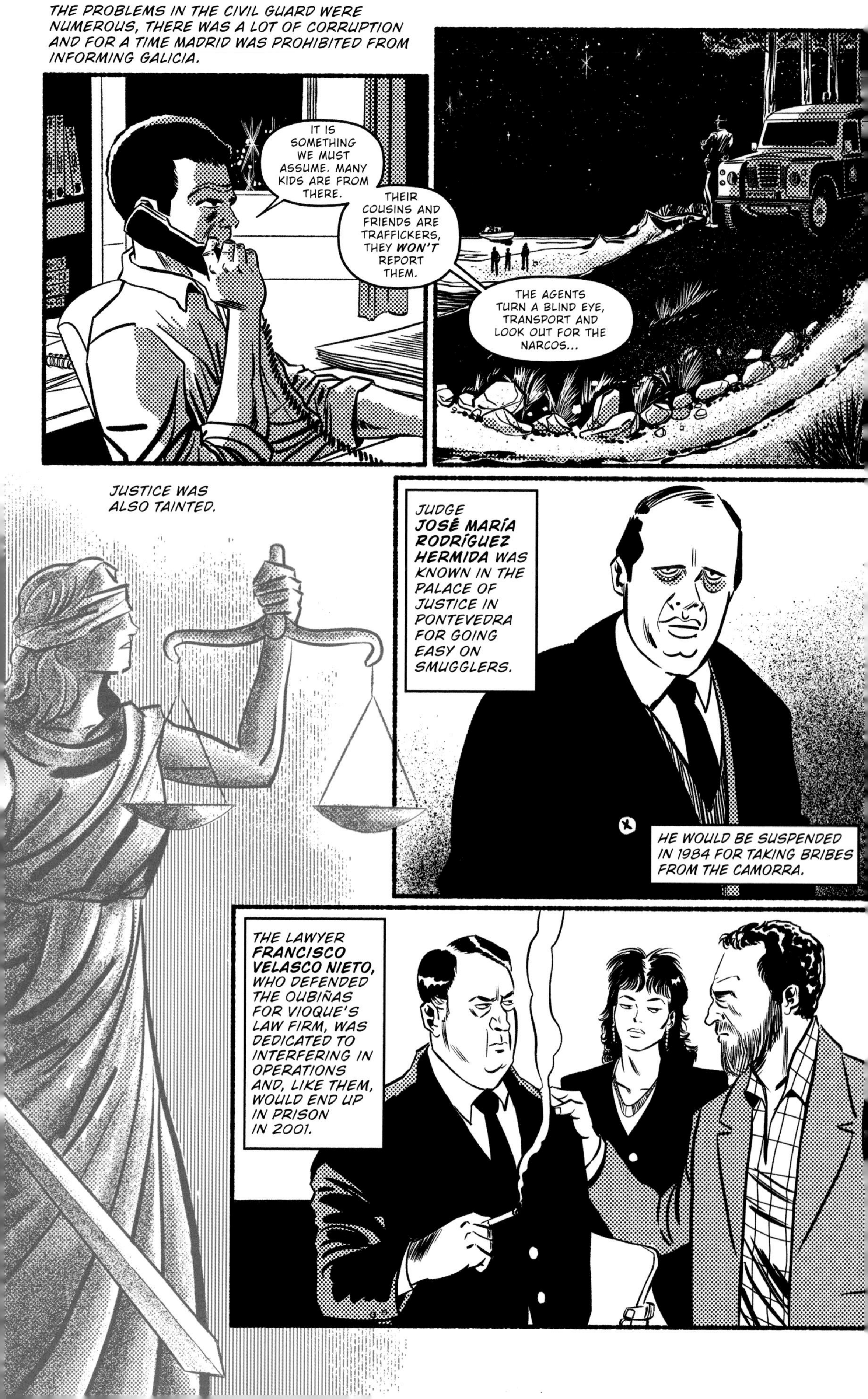
THE PROBLEMS IN THE CIVIL GUARD WERE NUMEROUS, THERE WAS A LOT OF CORRUPTION AND FOR A TIME MADRID WAS PROHIBITED FROM INFORMING GALICIA.
IT IS SOMETHING WE MUST ASSUME. MANY KIDS ARE FROM THERE.
THEIR COUSINS AND FRIENDS ARE TRAFFICKERS, THEY *WON'T* REPORT THEM.
THE AGENTS TURN A BLIND EYE, TRANSPORT AND LOOK OUT FOR THE NARCOS...
JUSTICE WAS ALSO TAINTED.
JUDGE **JOSÉ MARÍA RODRÍGUEZ HERMIDA** WAS KNOWN IN THE PALACE OF JUSTICE IN PONTEVEDRA FOR GOING EASY ON SMUGGLERS.
HE WOULD BE SUSPENDED IN 1984 FOR TAKING BRIBES FROM THE CAMORRA.
THE LAWYER **FRANCISCO VELASCO NIETO,** WHO DEFENDED THE OUBIÑAS FOR VIOQUE'S LAW FIRM, WAS DEDICATED TO INTERFERING IN OPERATIONS AND, LIKE THEM, WOULD END UP IN PRISON IN 2001.

# (HISTORIAS CRIMINAIS!) CRIME STORIES!

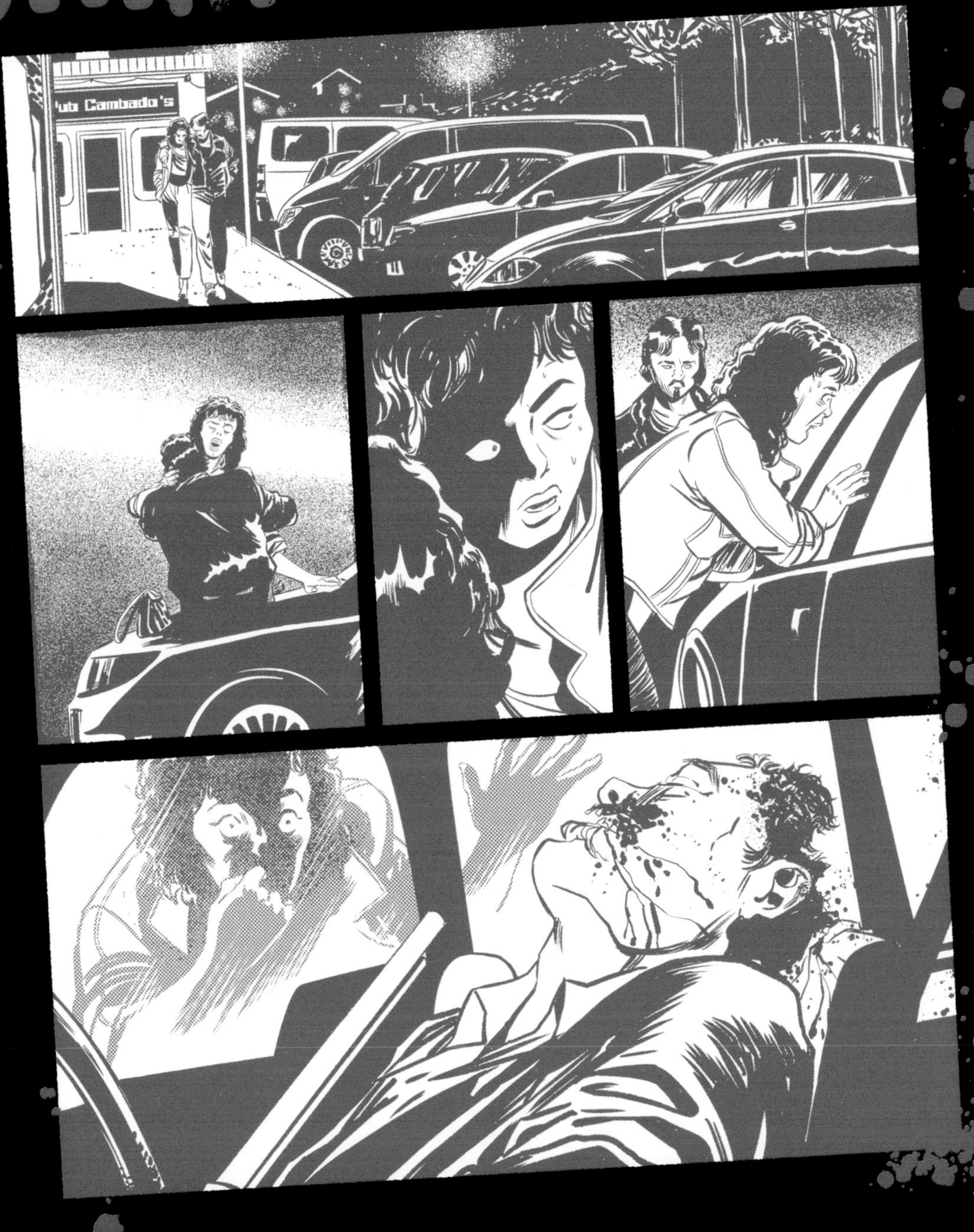
'ub Cambado's

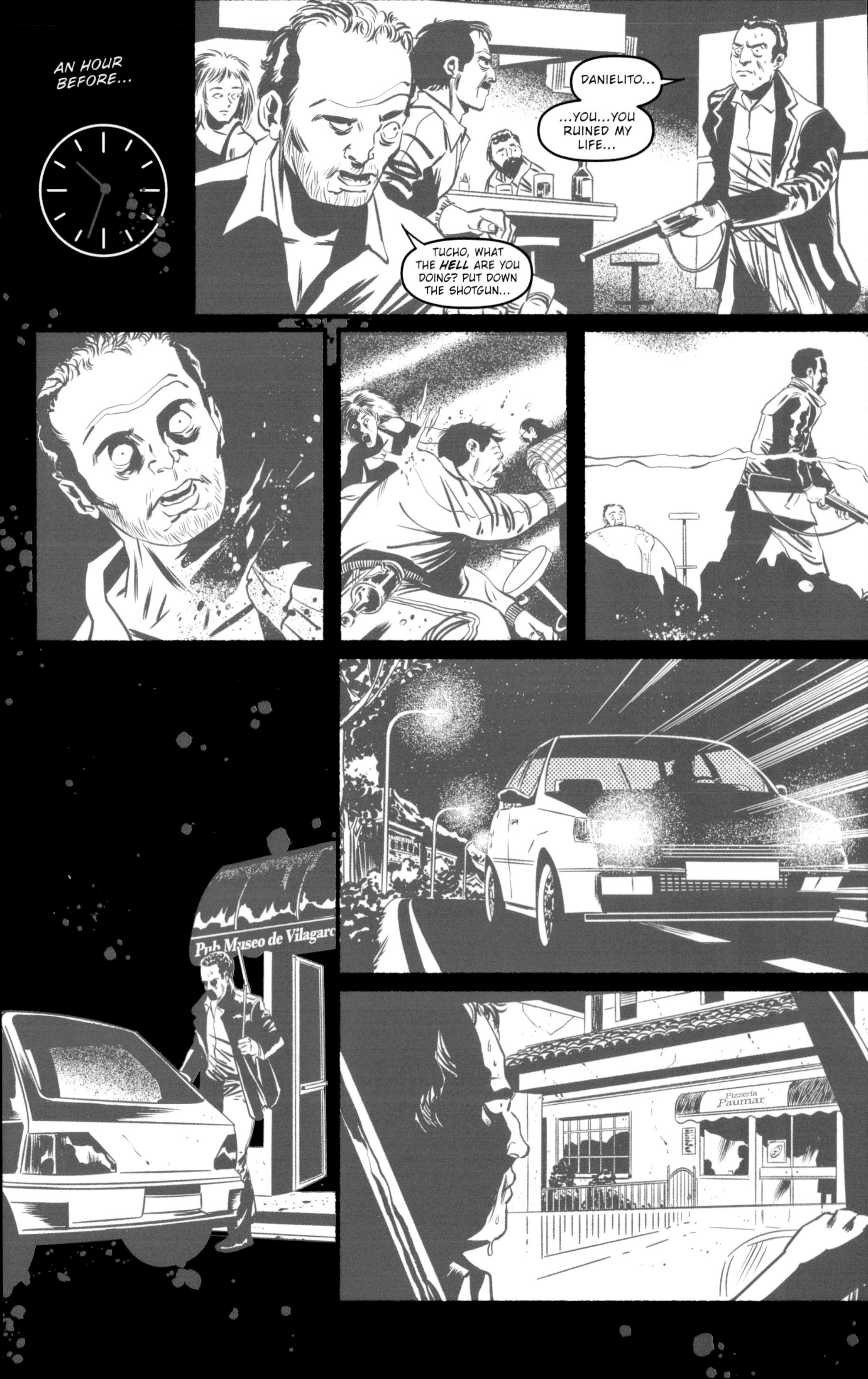
AN HOUR BEFORE...
DANIELITO...
...YOU...YOU RUINED MY LIFE...
TUCHO, WHAT THE **HELL** ARE YOU DOING? PUT DOWN THE SHOTGUN...
Pub Museo de Vilagarc
Pizzeria Paumar

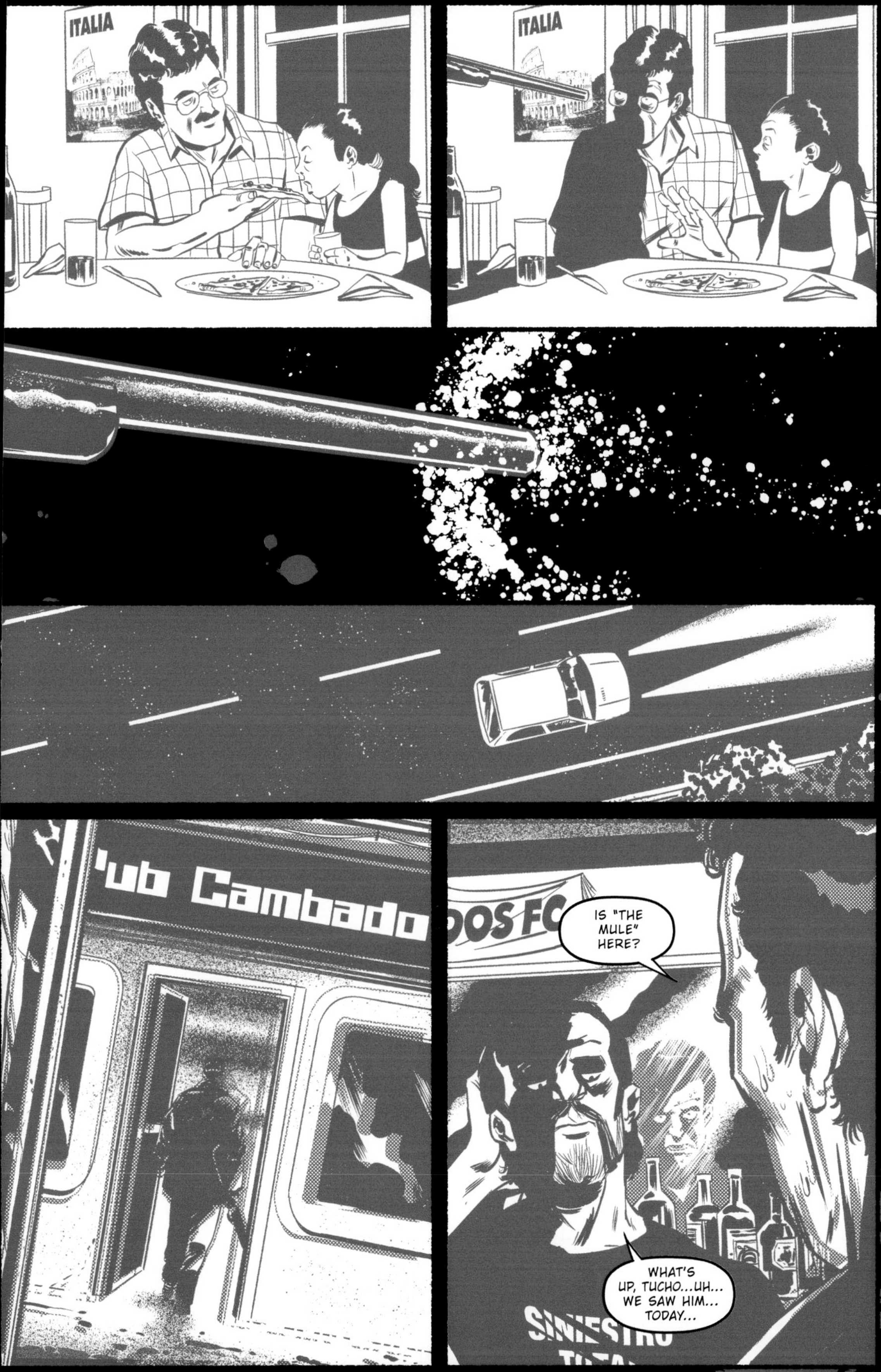
ITALIA
ITALIA
'ub Cambado
DOS FC
IS "THE MULE" HERE?
WHAT'S UP, TUCHO...UH... WE SAW HIM... TODAY...
SINIESTRO

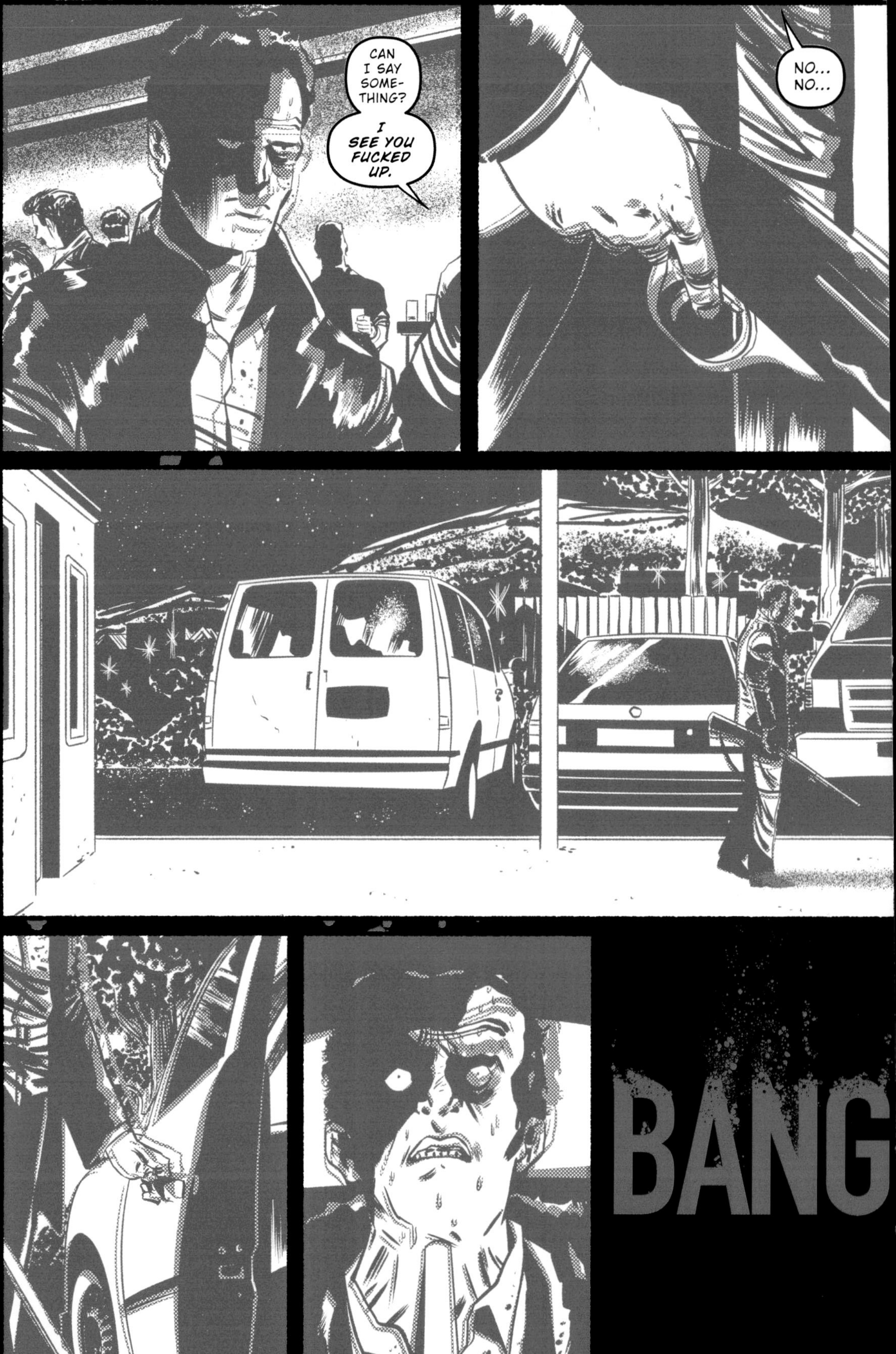
CAN I SAY SOME-THING?
I SEE YOU FUCKED UP.
NO... NO...
BANG

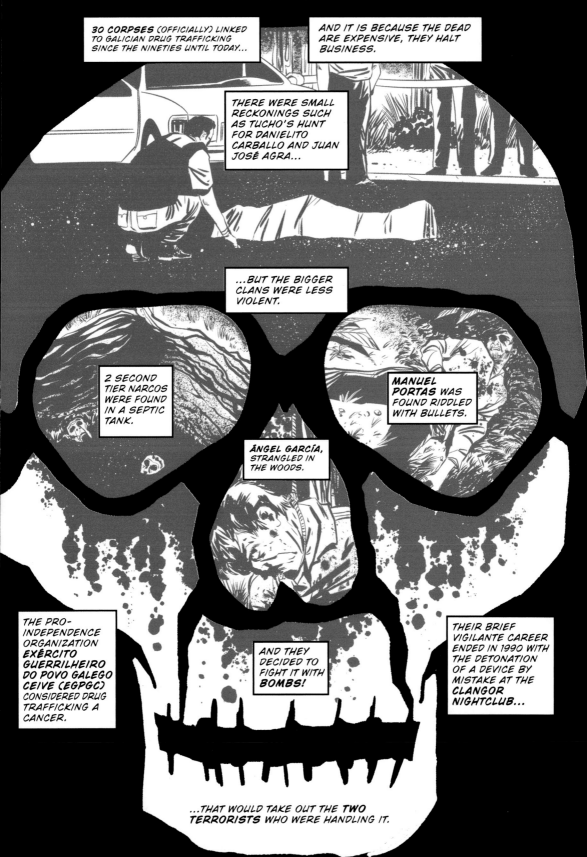

FOR THE AMOUNT OF DRUGS AND CLANS THERE WERE, LITTLE VIOLENCE OCCURRED.

30 CORPSES (OFFICIALLY) LINKED TO GALICIAN DRUG TRAFFICKING SINCE THE NINETIES UNTIL TODAY...

AND IT IS BECAUSE THE DEAD ARE EXPENSIVE, THEY HALT BUSINESS.

THERE WERE SMALL RECKONINGS SUCH AS TUCHO'S HUNT FOR DANIELITO CARBALLO AND JUAN JOSÉ AGRA...

...BUT THE BIGGER CLANS WERE LESS VIOLENT.

2 SECOND TIER NARCOS WERE FOUND IN A SEPTIC TANK.

MANUEL PORTAS WAS FOUND RIDDLED WITH BULLETS.

ÁNGEL GARCÍA, STRANGLED IN THE WOODS.

THE PRO-INDEPENDENCE ORGANIZATION EXÉRCITO GUERRILHEIRO DO POVO GALEGO CEIVE (EGPGC) CONSIDERED DRUG TRAFFICKING A CANCER.

AND THEY DECIDED TO FIGHT IT WITH BOMBS!

THEIR BRIEF VIGILANTE CAREER ENDED IN 1990 WITH THE DETONATION OF A DEVICE BY MISTAKE AT THE CLANGOR NIGHTCLUB...

...THAT WOULD TAKE OUT THE TWO TERRORISTS WHO WERE HANDLING IT.

Chapter Five

# THE AVALANCHE THAT DOES NOT STOP

ACCORDING TO JUDGE *JOSÉ ANTONIO VÁZQUEZ TAÍN*, BETWEEN 2001 AND 2003 THEY BROUGHT THROUGH GALICIA...

# 150.000 KILOS OF COCAINE

THAT **PERIOD** WAS VERY TURBULENT FOR GALICIAN DRUG TRAFFICKING.

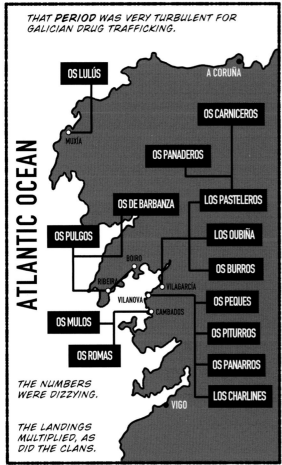

ATLANTIC OCEAN

OS LULÚS

A CORUÑA

MUXÍA

OS CARNICEROS

OS PANADEROS

OS DE BARBANZA

LOS PASTELEROS

OS PULGOS

BOIRO

LOS OUBIÑA

RIBEIRA

VILAGARCÍA

OS BURROS

VILANOVA

CAMBADOS

OS PEQUES

OS MULOS

OS PITURROS

OS ROMAS

OS PANARROS

VIGO

LOS CHARLINES

THE NUMBERS WERE DIZZYING.

THE LANDINGS MULTIPLIED, AS DID THE CLANS.

IT WAS DOG-EAT-DOG, EVERYONE AGAINST EVERYONE.

LEADING THE FIGHT WAS JUDGE TAÍN, PRACTICALLY A NEWCOMER TO VILAGARCÍA.

HIS STRATEGY WOULD MERCILESSLY ATTACK THE WORL OF THE TRAFFICKERS AND REACH AGREEMENTS WITH THE NAVY, WHO WOULD JOIN THE REST OF THE STATE SECURITY FORCES IN THE FIGHT AGAINST DRUGS.

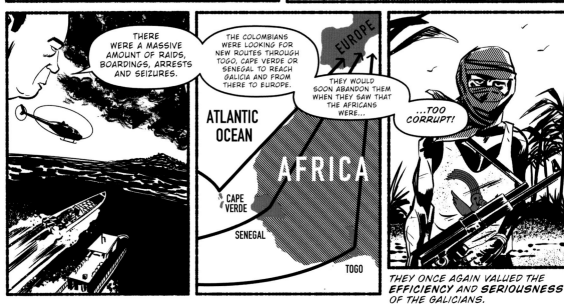

THERE WERE A MASSIVE AMOUNT OF RAIDS, BOARDINGS, ARRESTS AND SEIZURES.

THE COLOMBIANS WERE LOOKING FOR NEW ROUTES THROUGH TOGO, CAPE VERDE OR SENEGAL TO REACH GALICIA AND FROM THERE TO EUROPE.

EUROPE

THEY WOULD SOON ABANDON THEM WHEN THEY SAW THAT THE AFRICANS WERE...

...TOO CORRUPT!

ATLANTIC OCEAN

AFRICA

CAPE VERDE

SENEGAL

TOGO

THEY ONCE AGAIN VALUED THE **EFFICIENCY** AND **SERIOUSNESS** OF THE GALICIANS.

...AÍN WAS THE ONE WHO SENT THE **GEO** TO ...RREST "SITO MIÑANCO" IN THE CHALET ...N MADRID WHEN HE WAS PREPARING A ...HIPMENT OF 5,000 KILOS OF COCAINE.

...SINCE THEN, "SITO" HAS ...BEEN PROHIBITED FROM ...STEPPING FOOT IN GALICIA.

A FEW MONTHS BEFORE, **JOSEFA CHARLÍN**, THE PATRIARCH'S HEIR, HAD ALREADY BEEN ARRESTED.

LEGENDARY FOR BEING A DESPOT, SHE WAS A FUGITIVE IN PORTUGAL FOR 6 YEARS.

EXTRADITED AND SENTENCED, SHE WAS RELEASED IN 2012.

NOBODY SPOKE BACK TO JOSEFA.

I WANT TO OPEN A SAVINGS ACCOUNT FOR THE GIRL.

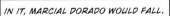

"LA CHARLINA" WOULD EVEN USE ONE OF HER DAUGHTERS, A MINOR, TO LAUNDER MONEY.

BUT THE BIG BLOW TO THE CLANS, WHICH TAÍN SET IN MOTION IN 2003, WOULD BE **OPERATION FLASHBACK**.

IN IT, MARCIAL DORADO WOULD FALL.

THE ONE WHO ALWAYS MAINTAINED THAT HE HAD NEVER TAKEN THE STEP FROM TOBACCO TO COCAINE.

A TERRIBLE BLOW FOR THE GALICIAN CLANS AND COLOMBIAN NARCO-GUERRILLAS, WHO TOOK A WHILE TO REORGANIZE.

THEY WOULD GET BACK TO BUSINESS, BUT IN ANOTHER WAY.

A NEW STAGE WAS BEGINNING.

# THE RELAY

THE CARTELS TRIED NEW PARTNERS AND DIFFEREN[T] ROUTES.

AFRICA, BULGARIA, RUSSIA, HOLLAND...

BUT, IN THE END, THEY NEEDED THE GALICIANS.

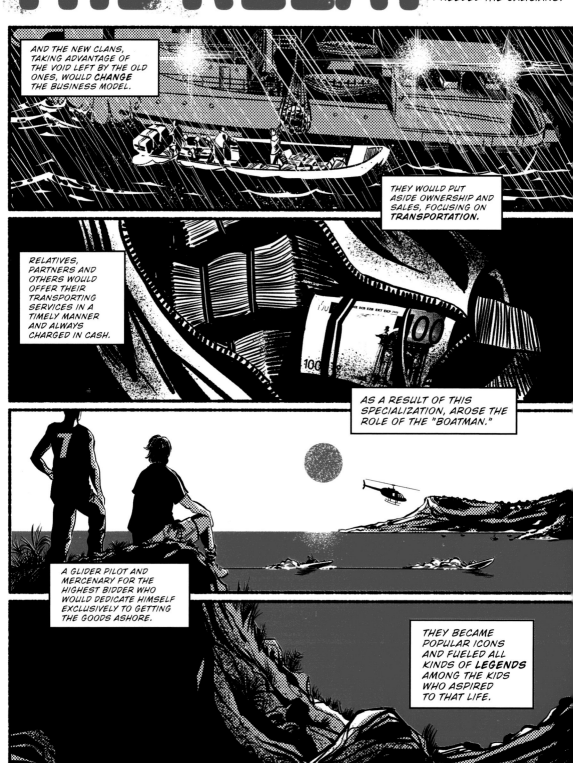

AND THE NEW CLANS, TAKING ADVANTAGE OF THE VOID LEFT BY THE OLD ONES, WOULD **CHANGE** THE BUSINESS MODEL.

THEY WOULD PUT ASIDE OWNERSHIP AND SALES, FOCUSING ON **TRANSPORTATION**.

RELATIVES, PARTNERS AND OTHERS WOULD OFFER THEIR TRANSPORTING SERVICES IN A TIMELY MANNER AND ALWAYS CHARGED IN CASH.

AS A RESULT OF THIS SPECIALIZATION, AROSE THE ROLE OF THE "BOATMAN."

A GLIDER PILOT AND MERCENARY FOR THE HIGHEST BIDDER WHO WOULD DEDICATE HIMSELF EXCLUSIVELY TO GETTING THE GOODS ASHORE.

THEY BECAME POPULAR ICONS AND FUELED ALL KINDS OF **LEGENDS** AMONG THE KIDS WHO ASPIRED TO THAT LIFE.

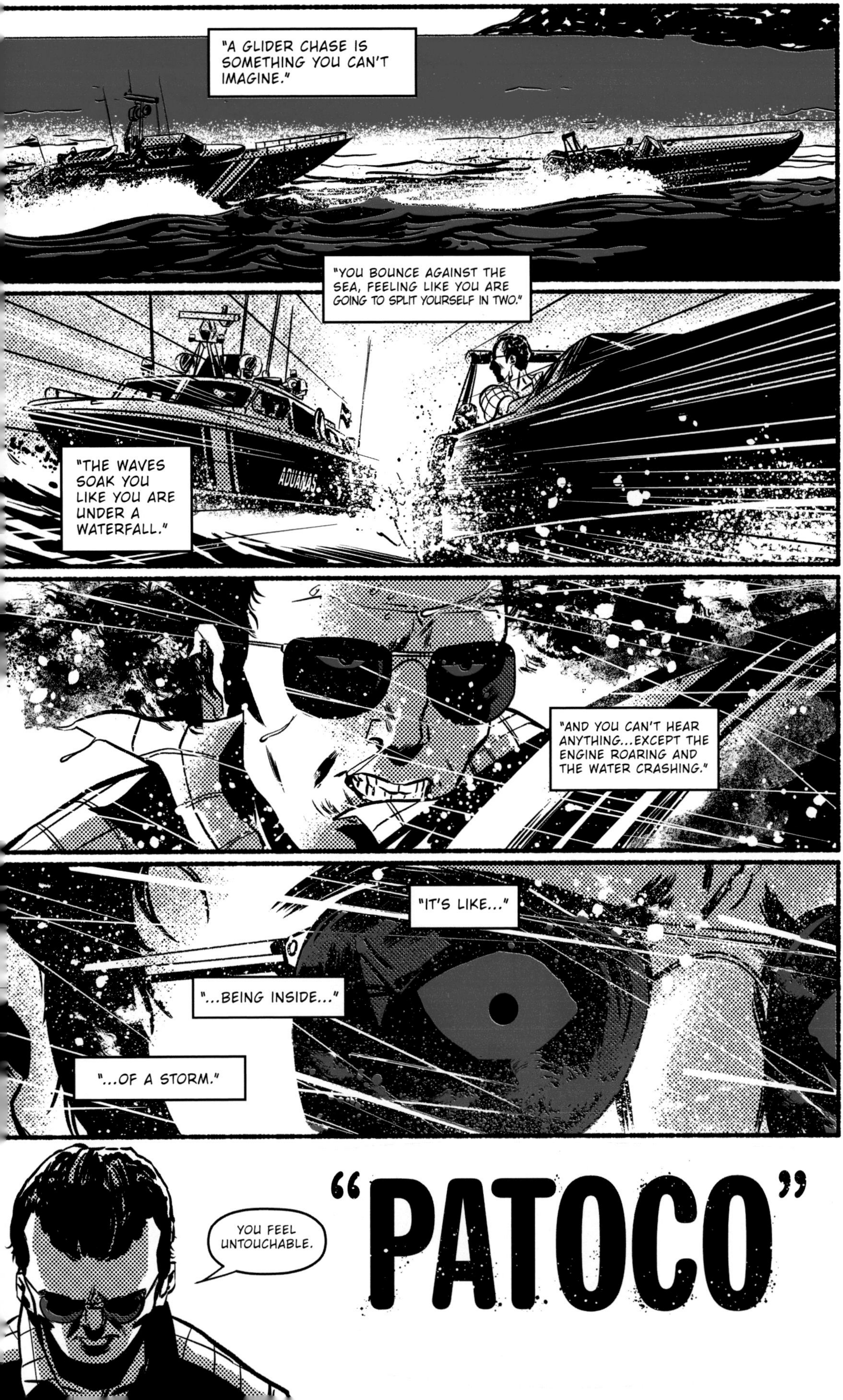
"A GLIDER CHASE IS SOMETHING YOU CAN'T IMAGINE."
"YOU BOUNCE AGAINST THE SEA, FEELING LIKE YOU ARE GOING TO SPLIT YOURSELF IN TWO."
"THE WAVES SOAK YOU LIKE YOU ARE UNDER A WATERFALL."
ADUANAS
"AND YOU CAN'T HEAR ANYTHING...EXCEPT THE ENGINE ROARING AND THE WATER CRASHING."
"IT'S LIKE..."
"...BEING INSIDE..."
"...OF A STORM."
YOU FEEL UNTOUCHABLE.
"PATOCO"

ALTHOUGH THE BOATMEN HAD EXISTED SINCE THE TOBACCO ERA...

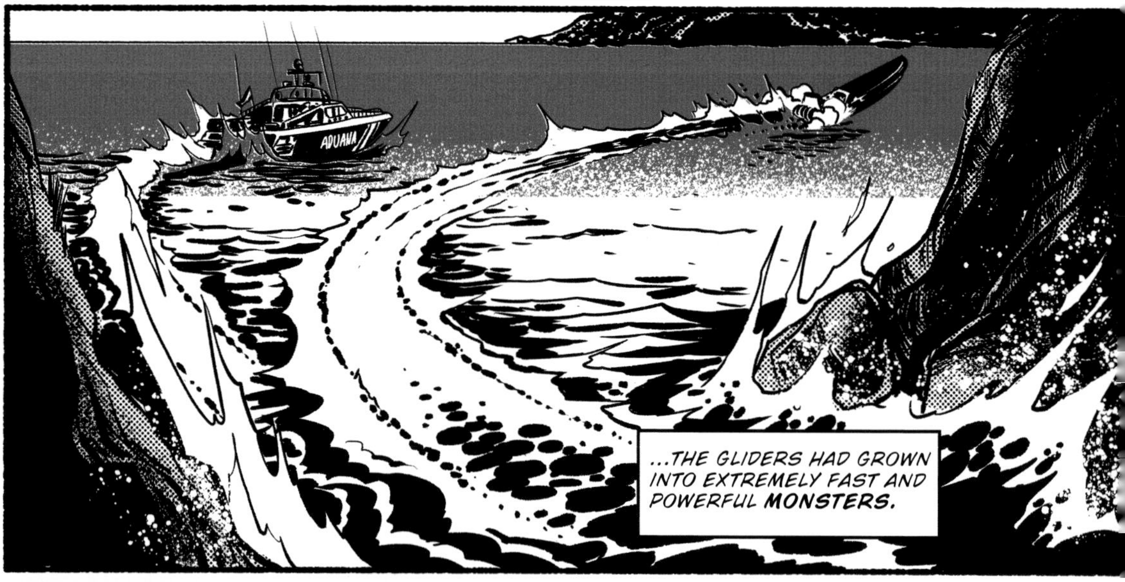
ADUANA
...THE GLIDERS HAD GROWN INTO EXTREMELY FAST AND POWERFUL **MONSTERS.**

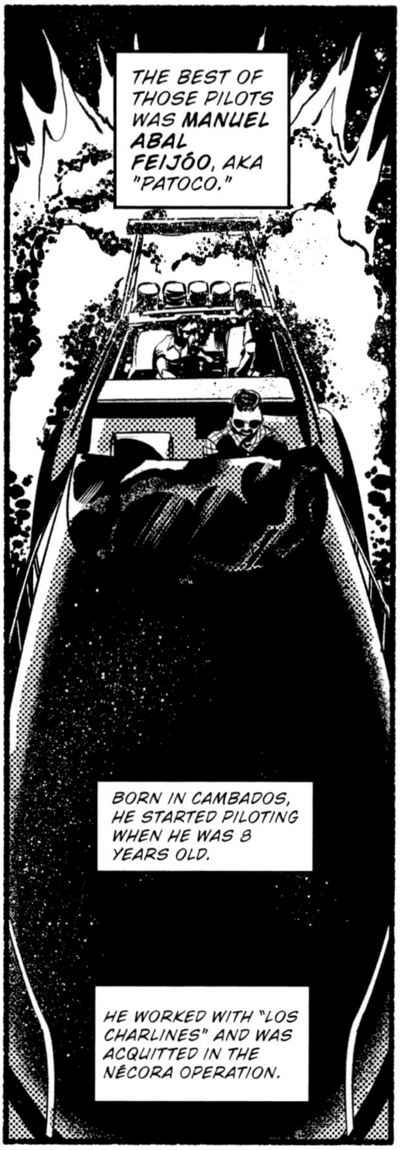
THE BEST OF THOSE PILOTS WAS **MANUEL ABAL FEIJÓO**, AKA "PATOCO."
BORN IN CAMBADOS, HE STARTED PILOTING WHEN HE WAS 8 YEARS OLD.
HE WORKED WITH "LOS CHARLINES" AND WAS ACQUITTED IN THE NÉCORA OPERATION.

SHORTLY AFTER, HE WOULD DESIGN HIS OWN FLEET, WHICH CULMINATED IN THE COMMISSION FROM A MILAN SHIPYARD IN PATOCA, THE MOST POWERFUL GLIDER THAT AROUSA SAW, FOR WHICH HE PAID **700,000 EUROS***.

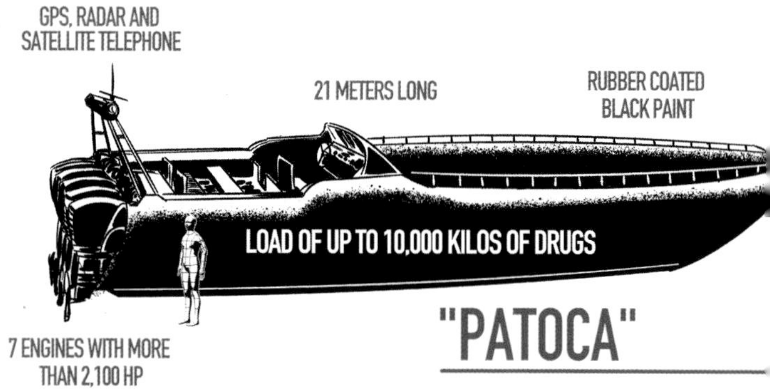
GPS, RADAR AND SATELLITE TELEPHONE
21 METERS LONG
RUBBER COATED BLACK PAINT
LOAD OF UP TO 10,000 KILOS OF DRUGS
7 ENGINES WITH MORE THAN 2,100 HP
"PATOCA"

AGAINST THAT MACHINE, THE CIVIL GUARD COULD NOT COMPETE.

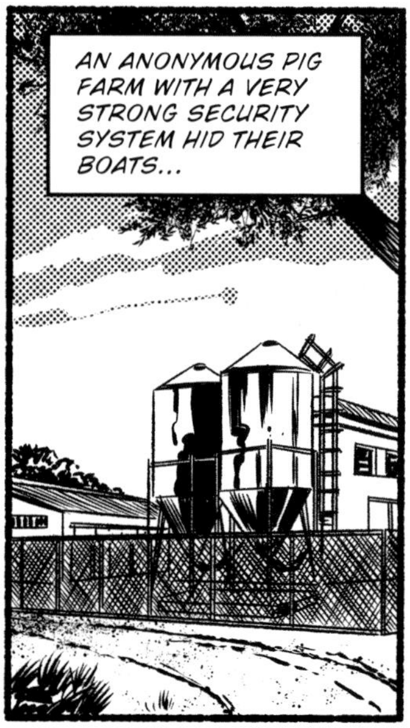
AN ANONYMOUS PIG FARM WITH A VERY STRONG SECURITY SYSTEM HID THEIR BOATS...

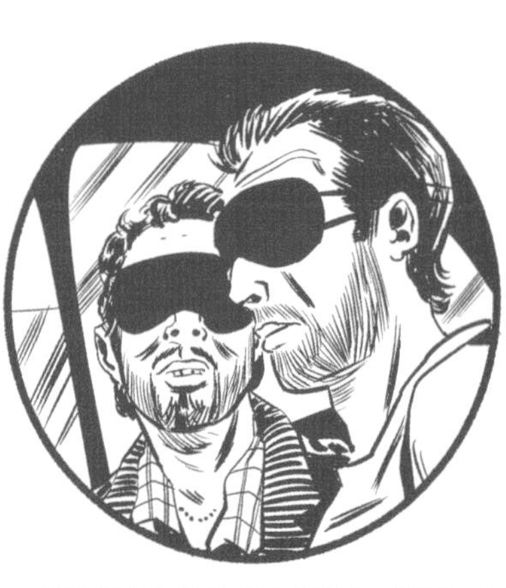

...WHERE FARM WORKERS WERE LED **BLINDFOLDED** BY "PATOCO'S" MEN.

*ABOUT $850,000 USD TODAY

HIS TWO CLOSEST PARTNERS WERE "O SARO" AND "YOYO." EACH COORDINATED A SECTION OF THE ORGANIZATION.

SURFING THE WAVES, DODGING RAFTS AND ROCKS AT FULL SPEED WAS SUICIDAL.

AS GOOD AS "PATOCO" WAS, HE SEEMED DESTINED TO FINISH HIS CAREER CRASHING AT 130 KM PER HOUR*.

WRRRRRRCOOMA

BUT NO.

IN AUGUST 2008, "PATOCO" DIED IN A TRAFFIC ACCIDENT WHEN HE HIT AN OLD MAN WITH HIS MOTORCYCLE.

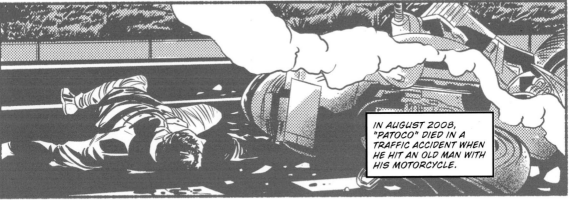

HIS **DEATH** OPENED A VOID THAT WOULD LEAD TO A CONFRONTATION BETWEEN FACTIONS, ENDING IN THE **DISINTEGRATION** OF THE EMPIRE CREATED BY THE "BEST BOATMAN GALICIA HAS SEEN."

* ABOUT 81 MILES PER HOUR

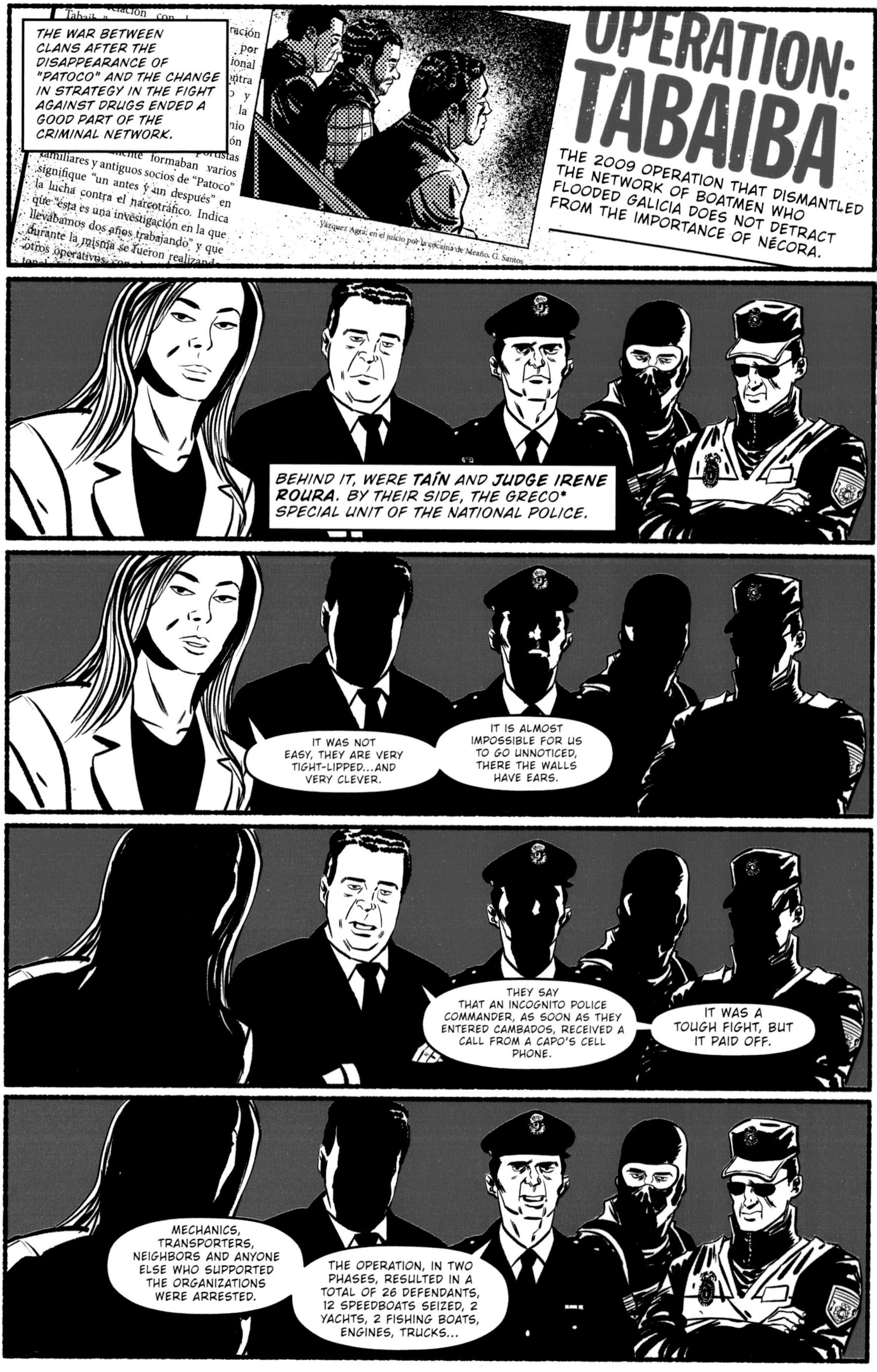
THE WAR BETWEEN CLANS AFTER THE DISAPPEARANCE OF "PATOCO" AND THE CHANGE IN STRATEGY IN THE FIGHT AGAINST DRUGS ENDED A GOOD PART OF THE CRIMINAL NETWORK.
familiares y antiguos socios de "Patoco"
signifique "un antes y un después" en
la lucha contra el narcotráfico. Indica
que "ésta es una investigación en la que
llevábamos dos años trabajando" y que
durante la misma se fueron realizando
Vázquez Agra, en el juicio por la cocaína de Meaño. G. Santos
OPERATION: TABAIBA
THE 2009 OPERATION THAT DISMANTLED THE NETWORK OF BOATMEN WHO FLOODED GALICIA DOES NOT DETRACT FROM THE IMPORTANCE OF NÉCORA.
BEHIND IT, WERE TAÍN AND JUDGE IRENE ROURA. BY THEIR SIDE, THE GRECO* SPECIAL UNIT OF THE NATIONAL POLICE.
IT WAS NOT EASY, THEY ARE VERY TIGHT-LIPPED...AND VERY CLEVER.
IT IS ALMOST IMPOSSIBLE FOR US TO GO UNNOTICED, THERE THE WALLS HAVE EARS.
THEY SAY THAT AN INCOGNITO POLICE COMMANDER, AS SOON AS THEY ENTERED CAMBADOS, RECEIVED A CALL FROM A CAPO'S CELL PHONE.
IT WAS A TOUGH FIGHT, BUT IT PAID OFF.
MECHANICS, TRANSPORTERS, NEIGHBORS AND ANYONE ELSE WHO SUPPORTED THE ORGANIZATIONS WERE ARRESTED.
THE OPERATION, IN TWO PHASES, RESULTED IN A TOTAL OF 26 DEFENDANTS, 12 SPEEDBOATS SEIZED, 2 YACHTS, 2 FISHING BOATS, ENGINES, TRUCKS...

*GRUPOS DE RESPUESTA ESPECIALIZADA CONTRA EL CRIMEN ORGANIZADO.

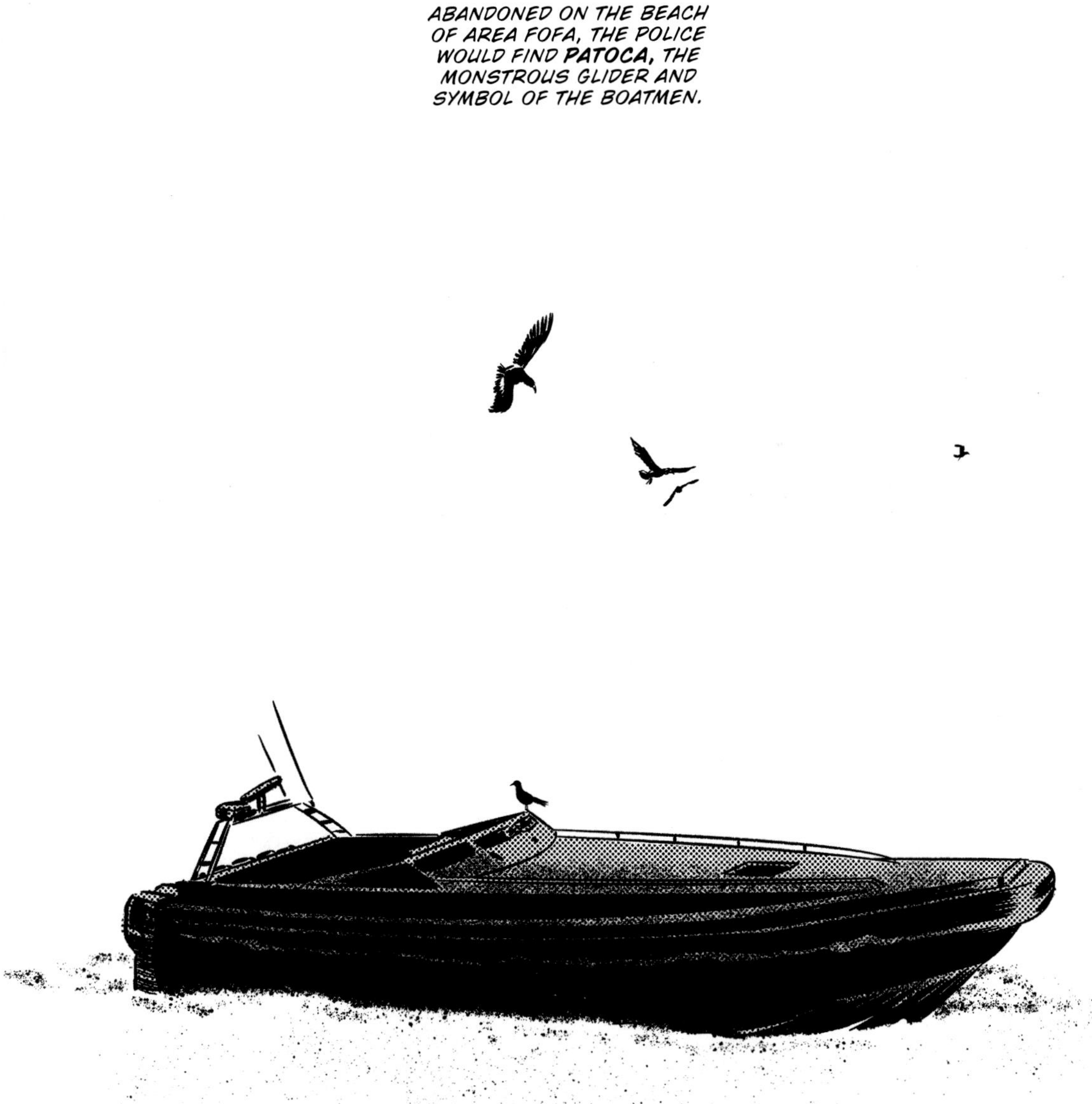
ABANDONED ON THE BEACH OF AREA FOFA, THE POLICE WOULD FIND **PATOCA,** THE MONSTROUS GLIDER AND SYMBOL OF THE BOATMEN.

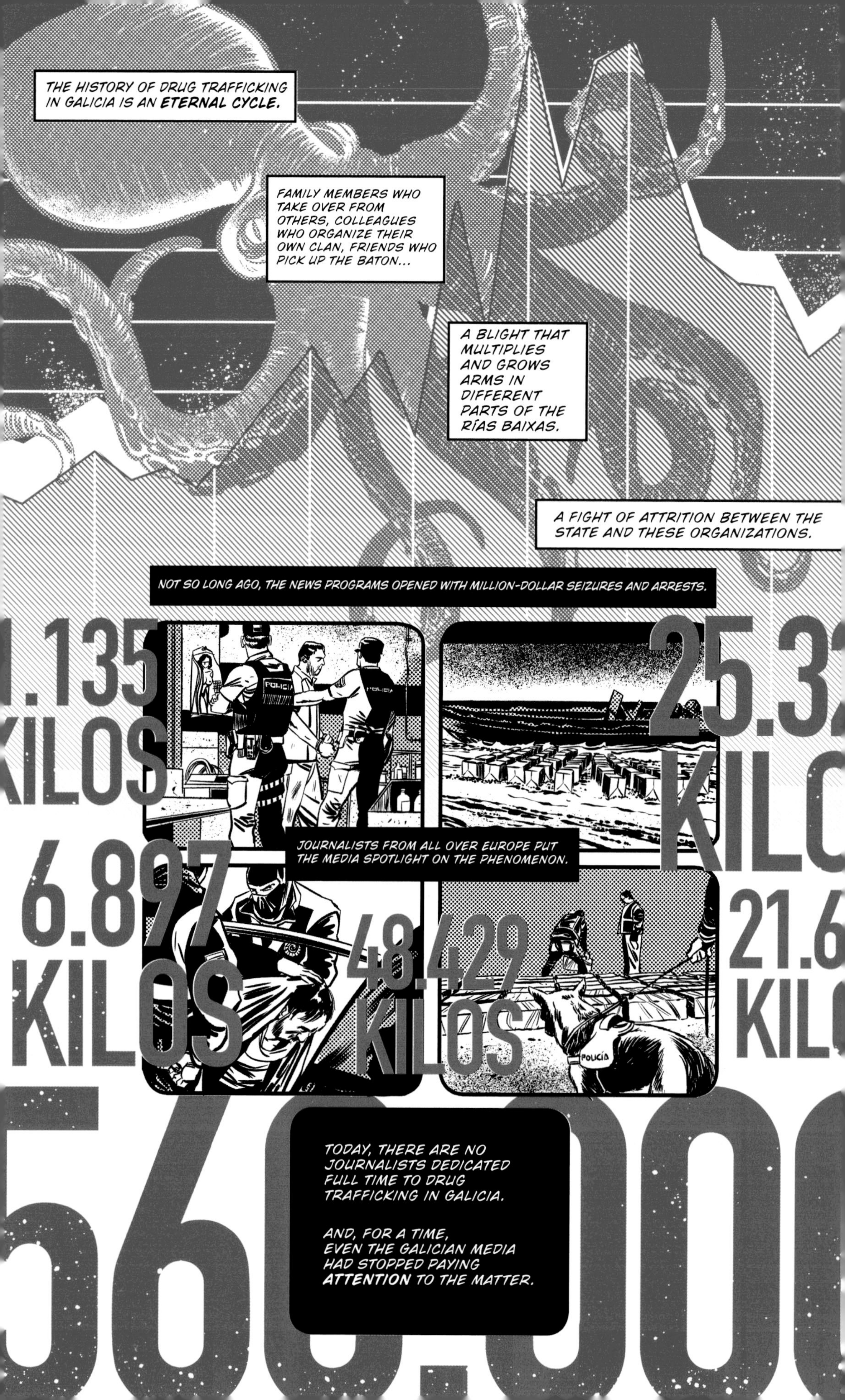

THE HISTORY OF DRUG TRAFFICKING IN GALICIA IS AN **ETERNAL CYCLE.**
FAMILY MEMBERS WHO TAKE OVER FROM OTHERS, COLLEAGUES WHO ORGANIZE THEIR OWN CLAN, FRIENDS WHO PICK UP THE BATON...
A BLIGHT THAT MULTIPLIES AND GROWS ARMS IN DIFFERENT PARTS OF THE RÍAS BAIXAS.
A FIGHT OF ATTRITION BETWEEN THE STATE AND THESE ORGANIZATIONS.
NOT SO LONG AGO, THE NEWS PROGRAMS OPENED WITH MILLION-DOLLAR SEIZURES AND ARRESTS.
JOURNALISTS FROM ALL OVER EUROPE PUT THE MEDIA SPOTLIGHT ON THE PHENOMENON.
6.897 KILOS
48.429 KILOS
TODAY, THERE ARE NO JOURNALISTS DEDICATED FULL TIME TO DRUG TRAFFICKING IN GALICIA.
AND, FOR A TIME, EVEN THE GALICIAN MEDIA HAD STOPPED PAYING **ATTENTION** TO THE MATTER.

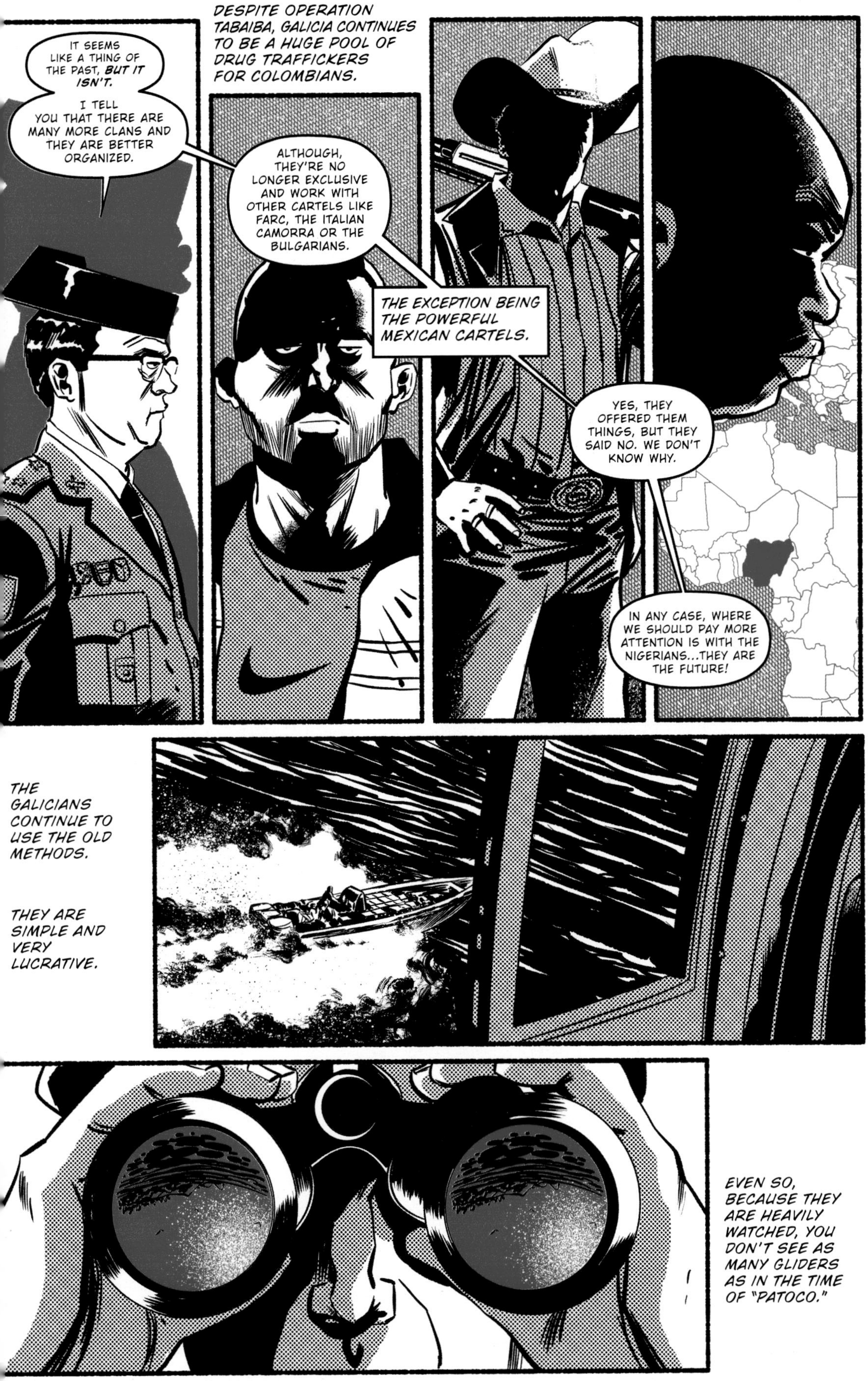
DESPITE OPERATION TABAIBA, GALICIA CONTINUES TO BE A HUGE POOL OF DRUG TRAFFICKERS FOR COLOMBIANS.
IT SEEMS LIKE A THING OF THE PAST, BUT IT ISN'T.
I TELL YOU THAT THERE ARE MANY MORE CLANS AND THEY ARE BETTER ORGANIZED.
ALTHOUGH, THEY'RE NO LONGER EXCLUSIVE AND WORK WITH OTHER CARTELS LIKE FARC, THE ITALIAN CAMORRA OR THE BULGARIANS.
THE EXCEPTION BEING THE POWERFUL MEXICAN CARTELS.
YES, THEY OFFERED THEM THINGS, BUT THEY SAID NO. WE DON'T KNOW WHY.
IN ANY CASE, WHERE WE SHOULD PAY MORE ATTENTION IS WITH THE NIGERIANS...THEY ARE THE FUTURE!
THE GALICIANS CONTINUE TO USE THE OLD METHODS.
THEY ARE SIMPLE AND VERY LUCRATIVE.
EVEN SO, BECAUSE THEY ARE HEAVILY WATCHED, YOU DON'T SEE AS MANY GLIDERS AS IN THE TIME OF "PATOCO."

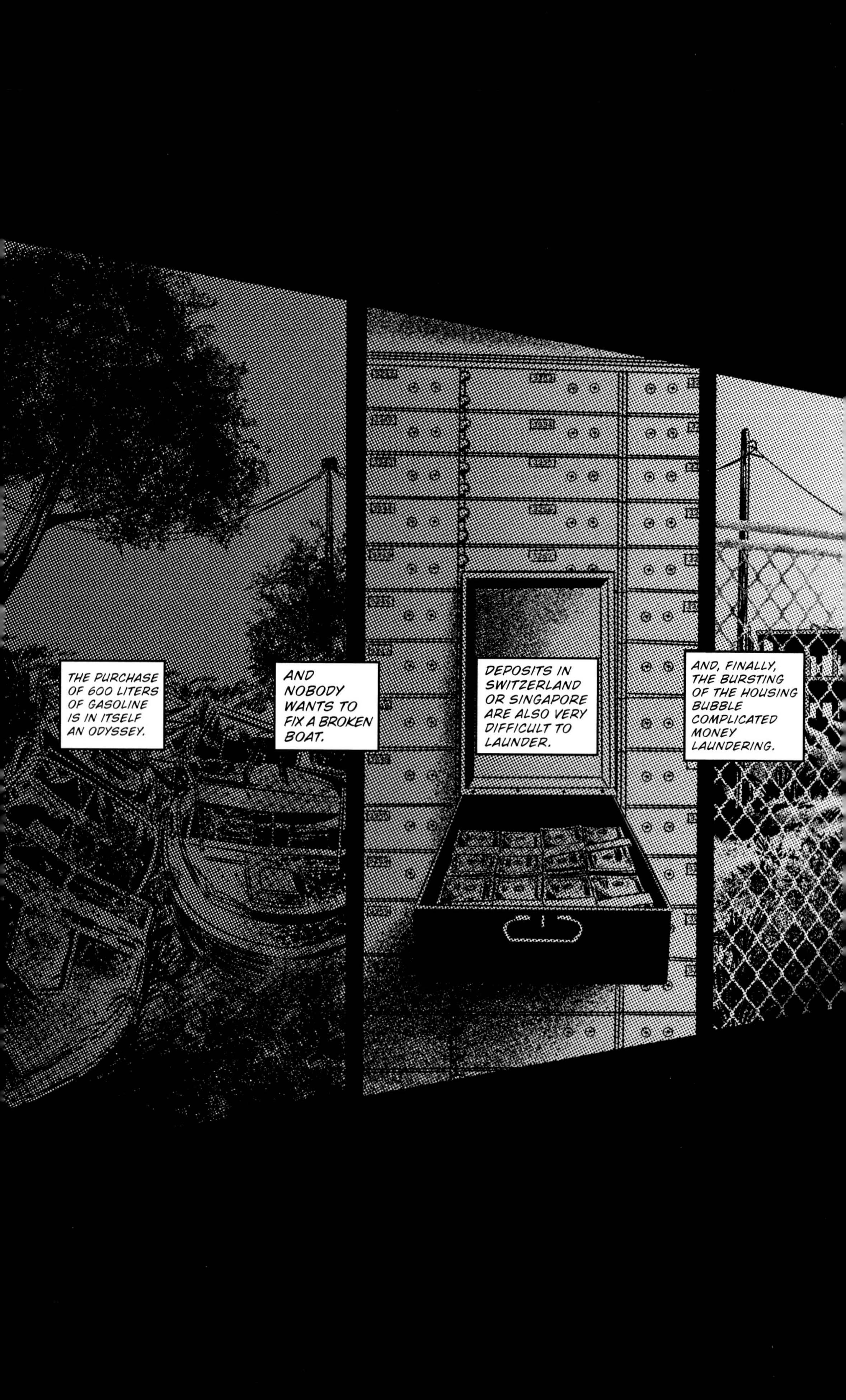
THE PURCHASE OF 600 LITERS OF GASOLINE IS IN ITSELF AN ODYSSEY.
AND NOBODY WANTS TO FIX A BROKEN BOAT.
DEPOSITS IN SWITZERLAND OR SINGAPORE ARE ALSO VERY DIFFICULT TO LAUNDER.
AND, FINALLY, THE BURSTING OF THE HOUSING BUBBLE COMPLICATED MONEY LAUNDERING.

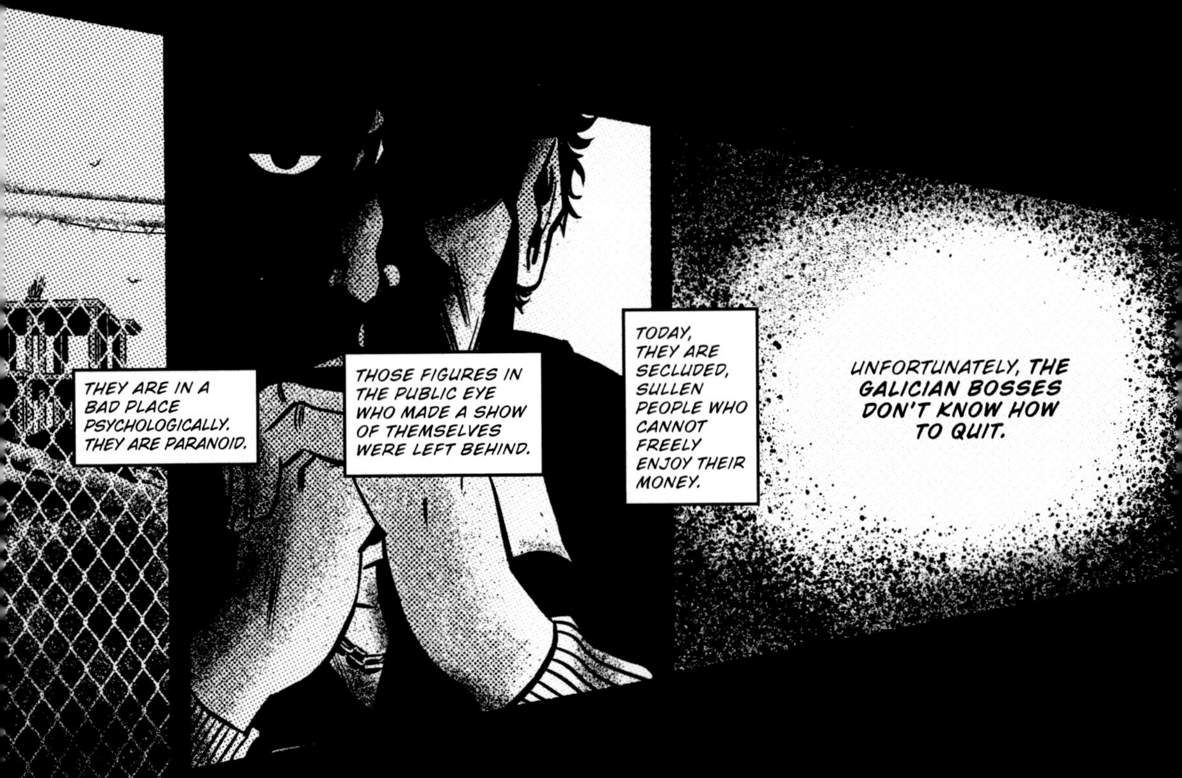
THEY ARE IN A BAD PLACE PSYCHOLOGICALLY. THEY ARE PARANOID.
THOSE FIGURES IN THE PUBLIC EYE WHO MADE A SHOW OF THEMSELVES WERE LEFT BEHIND.
TODAY, THEY ARE SECLUDED, SULLEN PEOPLE WHO CANNOT FREELY ENJOY THEIR MONEY.
UNFORTUNATELY, THE GALICIAN BOSSES DON'T KNOW HOW TO QUIT.

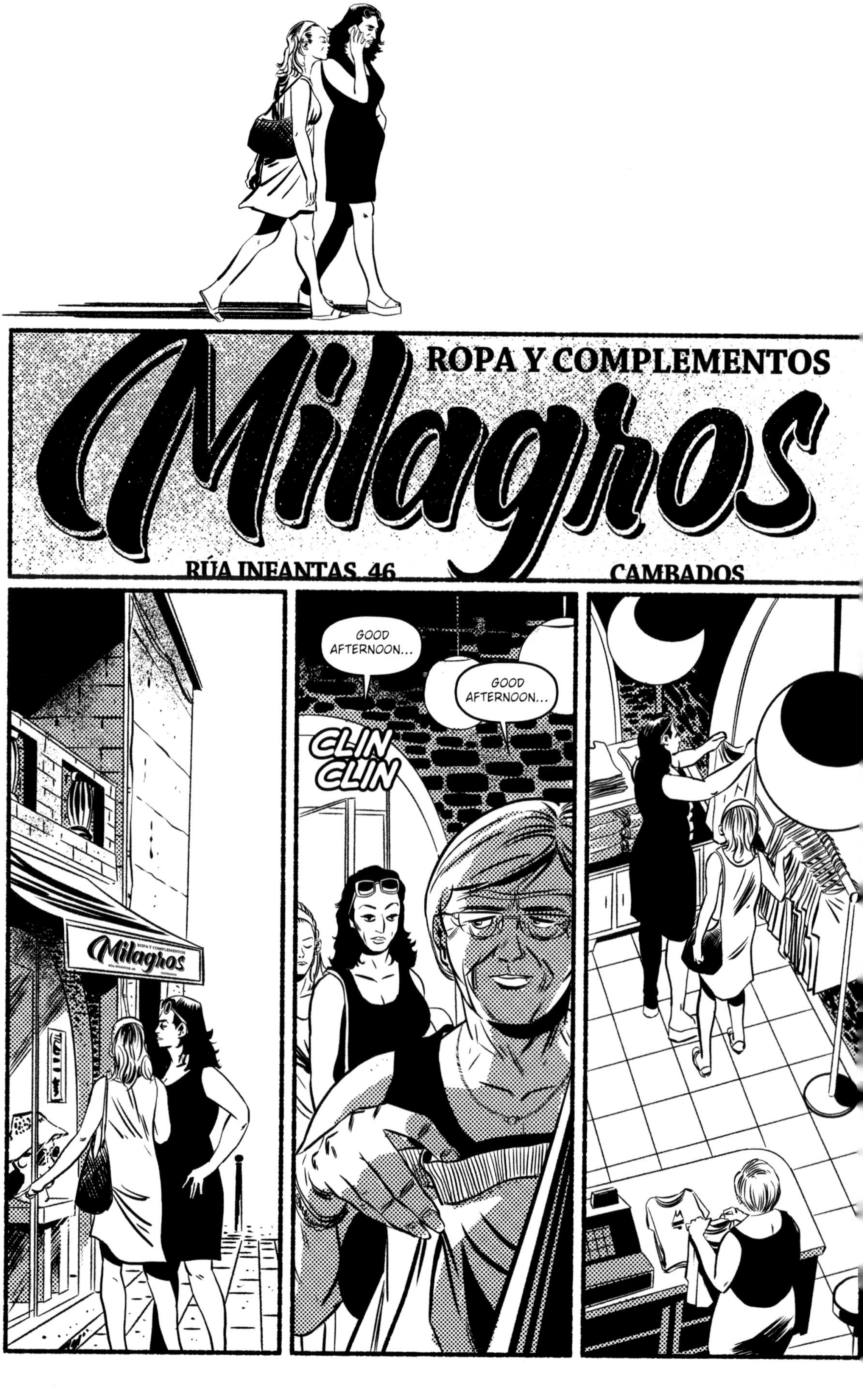
ROPA Y COMPLEMENTOS
Milagros
RÚA INFANTAS 46
CAMBADOS
Milagros
GOOD AFTERNOON...
CLIN CLIN
GOOD AFTERNOON...

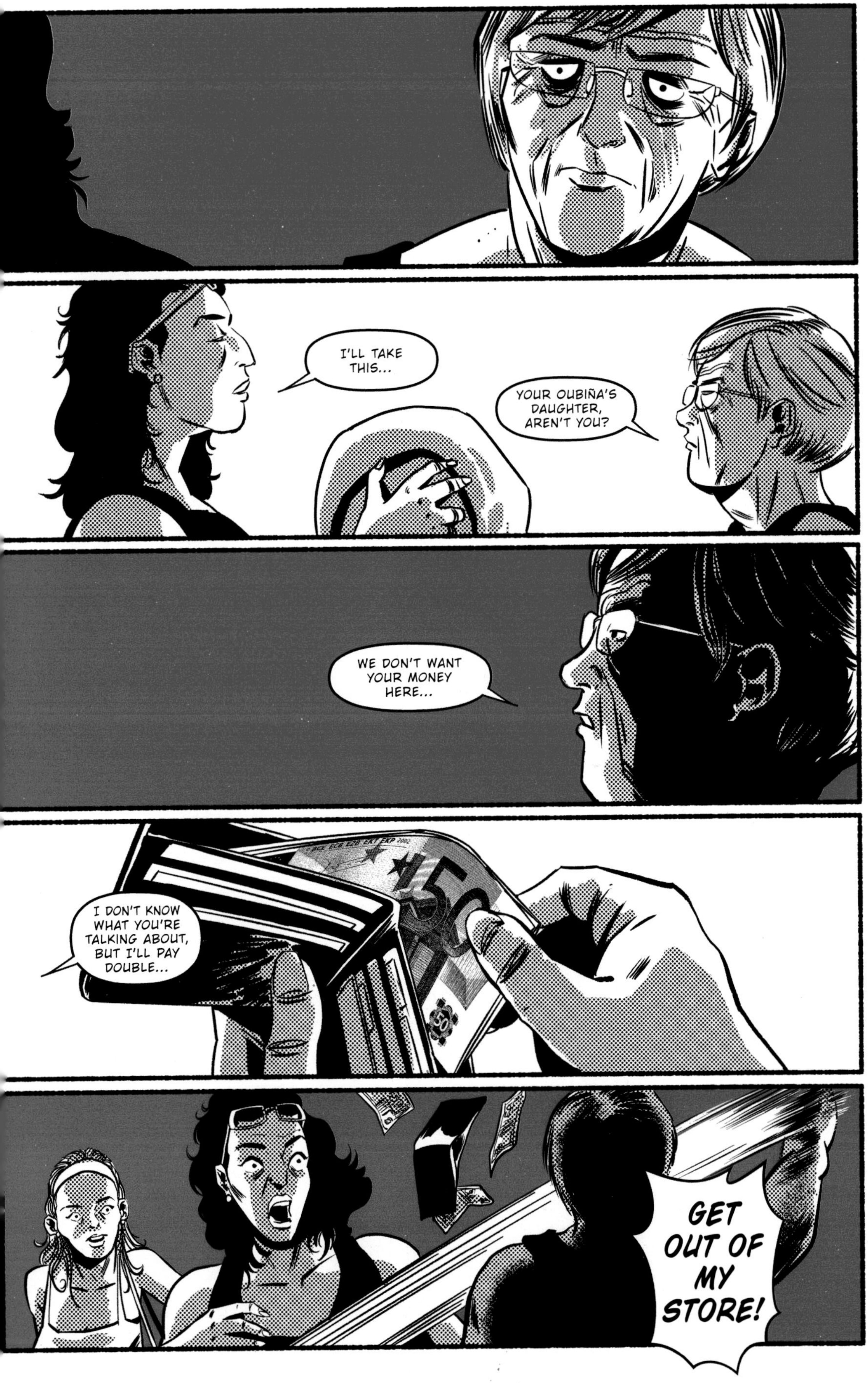
I'LL TAKE THIS...
YOUR OUBIÑA'S DAUGHTER, AREN'T YOU?
WE DON'T WANT YOUR MONEY HERE...
I DON'T KNOW WHAT YOU'RE TALKING ABOUT, BUT I'LL PAY DOUBLE...
GET OUT OF MY STORE!

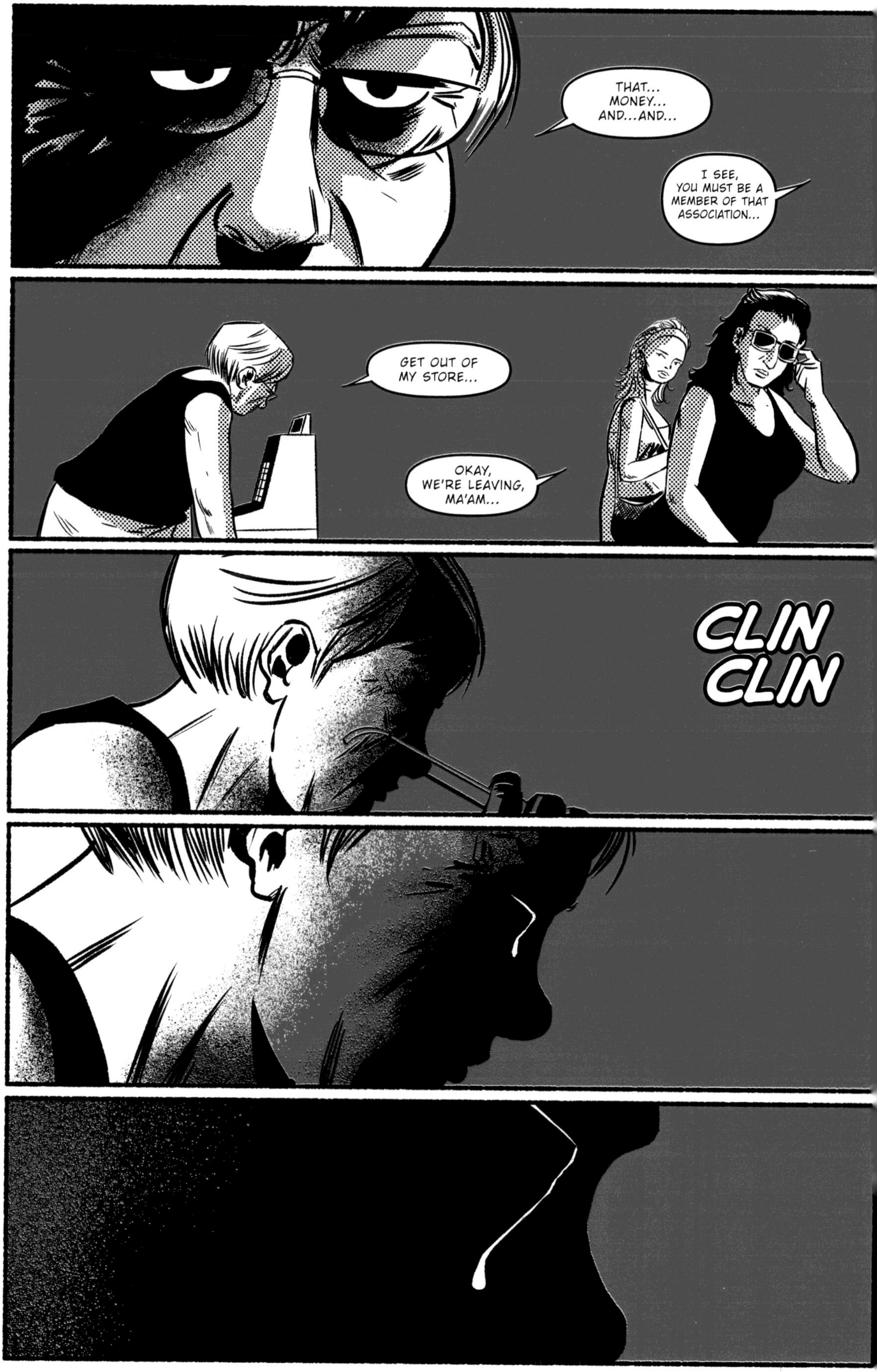
THAT... MONEY... AND...AND...
I SEE, YOU MUST BE A MEMBER OF THAT ASSOCIATION...
GET OUT OF MY STORE...
OKAY, WE'RE LEAVING, MA'AM...
CLIN CLIN

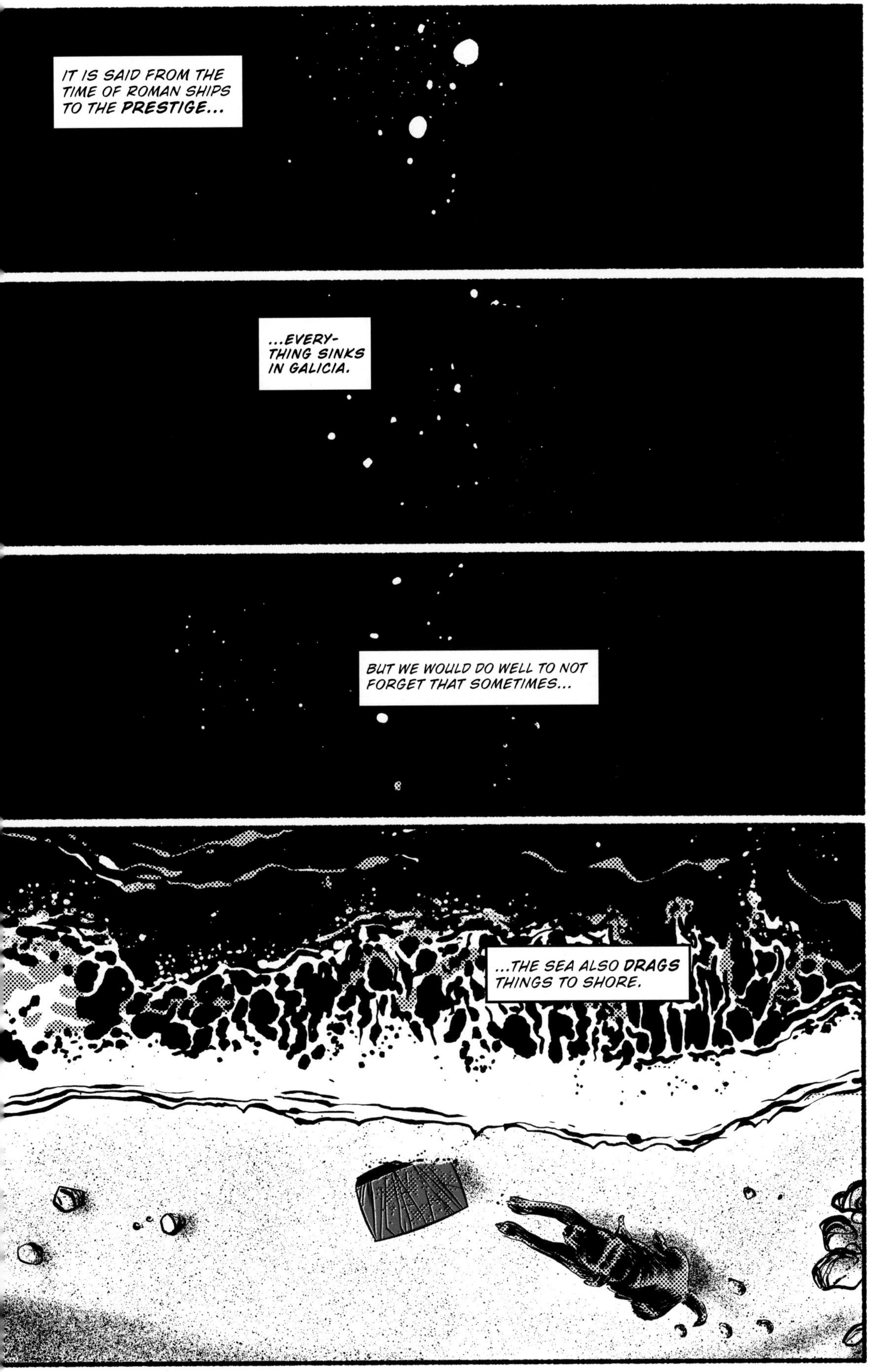
IT IS SAID FROM THE TIME OF ROMAN SHIPS TO THE PRESTIGE...
...EVERY-THING SINKS IN GALICIA.
BUT WE WOULD DO WELL TO NOT FORGET THAT SOMETIMES...
...THE SEA ALSO DRAGS THINGS TO SHORE.

# BEYOND *COCAINE COAST*

## Nacho Carretero

One sunny summer day, a Galician drug dealer invited me to eat at a restaurant on the Vigo estuary. Forget it, he isn't in this graphic novel. Nor does he appear in the original book, or in the TV series based on it. He is one of those narcos that the public doesn't know, that the police watch, but they have nothing on him to act, and thus has not been paraded before any court. Yes, beyond the Galician drug traffickers we know, there are at least as many others that we have not heard of. *There are, there are.* Those for whom business has gone well. They've retired on time, been smarter or have just been luckier. This one, the one who invited me to shrimp and hake in sauce, was one of them; one of the anonymous, those who read or watch reports on drug trafficking in Galicia with a smirk because the media focus is far from them.

This man confessed to me that he liked the book. In fact, and to my surprise, he asked me to sign a copy that he carried with him. Then, criticized the trivialization of drug trafficking: he complained that there would be t-shirts or sweatshirts with the names or faces of famous Galician drug traffickers. He said he was a bad example for children. I still don't know if he really thought this or if his ego was hurt by his anonymity. After all, narcos are people too, he would say.

By then, the book had just been released after an incomprehensible judicial hijacking. The ban, together with the premiere of the television series that adapted the story, made *Cocaine Coast's* popularity multiply. And that was already more than the publisher and I could have dreamed: *Cocaine Coast*, before the ban, had become a book that, without any marketing or promotional strategy, had sold forty thousand copies in ten editions and was already being translated into five languages. A little miracle.

Not only that: the publication of the book helped to shift the media focus, again, to the Galician narcos. And I say again because the media attention about the entry of hashish and cocaine through the Galician estuaries there had practically disappeared in recent years, even though business flourished. Oh yes, flourished…this is something that brave journalists who risked their lives to report, such as Elisa Lois, Julio Á. Fariñas, Benito Leiro, Felipe Suárez,

Ujué Foces, Susana Luaña, Perfecto Conde, Xosé Hermida and more, had been denouncing for a long time. The noise that *Cocaine Coast's* publication caused helped create this demand, and suddenly the newspapers and televisions were interested again in Vilagarcía, Cambados or Vilanova; publishers reissued books written in the early 1990s that had been abandoned and forgotten. If something positive came out of *Cocaine Coast's* publication it is, of course, the renewed attention from those who believed that this Galician cancer was removed or healed; to have stirred those who firmly believed that it was in the past, when in fact, it has not ended.

Yes, the excessive media focus, tends to have toxic effects: misinformation or exaggeration, which creates scaremongering and affects over and over again the same names and the same stories. But—and this is a personal opinion— amid the excess of concern and the zero interest, Galicia is much better off facing its ills.

The problem was that, over the months, *Cocaine Coast* began to take on a life of its own apart from me or the publisher. At times, it seemed that everything that happened in relation to the Galician drug traffickers, was related or due to the book. Dozens of media and production companies called asking for opinions, interviews, reactions. It was as if, with regard to Galician drug trafficking, there was nothing beyond *Cocaine Coast*, when there was obviously much more, starting with a large group of Galician journalists, some of them already mentioned.

Historical capos took to blame the book and the series for all their ills, as if life had gone well for them up to that point. "The blame for everything is from *Cocaine Coast* and Nacho Carretero," an old narco said while he busted the camera of a Galician photojournalist. The victim was there working because, days before, a group of drug traffickers had met with Colombians with the intention of exchanging views. It is clear *Cocaine Coast* was also to blame for that.

Everyone started talking about *Cocaine Coast* as if drug trafficking had not existed in Galicia before. Resulting in the traffickers themselves conveying their anger at not appearing in the book. This is true: some drug traffickers let me know their disappointment that their names were not mentioned in the pages of the book. "It is incomplete," they informed me.

The matter got out of hand when *Cocaine Coast's* hijacking was made public and, in parallel, the TV series premiered. We knew that the plaintiff, a guy who had been mayor of O Grove and had been affiliated with drug trafficking in the eighties, requested the book be stopped. But neither the publishers nor I were concerned with his filing. That man barely appeared in a paragraph of the book; a paragraph that, in addition and above all, contained factual information, that the courts would eventually recognize. Not to mention that I didn't think a book's release could be stopped.

In a decision that is still difficult to understand to this day, the judge approved the petition and prohibited the sale of *Cocaine Coast*. In a little over twenty-four hours from the announcement and its execution, more than ten thousand copies were fresh off the press before the judicial decision. The announcement caught up with me in Barcelona, where I was doing a report for *El País*, my newspaper. The avalanche was such that I decided to call my family and tell them that I was going to turn off my cell phone for a couple of days. Have you ever had your phone ring incessantly? Until you had to turn it off or throw it out the window.

I received calls and messages from judges, prosecutors, deputies, journalists… Some parties asked us for books to bring to Congress, from the nationalist spheres of Catalonia and Galicia they invited me to all kinds of initiatives to denounce the censorship and my social networks collapsed. This snowball grew steadily because, around the same time, a rapper named Valtònyc had been denounced for some lyrics in his songs and at the ARCO, a work of art had been removed. The public debate, suddenly, pointed unanimously for freedom of expression and, in the midst of the hurricane, Ramón Campos, executive producer of the TV series, called me to tell me that the network had decided to premiere the series that same week. Faced with such a pandemonium, the publisher and I decided to get away from it all, stay silent and wait it out. It was not easy.

Many people told me that "the prohibition" was the best thing that could happen to me and the book. I don't disagree: sales soared thanks to the order. But that does not invalidate the bad taste that we had to endure for a few months. As a journalist, a judge prohibiting my work for a paragraph that was truthful frustrated me, hurt me and made me enormously angry. The message that judge was sending about my work was that my research was unreliable, it was not rigorous. And that affected me. In addition, the moment that both the publisher and me had been waiting for, the premiere of the TV series, a milestone that we wanted to enjoy and that we were very excited, was upended with the prohibition of the book. Seeing the TV episodes airing each week was a reminder that the book was banned.

If I could go back in time, I would choose not to have spent those months excessively in my own head and in silent frustration, while our plaintiff walked around television sets and posed for covers disguised as a baker and declaring that I'd put a bullet in his head.

After our meal in the beautiful Vigo estuary, during dessert, my host paradoxically began stating that an unjust stigma was being attached to Galicia. That drug trafficking was in all of Spain (I knew this, of course) and it seemed that now it only existed in the estuaries. It seemed a little surreal to discuss this with my host, but in that moment my options were limited.

In my opinion, the phenomenon to which *Cocaine Coast* has contributed is nothing more than exposing a reality. A harsh unpleasant reality, which has been present in Galicia for years and which, for a time, was covered by the media with great skill and courage, but lately it seemed to have become something of a taboo. It even came to give the impression in Galicia that drug trafficking only existed if it was invoked, so that, in order not to see it, it was better not to mention it. Defensive reactions were avoided from the school of "This feeds the stereotype," "They are prejudices," "It is trivializing," and the like. In this way, like so many others things, it seemed to be kept in a drawer and swallowed with the prevailing message: "It has already happened and, if anything, it is a matter of foreign drug traffickers."

Since I was young, I have seen how in other places with similar criminal phenomena it has been used to make a cultural exploitation of them without this coming into conflict with respect and sensitivity towards them. Like how Italy is branded with the Mafia scourge in movies, TV series, and book. Latin America and the United States are other good examples.

Nobody there even considers that doing so is to detract from seriousness or concern about the matter. Why don't we do it in Galicia? I started from this question when writing my book.

I think that *Cocaine Coast* has helped change all this a bit. The narco, our narco, that misfortune that we had kept in a drawer, has been put on the table and has been culturally exploited, which has allowed talk about it openly again, debated, become folklore and its visibility helps raise awareness. There is nothing disrespectful about using the channels of culture and communication to examine a reality. And Galician society has understood this, has shown exemplary maturity and has managed to reconcile folklore with sensitivity and conscience. It is a step forward.

Granted, in folk exploitation there are always excesses. Like the drug dealer who invited me to eat, I don't find it too moral to wear the face of a drug lord on a T-shirt. But that doesn't invalidate everything else. Even less so if the one who complains about it is a drug dealer!

And things in Galicia have changed. The narrative possibilities of the old bosses, their romamtic and ostentatious lives, no longer exist. Or, if they exist, they are invisible.

Months after that meal, and as a result of a report that he prepared last year, I had a long coffee with one of the top drug agents of the National Police. The meeting took place in Madrid, although he had worked before, for many years, in the GRECO of Galicia, so he was a great connoisseur of the reality of the estuaries.

He gave me three names. Or rather, three nicknames: *O Burro*, *El Pastelero* and *Os Lulu*. Three groups of Galician drug traffickers who are among the current priority objectives of the police forces in Spain. The first is a Galician businessman, well connected on a political and business level, who lives in Colombia. According to the police, he introduces tons of cocaine into Galicia from Colombian drug trafficking groups. The second is, perhaps, the most powerful narco Galicia has ever known. The current king of the estuaries. Without being so well connected or playing the role of businessman, El Pastelero squanders his life between mansions watched by security cameras, luxury cars that he drives in tracksuits and nightlife at the stroke of a checkbook. All without any information being known about him. The Lulus are a clan from Costa da Morte who controls everything that enters this area of Galicia. It is headed by two brothers who are, themselves, part of the historical ones and already had problems with the law in the nineties.

There are some other heavyweights, but none in Galicia has the contacts and trust of Latin American cartels like these three groups. The police are convinced that they continue to introduce huge amounts of drugs through Galicia. The difference is that they are hidden. In fact, for the general public, absorbed by the adventures of the old capos of the eighties, they are invisible.

And they are, in large part, thanks to the Nécora Operation, whose echoes still resound in the Galician estuaries. In 1990, a young judge named Baltasar Garzón decided to carry out a macro-assault against the clans of the Galician narcos. The secrecy to achieve it had to be absolute, with hundreds of police mobilized from Madrid and without a drop of information slipping to Galicia. Any crack would inform the kingpins, who had eyes and ears in every square meter of Galicia.

One early morning in June, vans, cars and even a helicopter stormed Vilagarcía de Arousa and surprised the heads of the main Arousan gangs. Los Charlines fell, Oubiña fell, the Baulos fell and Sito Miñanco would fall months later. And although the penalties that were handed down were insufficient and, in some cases, even non-existent, that day something changed forever in Galicia. For the first time, the state had shown signs of life. For the first time, the authorities had moved against drug traffickers, who were until that moment untouchable, popular, accepted. From then on, there was no longer impunity. Drug trafficking continued, sure, but it mutated. The capos understood, the hard way, that the life of excess and flashiness had turned against them. And to preserve the success of their business, they needed to be discreet. A discretion that has not stopped growing since then.

However, it would be unfair to only give credit to this change to the Nécora. This also happened because a brave part of Galician society woke up and shouted against the impunity. Led by dozens of mothers fed up with seeing their children dying due to overdose, residents of the Galician coast organized and began to confront the clans face to face, in a dark and turbulent time, in which shouting against Sito Miñanco was equivalent to opening a dark and gloomy attic and turning on a flashlight. Those mothers carried out eschraches (a demonstration involving publicly shaming well known figures) against the narcos when this word did not yet exist. They were planted at the gates of their pazos and yelled at them, went to the trials and attacked them with umbrellas. Politicians were blushing because of their own inaction. They pressed in such a way that it forced the state, finally, to act. Galicia owes them the sanitation of its narco landscape. Yes, there are still many capos, but at least they don't flaunt their embarrassing successes in front of their neighbors' faces.

It is the before and after of the Galician drug trafficking. The impunity with which Sito Miñanco, Laureano Oubiña or Los Charlines moved, it became almost total. The result: romantic and ostentatious lives typical of a book, series, or even graphic novel.

Around the aforementioned current kings of drug trafficking in Galicia, there are still numerous minor clans ready to collaborate in some offloading or initiate one of their own. Many of these clans are the children and even the grandchildren of historic traffickers and smugglers. A narcoculture survives in some areas of the Galician estuaries in which a handful of groups, almost always with family ties and linked to the sea, still plan, brag and enrich themselves by introducing kilos of cocaine down the coast. They tend to fare worse: their power and influence are minor and most end up paraded before a judge.

The curious thing about Galician drug traffickers is that they resist the classic methodology of the place. Although in danger of extinction, unloading is still carried out by means of gliders, speedboats with enormous power and capacity that cut through the sea into the middle of the Atlantic Ocean to carry the bales and unload them on some remote beach on the Galician coast.

Sito Miñanco was one of the proper names of this old school. The historic kingpin was released from jail in 2017 and months later he was arrested again for planning an offloading. Investigators discovered that Sito had his own fleet of gliders and that the shipyard where he manufactured and kept them was in the Arousa estuary itself. The police believe there are still a dozen gliders in Galicia, but their activity is limited, since they are under major scrutiny. Any movement (the purchase of large quantities of gasoline, for example) is quickly detected.

So the Galician drug lords are becoming more and more friendly with the method that prevails in the rest of Spain: introducing cocaine in maritime containers. Sometimes the cocaine travels in a container of a fictitious export company or front, belonging to criminal groups in Latin America. Other times, cocaine is smuggled into a container from a legal company and extracted when it is already in a Spanish port. Those chosen are usually, in order of preference, Algeciras, Valencia and Barcelona.

In reality, the big drug traffickers, the masters of Europe, are the Dutch Arab gangs who live on the Costa del Sol and control the port of Algeciras, while the media focuses on the gypsy clans that traffic hashish in La Línea de la Concepción. These gangs based in Marbella are introducing tons of cocaine every year and they are violent and dangerous. They work with gangs of Albanians and Kosovars and sell their merchandise to British, Italian, Russian or Irish groups who distribute it throughout Europe. Spain is, today, and with the permission of the Netherlands, the gateway for cocaine to the old continent. If a gunshot fatality appears every now and again in southern Spain, it is not by chance.

When we finished the meal, the Galician narco offered me his help and encouraged me to write *Cocaine Coast* II: "Let me know." I never saw him again and I have no intention of writing a second part. In any case, if it existed, it should be about how Galicia continues to look the other way when we talk about drug money. How almost no one on the Galician coast cares if the hotel where they stay, the restaurant where they eat or the store they enter belongs to or exists because of drug traffickers. If you could measure the businesses in the Rías Baixas that, directly or indirectly, exist thanks to drug trafficking, the result would be scandalous. But nobody seems to care. Other times it is simply impossible to find out. And, many others, neighbors have no choice but to go to a shop with ties to the cocaine due to the fact that there is none closer. It is the Galician narcoculture of the 21st century.

In any case, may this graphic novel serve as a new channel for cultural exploitation. And not just any one. The work of Luis Bustos has now become part of the illustrated history of Galicia. I confess: my knowledge of the world of graphic novels is limited. Despite having enjoyed (and learned) from the works of Guy Delisle, Joe Sacco and Art Spiegelman, my experience has more to do with comics than with work adapted from journalism. And this book with Luis has educated me. A graphic novel like this is, above all, a brilliant journalistic piece. And, told in such a masterly way as Luis Bustos carries out, it makes one understand how little journalism is using a channel as effective and engaging as the graphic novel.

A story like *Cocaine Coast*'s, such an important chapter, has had the privilege of being graphically captured. And this is something even more important when we are talking about a phenomenon, that of drug trafficking, which continues to exist and damages Galicia and that needs to be recounted as many times as necessary. And in as many ways as communication allows us.

**Nacho Carretero** (A Coruña, 1981) has written for various media outlets in Spain like *Jot Down, XL Semanal, Gatopardo* and *El Español*. He has dealt with topics such as the genocide in Rwanda, Ebola in Africa and the war in Syria, among others. He is currently a reporter for *El País* newspaper in Spain.

**Luis Bustos** (Madrid, 1973) is a cartoonist, illustrator and graphic artist. He has a versatile style and has done work in various genres and formats ranging from the traditional comic book to the European album format. His books include *Endurance, Versus, POP. I Can't Get That Song Out of My Head!* and *Garcia!*, with Santiago García.

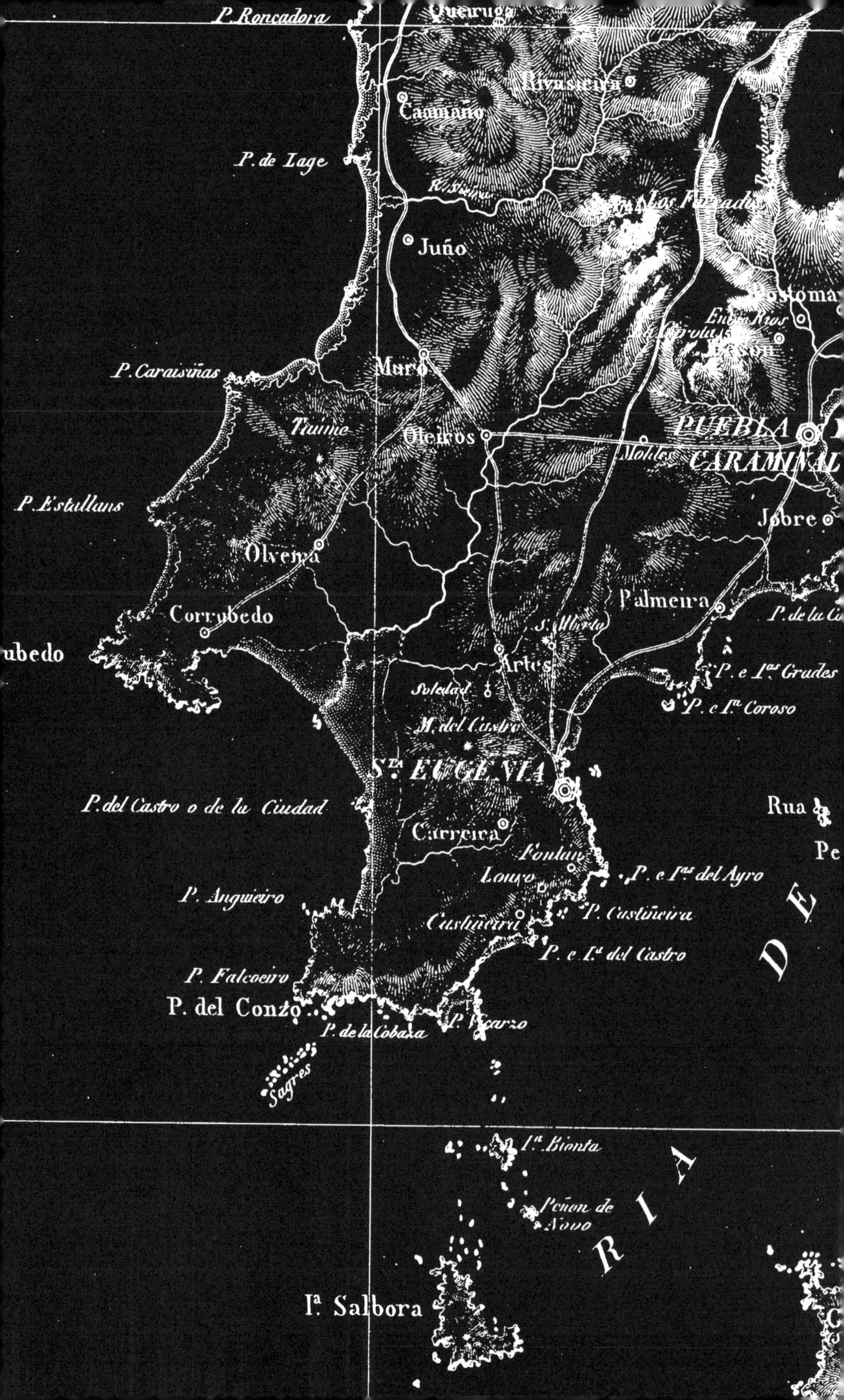
P. Roncadora
Rivasieira
Camaño
P. de Lage
Juño
Entre Rios
P. Caraisiñas
Muro
Oleiros
PUEBLA
CARAMIÑAL
P. Estallans
Olveira
Jobre
Corrubedo
ubedo
Palmeira
Artes
Soledad
P. e Iª Coroso
M. del Castro
Sª EUGENIA
P. del Castro o de la Ciudad
Rua
Carreira
Fontan
Louro
P. e Iˢ del Ayro
P. Anguieiro
Castiñeira
P. Castiñeira
P. e Iª del Castro
DE
P. Falcoeiro
P. del Conzo
P. de la Cobaza
Sagres
Iª Bionta
Peñon de Novo
RIA
Iª Salbora